D1241169

I WAS THERE
WHEN IT HAPPENED

I WAS THERE
WHEN IT HAPPENED
MY LIFE WITH JOHNNY CASH

MARSHALL GRANT
WITH CHRIS ZAR

CUMBERLAND HOUSE
NASHVILLE, TENNESSEE

I Was There When It Happened
Published by Cumberland House Publishing, Inc.
431 Harding Industrial Drive
Nashville, TN 37211-3160

Cover design: James Duncan Creative
Text design: John Mitchell

Library of Congress Cataloging-in-Publication Data

Grant, Marshall, bassist.
   I was there when it happened : my life with Johnny Cash / Marshall Grant.
     p. cm.
   Includes index.
    ISBN-13: 978-1-58182-510-7 (hardcover : alk. paper)
    ISBN-10: 1-58182-510-2 (hardcover : alk. paper)
   1. Grant, Marshall, bassist. 2. Cash, Johnny. 3. Country musicians—United States—Biography. I. Title.
    ML419.G725A3 2006
    781.642092—dc22
    [B]

                                                                          2006022195

Printed in the United States of America

1 2 3 4 5 6—11 10 09 08 07 06

*To all the fans who have supported
Johnny Cash and the Tennessee Two
for all these years.*

Contents

Part Three: The Seventies

Part Four: The Eighties

Part Five: The Nineties and Beyond

Foreword I

Johnny Cash was a good friend, a respected mentor, and for eight and a half years of our early career, our employer. He gave us that proverbial big break that all show business aspirants search for desperately, and in giving us that break, gave us a steady job with his touring company and got us our first recording deal with Columbia Records. And that's about all we're going to say about John, because in this book you'll find out all you ever need to know about the Man in Black from the Man in Back—Marshall Grant, the man who stood beside John on and off stage for decades.

We came along in John's life and career in 1964, but Marshall was there from the beginning, ten years before. He and only he knows all the stories from the very start of John's career. Sadly, as we look back on those times, we see that most of those who were closest to John in those glory years are gone. Luther Perkins and Carl Perkins were very much a part of that traveling show we all made history with so long ago, and both have passed on. So have

Mother Maybelle Carter and her daughters Helen and Anita, who brought history and great sweetness onstage every night. And, of course, John and June are no longer around to talk to and reminisce with. Marshall and we three original Statler Brothers are about all that's left from those early days. And if there ever was a man qualified to set the legend of Johnny Cash straight and place the truth at the feet of the people, it's Marshall Grant.

We parted ways with John as friends at the end of 1972 because our collective career was growing so quickly that it demanded more and more of our attention, and he was the first person to notice that. About ten years later, Marshall, who was always a friend and whom we had stayed in touch with, joined our organization as our representative and remained with us for the next twenty years, until we all decided to retire and sleep late. We were with Marshall through the happiest and saddest days of his relationship with John. We've stood on countless stages throughout countless concerts with him behind The Man—and later stood for what seemed like countless hours with our arms around one another as we stared down at that same man lying peacefully in his final rest.

There were so many wonderful days and memories in between, and we can honestly say there is no one better equipped to write about them than Marshall. There was a special bond between these two men, which we're sure you'll discover as you read their story. We were honored to have been there and to have seen it all firsthand.

To John and Marshall, we love you both.

— The Statler Brothers
Harold Reid, Phil Balsley, Don Reid

Foreword II

Truth is subjective. Every experience has its own individual interpretation, no matter how many people witnessed the same event at the same time and place. I would venture to say, however, that if a purely objective witness exists to document the evolution of Johnny Cash and the Tennessee Two, then that person is Marshall Grant.

Marshall is the one I go to when I want to know the real facts about some moment in the life of my parents, or if I want to know the back story of a more public event in my dad's career. He is a living archive and a meticulous historian. He is the record-keeper, not just of dates, facts, albums, shows, tours, and songs, but also of the emotional life that went into the creation of the music. Marshall was a witness, but he was also part of the story, and so he knows not just what it looked like, but how it felt.

Marshall loved my father deeply and loyally. Any differences that may have arisen between them, after nearly an entire lifetime of friendship and collaboration, were resolved completely, until the only thing that remained between Marshall and Dad at the time of my father's death was the mutual love of brothers.

I also love and respect Marshall and dear Etta so deeply. They knew my parents before they became my parents. They knew my father before he became Johnny Cash, and they knew me from the moment of my birth until now, and have always treated me like a beloved adopted daughter. As long as Marshall lives, I know there is someone on the planet who not only knows the truth about my father's greatness, but also about his humanity. There is so much comfort for me in that.

This book is as close to the "real" story of Johnny Cash and the Tennessee Two as you are ever likely to read. When I think of Marshall, I think of Dad's song "I Was There When It Happened." To paraphrase, Marshall was there when it happened, so I guess he ought to know.

— Rosanne Cash
New York City
May 2006

Preface

For several years people from all walks of life have encouraged me to write a book about my experiences with music legend Johnny Cash. The story of Johnny Cash and the Tennessee Two is an unbelievable one that I had purposely put off writing for years. But if I was ever going to do it, what better time to start than on February 26, John's birthday?

Many things have been written over the years about John, his band, and those around him. Some of them don't make any sense, and some are just plain distortions, so I have decided to set the record straight the best I can in order to preserve the history and the legacy of Johnny Cash and the Tennessee Two.

For the sake of our families—mine, John's, Luther's, all the others who were involved, and for our grandchildren, great-grandchildren, and on down the line—I believe this is a story that must be told. I've kept everything authentic, since there is no reason for me to distort anything.

Acknowledgments

Many people deserve special thanks for their contributions over the years to Johnny Cash and the Tennessee Two. Roy Cash introduced me to John, which started it all. I can't say enough about Luther Perkins, who was the one who made it all happen. My brother Hershel brought me to Memphis, which was the turning point in my life, and he was 100 percent responsible for me meeting my wife, Etta, and everything that came along after that. Sam Phillips gave us a chance and heard something that no one else could hear. And I'll never forget Carl Perkins, one of the best friends I ever had, and the times we had together.

Thanks also to Bob Wootton, the only person who could come close to Luther Perkins, and who did it so very well; Chris Zar, who took my words off the tape and put them on paper; and David Caywood, my attorney and friend, who understood me and what I stood for.

I can't put into words my feelings for the Statler Brothers, so I will simply say, "Thank you, guys."

Special thanks to John and June's children. I wish I could have done more. Etta and I will always be here for you.

To Vivian Liberto: I'm sure the hell you went through here on earth has earned you a place in Heaven.

To my son, Randy: You are what you are because of your mom, and that's good enough for me. I'm truly sorry for the time we spent apart.

And finally, to my wife, Etta: You are truly a great lady, and no one could have done more. You were and still are the cornerstone of my life. Thanks for everything it took to make it work; you were right in the middle of it all. As I look back to day one, it scares me to think what would and could have happened without you.

Introduction

In the spring of 1947, my wife, the former Etta May Dickerson, a lovely girl from Memphis, and I settled in the Bluff City to make our home. I'd spent a good deal of time in the months following World War II traveling between my family home in North Carolina and Memphis as I courted Etta, and on November 9, 1946, we'd gotten married. After living in North Carolina for a short while, we decided to move to the bustling city overlooking the Mississippi River.

I didn't have a job or a trade, so the only thing I knew to do was to hit the streets and see what kind of work I could find. I was willing to take any job, for almost any salary, just to get some money coming in. One day I decided to start on Union Avenue, going into every business one by one and asking if they had an opening.

When I came to 678 Union, the C. M. Booth Motor Company, a Desoto-Plymouth dealership, the shop foreman, Don Sharp, told me the company was planning to add another person in a month or so. I thanked him for his help and then walked right across the street to Wagner Brake Service, where I was able to land a job. A month or so later, Don walked into the shop and told me the position at C. M. Booth was available. I gave my notice at Wagner and soon went to work at the car dealership.

I was hired to run parts for the mechanics, clean the shop, and sweep the floor, but whenever I didn't have anything to do, I would hang around the mechanics and was soon helping them work on vehicles. After about six months, Don Sharp came up to me and said, "Marshall, I've been watching you, and you've really got the knack for repairing cars. I think you could make it on your own if you wanted to go on as a full-time mechanic." I jumped at the chance. I didn't have any tools, so my father-in-law, V. A. Dickerson, gave me a toolbox and a handful of tools to get me started.

The back of the dealership at 678 Union opened onto Marshall Avenue, and each day at lunchtime I would cross Marshall, turn right, and walk down to the corner to Taylor's Restaurant to eat. On the way, I passed a small brick building with no signs out front and blinds that were always drawn. I had no idea what was inside. The building almost looked unoccupied, but I knew that wasn't the case because I would occasionally see a car pull up and someone go inside for quite a while. For almost a year, curiosity just ate me up as I wondered what could possibly be going on there.

I'd been working at C. M. Booth for about a year when they hired a new mechanic, A. W. "Red" Kernodle. As we got to know each other, Red and I discovered that we both liked country music and both played an instrument. I played rhythm guitar, and Red played steel guitar, and even though he didn't have an instrument of his own, he played pretty well. One day when I was in the local Sears store, I saw a little steel guitar, what I call a Hawaiian guitar, and an amplifier, which I bought so that Red would have something to play.

Red and his wife and three daughters were a close-knit family, and occasionally we'd get together, sometimes at his house and sometimes at mine. We knew a couple of other guys who did a little picking, and we'd invite them over for some family fun.

As time passed, Red needed more money to support his family, so he took a job at Automobile Sales a few blocks down the street at 309 Union. About once a week, while test-driving a car, Red would stop by the C. M. Booth shop to visit me. One day in 1951 he came in and said, "Marshall, you need to come down to Automobile Sales. They need a mechanic, and you can make a lot more money down there than you can here."

I went over and met the shop foreman, Floyd Ward, and about a week later he hired me. Floyd took me back into the shop and introduced me to the mechanic who would be working by my side. His name was Roy Cash.

PART ONE
THE FIFTIES

utomobile Sales at the time was the world's largest Desoto-Plymouth dealership, with twenty-three mechanics working in the service department. In the summer of 1953, the company hired a mechanic—a tall, slim, black-headed guy, who went to work on the opposite side of the shop. After a couple of days, I decided I would go over and introduce myself. "Say, man," I said, "I been seeing you over here, and I've intended to come over and introduce myself, but I just haven't gotten around to it. My name is Marshall Grant." The lanky fellow stuck out his hand. "My name's Luther Perkins. Glad to meet ya."

Red Kernodle and I were still getting together with some of our buddies to play music, and when we discovered that Luther also played guitar, we invited him to join us. As it turned out, he was probably the best musician of us all.

Luther and I decided one day to take our guitars to work, and when we didn't have anything else to do, we'd go back to the dressing room and pick and sing while the other mechanics gathered around to listen. We weren't the greatest singers in the world, but we really didn't care—we were having fun, and that was the important thing.

Almost every time we'd go back to the dressing room, Roy Cash would join us, listening and laughing as we strummed our guitars and sang. He loved country music with all of his heart. One day as we were heading back to work, Roy said, "You know, Marshall, I got a brother in the service, and he plays guitar, too, and he sings just like Hank Snow." I jokingly said, "Well, we need him, because we really need a singer."

Roy kept talking about his brother, who was about to be discharged from the Air Force, and one day in mid-July 1954, he came over and said, "Grant, I'll be back in a few minutes; I'm going up to pick up J. R." The bus station was just two blocks up the street, so Roy walked there, but the bus must have been running late, because he was gone almost an hour and a half.

When he finally returned, I was standing under a lift, working on the back end of a car. I looked toward the big overhead door at the end of the shop and saw two men walk in. I knew one of them was Roy, so the other had to be his brother. He was a tall, slim guy, probably six feet two, 165 pounds, and as trim as could be. It was a moment I couldn't forget if I tried, for a funny feeling—kind of tingling—come over me, and it grew stronger as they got closer. By the time they'd crossed the shop, the tingling had crawled up my spine, and it felt like the hair on the back of my neck was sticking straight out. I didn't know what to think about that.

As I stepped out from under the lift, Roy said, "Marshall, this is my brother I've been telling you about, J. R." Turning to the tall man, he added, "J. R., this is Marshall Grant." As we shook hands, J. R. said, "I hear you do a little pickin'." "*Very* little," I replied, and he laughed and said, "Me, too." We talked for a few minutes, and just as it had been when I met Roy, we became friends right on the spot.

"I got a couple of other pickin' buddies in the shop," I told him. "Come on over and I'll introduce you." Red was out at the time, so J. R. and I walked over to where Luther was working under the dashboard of a car. I kicked him on the bottom of his foot, and said, "Luther, I got someone I want you to meet." He slid out from under the dash, then took time to comb his long black hair into place. I said, "Luther, this is J. R. Cash. J. R., this is Luther Perkins."

The first thing John said was, "I understand you do a little pickin', too." Luther nodded and said, "Yeah, Marshall and I get together, and another buddy here, Red Kernodle, plays steel guitar a little bit. We get together and we have a lot of fun. If you want to join us sometime, well, feel free, 'cause we really need a singer, and I understand that you sing like Hank Snow." J. R. laughed and said, "Well, I try to sing a little bit, but I don't know who I sound like."

———

We stood around and talked for a while, but J. R. was in a hurry to get to Dyess, Arkansas, to see his mother and dad and the rest of his family. Another reason he was anxious to get home was that he was chomping at the bit to get married. J. R. was engaged to Vivian Liberto, who lived in San Antonio, Texas, where he had been stationed before being shipped overseas.

The way John later explained it to me, he'd met her one night at a skating rink when he accidentally ran into her and knocked her down. She wasn't hurt, and he picked her up, brushed her off, and they began to talk. He walked her home later that evening. A short time after that, John was sent to Germany, and he and Vivian wrote to each other almost every day. During that time, they became engaged.

John stayed with his family in Dyess for a few days. He hadn't received his final pay from the Air Force, so he didn't have a lot of money and was getting by as best he could. He still wanted to get married, though, so Roy loaned him his car, and John drove to San Antonio, where, on August 7, 1954, he and Vivian Liberto were married.

The couple came to Memphis after they were married and rented a little apartment off Summer Avenue. John wasn't working yet, and he would come by the shop almost daily. We'd sit around and talk, and we became very good friends. That wasn't hard to do, because John was very friendly and he loved companionship.

One day he came in and said that he'd found a job as a door-to-door salesman for Home Equipment Company. John wasn't very good at selling, and it wasn't something he wanted to do, but he knew that and often joked about it.

One day I asked John just what the company did. With a name like Home Equipment, I thought they might do other things in addition to selling appliances. "Oh, we're involved with a lot of other things," he said. "We remodel houses and all kinds of things." I told him I was thinking about adding a garage behind my house and said he might want to come over and work up an estimate. He said he'd be glad to do that.

John had never been to my house at 4199 Nakomis, right off Park Avenue in southeast Memphis, so I gave him directions. He stopped by one day to look at where I wanted to put the garage, and he brought Vivian with him. This was the first time that Etta and I had met her, and we all sat around and talked for a while. Vivian was such a nice lady, and she and Etta immediately established a warm relationship—just as John and I had done. As we sat around talking and drinking coffee, it became apparent that we'd all made some really good friends.

A few days later, a woman came into Home Equipment looking to buy a used refrigerator. There was one in stock, and John showed it to her. When she asked the price, he went into the back to check and came back out and told her. Then he added, "That's too high for that refrigerator." As they continued to talk, the woman told him she was converting her house into a duplex and was planning to rent out one side. John asked if it would be all right if he came by and looked at it, since he and Vivian were looking for a place to live. I think the woman bought the refrigerator, and it wasn't long before the newlyweds moved into the newly converted duplex. The lady who became their landlord was Pat Isom, and she lived in the other side of the house with her husband, Charles.

We four budding musicians—Luther, Red, J. R., and I—
decided to get together one night to do some picking. I
invited them all to our house one Friday night, and
everyone brought his wife along.

J. R. brought in his old guitar, which was the worse thing to try
to play I'd ever seen. He said he'd given $5 for it while he was sta-
tioned in Germany and it was the only thing he had. I was very fortunate; I had a real decent Martin guitar that Etta had given me for
my birthday some years earlier. Luther also had a nice instrument,
and Red had my steel guitar that he played through the little Silvertone amplifier. As the men sat down in the den, the girls went
into the kitchen and started a card game.

We tuned our instruments the best we could and started strumming a bit, then a little more, until we finally decided to sing a song.
J. R. asked, "Do y'all know any gospel songs?" I said, "I know about
all of them; I'm a big gospel music fan." He grinned and said, "Well,
I am, too!"

We started playing some gospel songs, and I sang harmony with J. R. He was a decent singer, not a great one, but there was power and presence in his voice. We both loved Ira and Charlie, the Louvin Brothers, and while we couldn't sing as high or in the same key as they did, we knew most of their songs.

I have to say we weren't very good, the four of us. Red would do a little fill on the steel guitar and play a break or two, and Luther would play rhythm guitar. You could tell Luther wanted to play some lead, but he didn't know much about it. As a result, John, Luther, and I all ended up playing rhythm. We got along so well and had so much fun that we decided to get together again.

Our weekend picking sessions soon became a routine. After work on Friday, everyone would head home, get cleaned up, and then come over to my house where we would play music for hours while our wives played cards in the kitchen. Sometimes we'd go to Luther's place, but he didn't have quite as much room there. Luther's wife, Bertie, was a little slow to come around, but she eventually joined the other girls, and soon they were all laughing and having a great time. We became so close, we were just like brothers and sisters.

I think that of all the things we tried to do, we were better at playing gospel music than anything else. John would sing Ernest Tubb and Hank Snow songs, and he and I would harmonize on Louvin Brothers songs. We'd play all the gospel songs we knew and eventually got to where we could do them pretty well. We weren't the quality of singers that we were hearing on the radio, of course, but we were having a lot of fun making music. And we were proud of what we'd been able to accomplish by just sitting down and saying, "Hey, let's do this one," and then figuring out a way to do it.

Instrumentally speaking, we weren't very well balanced, with three rhythm guitars and a steel guitar. But we didn't take that very seriously—we were having fun, and looking back, it was just a fantastic time in our lives.

⸻ ⁘ ⸻

In the latter part of July 1954, Elvis Presley cut his first record and the music world would soon begin to change. One evening, as we were sitting around listening to Elvis's mellow voice on the radio, one of our group said, "Maybe we ought to try and do that." We knew that Elvis had recorded for a company in Memphis, because the disc jockeys were talking about it, but we didn't listen closely enough to find out which label it was.

I said, "Guys, that would be great, but we can't go in for an audition with three rhythm guitars and a steel. I mean, we're gonna have to change up our instruments somehow or other if we're gonna to try to do that. We're not the greatest thing in the world anyhow, and to go in there with this instrumentation, we'll probably get laughed out of the studio."

We thought about that for a while, and finally Luther said, "Hey, I know where I can borrow an electric guitar." That was well and good, but just because Luther could find an electric instrument didn't mean he could play lead guitar. He was a pretty good rhythm player, probably the best of the three of us, but he couldn't play lead and didn't even try. Sometimes he might kick off a song, but he didn't try to play the breaks. Red did most of that on the steel guitar, and Red was pretty good.

I said, "Well, if you get an electric guitar, and, John, you do most of the lead singing, I'll get a bass and see if I can learn to play that sucker. That way we'll have a lead guitar, a rhythm guitar, a bass, and a steel guitar, and we'd be balanced out pretty good."

The following Monday, Luther went to the O. K. Houck Music Store on Union, which was run by a fellow named Sid Lapworth. I knew Sid because I bought strings and other stuff from him, and I'd go to his store about once a month just to look around and see what he had. Sure enough, Sid loaned Luther a Fender Telecaster, and Luther brought it down to the shop and showed it to all of us. It was worn out, beat up, and ragged, but it was an electric guitar.

"You know, Marshall," Luther said, "he's got a big ol' upright bass you might be interested in." When I went to the music store and asked Sid about it, he said, "Yeah, I got a used one back there, but it's kinda beat up." We went into the back and pulled the bass out of stock, and Sid was right: it was beat up, but it had all four strings. I asked, "What do you want for this thing, Sid?" He said, "I'll take twenty-five dollars for it." I still have the receipt today.

Now that Luther had an electric guitar and I had a bass, we were pretty excited. I called John and said, "Let's get together and work with these instruments tonight." That evening, John and Luther came over to my house, but Red didn't show up. Luther pulled out his guitar and plugged it into the little amplifier that Red had been using. The guitar was pretty much a pile of junk. Both the volume and tone controls were wired wide open, so Luther had to set the volume and tone on the amplifier. But when he turned it to a low level, it sounded pretty good.

Then came the problem: none of us knew anything about playing bass. Unlike a guitar, the instrument has no frets, and we had no earthly idea how to tune the thing. About the only thing we could do was thump on it.

With John and I playing our acoustic guitars and Luther playing his "new" electric, we ran through several songs for about an hour or so, and everything went very well. I said, "Guys, I'll find out tomorrow how to tune the bass. Gene Steel is a salesman at work, and he's got a band. He plays gigs around town, and I'll bet he'll know."

I spotted Gene on the showroom floor the next morning. "Gene, how in the world do you tune a bass?" I asked. "I just bought one, and I don't know how to tune it." He said, "Well, I don't either, but we're doing a gig down in Grenada, Mississippi, tonight, and I'll ask my bass player and I'll let you know tomorrow." The next morning, Gene walked into the shop holding a piece of paper in his hand and came over to where I was working. "Marshall, I asked my bass player, and here's what he gave me," he said, handing me a drawing of a bass neck with four strings and instructions to tune them to G, D, A, and E.

"Gene," I said, "that's just like the top four strings on a guitar." He said, "Yeah, that's right, but I didn't know that." I said, "I didn't either, but now we know, don't we?" We laughed, and then Gene asked, "What are you going to do with a bass?" I told him, "Well, Luther and myself and Roy's brother are playing a little music, and we decided we'd change our instruments up a little bit, so I want to learn to play the bass." He chuckled a little, shook his head, then turned around and walked back to the showroom.

I hurried over to the other side of the shop where Luther was working and said, "Hey, Luther, lookie here. Here's how you tune a bass!" I showed him the drawing, and he looked at it real close and said, "Well, it's just like the top four strings on a guitar, isn't it?" I said that it was. "But we didn't know that, did we?" he said. "No, we didn't, but we found out," I replied. Then I said, "Let me see if I can get ahold of J. R., and we'll get together tonight."

I called John at Home Equipment Company and told him about the tuning diagram and asked if he wanted to come over that evening. He laughed and said, "You sure you can play that thing?" I told him, "No, no, I'm not, but we at least can tune it, and we'll go from there. You gotta start somewhere."

Luther and Bertie and John and Vivian showed up at the house that evening. While the girls went into the kitchen to play cards, we guys went to work trying to tune the bass. This wasn't easy, because none of us knew anything about the instrument. I'd never even touched an upright bass before, and I'm sure they hadn't either. Finally, after about thirty minutes and lots of laughter, we got it tuned pretty well, although we still didn't have any idea where to go from there.

"Well, guys," I said, "we gotta start somewhere. Luther, we'll start on the G string and we'll go all the way through A, B, C, D, E, F, and G. Every time we can find a note on this thing, we'll get a piece of adhesive tape and put it on there and write it on each of the four strings." After about an hour or so, we finally figured out all the notes and then sat back and looked at our handiwork. The bass was a mess. It looked so funny, with its neck all covered with adhesive tape and those little letters, that we sat there and laughed at it for a while before I stood it up and began plucking out a few notes.

"OK," I said, "let's play something!" John said, "What?" I said, "I don't know, let's just play something." Luther asked, "What key?" I said, "I don't know; I have no earthly idea. Let me fool around with this thing a little bit and see if I can figure out a key I might be able to do something with."

Finally, I said, "Luther, I'm not too sure, but E looks pretty good; let's play something in E. Now don't play fast! Just start a little tempo in E, and let me picture this thing in my mind as being a guitar and maybe I can join in. Y'all just play a real slow tempo in E and don't change chords, and I'm going to join you." They started a slow rhythm in E, and when I got up the nerve, I hit the E string, and then I slapped it. Back and forth and back and forth, I'd hit and slap the string, hit and slap the string. That seemed so funny to us that we had to stop and laugh.

John said, "Marshall, if you're going to play that bass, can I borrow your guitar?" His was pretty awful, and I was happy to let him borrow my Martin. (John would continue to use that guitar—it was the one he played on every recording we made with Sun Records, and he also used it while writing every song he wrote while we were with the label. That little Martin guitar made a lot of history.)

Luther's guitar had no volume control, so he had to lay the palm of his hand across the strings to muffle them while we played.

I said, "OK, guys, let's try something else. Still, don't change chords on me; I can't change chords. But let's get the tempo going a little faster and get a little bit of rhythm going here and hang onto it for a few bars." Luther started playing *tick-tack-tick-tack* on his guitar, and John joined in on the rhythm while I began to hit and slap a string on the bass. "Just keep it going there," I said. "Don't change chords on me; just keep it going."

We sat there playing in E and didn't try to change chords. Luther played *tick-tack-tick-tack* on his muffled guitar; I'd hit the string and slap, hit the string and slap; and John played this awkward lick (he always played that lick—never got rid of it, never tried to). We had a lot of fun and did a lot of laughing, and before the night was over, we could play some simple songs that had just two or three chord changes. We were very encouraged, but we still didn't like the way we sounded, didn't like it at all. However, we found out real quick that it was the only thing we could do. After all, we were two mechanics and an appliance salesman playing unfamiliar instruments.

But we thought we could work with it, and as time went along, change things around as we got used to our instruments. We wanted to sound like the musicians who played on the records by Ernest Tubb, Hank Snow, the Louvin Brothers, and Webb Pierce—that's who we wanted to sound like.

Luther was now playing an electric guitar, but he'd never played lead or even kicked off a song. He was still playing rhythm, but come to find out, that little *tick-tack-tick-tack* riff he did when he muffled the strings consisted of exactly the same notes that I was hitting on the bass.

That simple *tick-tack-tick-tack*, back and forth, would become very important as time went on. We didn't know it then, but before long it would become our trademark. In fact, the sound we were developing would soon be known around the world as "Johnny Cash and his boom-chicka-boom sound." But on that first night, we were just trying to learn to play our new instruments well enough so we could have more fun.

We got the rhythm section going pretty well. We could play just about anything we knew—but it was all rhythm. Luther decided he wanted to learn to play lead, take breaks in the songs, and kick them off. That was a real problem for him, so we took a couple of simple songs that he liked and started working with him so that he could kick them off, play along with the rhythm, and then do a little break after the chorus. He just wanted to be able to do a turnaround or play the melody line of a song, but that was easier said than done. Luther was very determined and worked hard; however, things came very, very slowly.

At the same time Luther was trying to learn to play lead guitar, I was struggling with that big ol' bass. In terms of learning our respective instruments, we seemed to be running neck and neck. Playing an upright bass is not as simple as you might think, especially since we didn't have a drummer and I was trying to supplement the beat by slapping the strings on the bass.

Red Kernodle didn't sit in on all of our jam sessions, as his family often wanted to do other things on the weekend. But almost every weekend without fail, John, Luther, and I would get together and have fun working with our instruments and trying to get better. We just kept at it, and after several months, the three of us decided it was time to go looking for the company that was recording Elvis.

I t didn't take long for us to discover that the little brick building near the corner of Union and Marshall was the Sun Records studio, the very place where Elvis Presley was recording.

There are many conflicting stories about how we got to know Sun's owner and chief producer, Sam Phillips. The simple truth is, we just showed up one day—no appointment, no nothing. We just walked in, introduced ourselves to Sam, and said we wanted to make a record. He asked us what we did, and after we told him, he said, "Well, come on down sometime and bring your instruments, and let's hear what you have to offer." This was very encouraging, to say the least.

We had a couple more practice sessions at home and came up with a few gospel songs that we wanted to record. One of them was "I Was There When It Happened and so I Guess I Ought to Know," which John and I were going to sing for one side of the record. We got in touch with Sam and made an appointment for what would essentially be our audition. A few days later, the four of us—

Luther, Red, John, and I—went to the Sun studio for our first recording session.

——⟨⟩——

It was in the middle of the day, and we had already been to work. Red, Luther, and I cleaned up a little bit, changed our clothes, and drove over to Sun Records. John was already there. I brought along the steel guitar and amplifier, which Red and Luther would both play through. As we started tuning our instruments, Red began to get really nervous. The poor guy was shaking all over!

After a few moments, John, Luther, and I were ready to go, but Red kept on trying to tune. He was so nervous and shaking so badly that he couldn't turn the tuning pegs accurately, and kept going a little above, then a little below the correct pitch, back and forth. Finally, he stood up and laid the steel guitar on his chair, turned to me, and said, "Grant, I can't do anything but hold y'all back. I'm going back down to the shop and go back to work."

Red's leaving didn't make a lot of difference to our audition, because he wasn't featured on any of the songs and was just doing some fills on "I Was There," but we were very concerned about him because we'd never seen a man so upset.

After a few minutes, John, Luther, and I were set up and ready to go. The Sun studio was a small place, with a limited number of microphones and a very small mixing board, which was located in an adjoining room behind a glass window. We used just three microphones: John had one for his guitar and sang through another, while the third mike was positioned near Luther. Since I was going to sing with John on the gospel song, Sam moved me over close to him. He then set Luther's amplifier in a chair on one side of the mike and put me on the other side, then pushed me close to the microphone.

"Now, you gotta play loud," Sam told me, "or this electric guitar will override your bass, and we don't want that to happen. So I set you in close and we'll move the guitar back a little bit, and that's the way we'll get our mix here." Then he stepped back and said, "OK, guys, let's see what you got."

Luther did the intro to the song, and we began singing "I Was There When It Happened and so I Guess I Ought to Know." We went all the way through the song, and I thought it turned out really well for our first audition.

Sam came into the studio with a slight smile on his face, as if he was somewhat pleased, but he didn't say much of anything. He readjusted my mike to improve the balance of the sound, then told me, "Marshall, when you play now, slap the hell out of it!" and he laughed. "You mean hit these things harder?" I asked. "Yeah, hit 'em harder, because you're not coming through real good and we'll get a better mix. I know you're sort of in a bind here, but that's really very important." I said, "O-o-o-K." Then he asked us to play the song again.

After that take, Sam came back out into the studio and said, "Guys, let me tell you something. We can't sell gospel music, so we can't record a gospel song. However, there's something about you guys that's very intriguing, that I'm very interested in. You're not like the everyday run-of-the-mill people that come in here. I'd like you to come up with an original song, whatever that may be, and come back in here and see me."

We were pleased with that, even though Sam had just refused to record a gospel song. He said, "I want you guys to go back home and work on it very hard and come up with something original."

After a week or so had gone by, John stopped by the shop one afternoon. "Guys, I've wrote a song," he said. "We need to get together and see what we can do with it. Well, It's not really a song; it's more like a poem. But I think if we get together, we can make something out of it."

The next Saturday night, we all got together and John showed us the poem he'd written, called "Hey Porter." We messed around with it for about an hour, first adding rhythm and finally a melody line. With Luther playing his electric guitar in the rhythm mode, me slapping the bass, and John strumming the old guitar, the song started to come together. We got to where we could play it all the way through, and then we started working on an intro for Luther and a break that he could play. This was going to be a problem, to say the least, because, with all due respect to Luther, at the time he just didn't have the musical skills to do it.

The intro we came up with was pretty simple, as far as intros go. It was just us hitting a note, stretching it out, and then getting right into the song. When it came to the break, Luther never did try to play the melody line, because he knew he couldn't, and that's where the work really started.

We accomplished quite a bit that night. We could at least play the song all the way through, and Luther could do the intro. So we decided to get together the following week and work on it some more, because we were awfully excited about the possibility of being able to cut a record.

We got together about three more times, and Luther began to put together a break for the song. He did it note by note. He'd play a little bit, then start over and add another note, then start over and add another note. . . . This went on literally for hours.

We still couldn't play the song with the breaks all the way through, so we got together again. We were still having fun, but there was more pressure on Luther than anyone else because his playing was going to be featured on the song. The way the record turned out, he was featured all right! In fact, what none of us knew at the time was that Luther was developing a unique style of guitar playing that would be copied by musicians for generations to come.

You know, most times an inability to do something can stop you from achieving whatever goal you may have set. But in our case, our *inability* to play our instruments was suddenly becoming a positive.

After about a week, Luther got to where he could play the breaks all the way through, and we had a complete song. Luther would kick it off, John would sing, Luther would do a break, John would sing another verse and chorus, Luther would do a break, John would sing another verse and chorus, and then we'd end it. I can't tell you just how excited the three of us were the first time we were able play "Hey Porter" all the way through.

We worked on that song over and over. We'd play it all the way through, stop and talk about it a bit, and then do it again. And each time it got a little tighter and a little better. We worked very diligently for about ten days on that one song, then we called Sam Phillips and set up another appointment to record.

When the three of us returned to the Sun studio, the setup was a little different because I wasn't singing on "Hey Porter." Sam put quite a bit of distance between Luther and me, although he used just one microphone for the two of us, placing my bass on one side of it and Luther's amp on the other. "OK, guys," he said, "let's try it now and see what we got."

We were all a bit uptight, and it took us two or three tries before we were able to get completely through the song. Sam didn't seem to mind; he knew that everything was mechanical at this point and that we weren't natural musicians. When he came back into the studio this time, he had a grin on his face. "Guys," he said, "I like that song, and I like the way you do it. I like the sound. I like the style. I like everything. But we gotta have another song." We wanted to put "I Was There . . ." on the other side, but Sam just wouldn't do it, so we worked some more on "Hey Porter" and finally recorded it that day.

After we finished, Sam told us, "OK, it's time for you to go back home and see what else you can come up with. When you get another song, give me a call and come back in."

<hr>

Talk about déjà vu! A week or so later, John stopped by the shop and said, "Guys, I got us another song—at least I got the words—we'll have to make it come to life a little bit." The next Friday night at my house John showed us what he'd written—a poem called "Cry, Cry, Cry."

By then, we'd had enough experience putting a song together that it didn't take us long to whip "Cry, Cry, Cry" into shape. The break Luther did wasn't as complicated as the one on "Hey Porter," and he felt a little more confident playing it. After three or four nights, we pretty much had everything worked out.

We gave Sam a call and told him that we'd come up with another song and were ready to record it. "Come on up," he told us. We went to Sun the very next day, and after we were all set up in the studio, Sam said, "OK, let me hear it. Let's see what we got."

When we finished our first run-through of "Cry, Cry, Cry," he walked into the studio and said, "I like this. I like it a lot. You guys have got something different and it's very unique, and I'm real excited about this thing. Let's do a take on it." I think it was on the third take that we finally recorded the version of "Cry, Cry, Cry" that Sun Records released. It was May 1955, and although we didn't know it yet, we had just taken our first steps toward making musical history.

That wasn't the only musical history made that month, though. On May 24, Vivian gave birth to a beautiful baby girl she and John named Rosanne, who would later make her own mark on the entertainment business.

—————

I don't think any of us really thought seriously about being successful in the music business, but we were extremely excited about having cut a record and were hoping that someday we might hear ourselves on the radio. But we certainly didn't quit our day jobs! John kept working as an appliance salesman for Home Equipment Company, and Luther and I kept working as mechanics for Automobile Sales. Everyone around the dealership was asking us questions. What were we going to do? Were we going to be successful? We couldn't answer those questions, but it sure was an exciting time.

We hadn't given much thought to recording another song with Sun. In fact, we didn't even know when—or if—the label was going to release the first one. Occasionally we'd go back and talk to Sam, but he never indicated what he was going to do and we didn't push him. We didn't know much about the music business, so we really had no idea what to expect.

We didn't even have a name for our group. The three of us eventually decided to call ourselves the Tennessee Three, but one day Sam called us in and said, "Guys, I see nothing wrong with the Tennessee Three, but why don't we change that to Johnny Cash and the Tennessee Two? It would have a better ring, and I think that since John is doing most of the lead singing, we should just call it Johnny Cash and the Tennessee Two. What do you think?" We agreed immediately that Johnny Cash and the Tennessee Two had a good ring to it, so we told Sam, "Let's go with it!"

T he key to success in the music business in the 1950s, much more so than today, was radio airplay. If a disc jockey played a record and listeners called the station wanting to hear it again, that was a sign to the recording company that the artist might have what it takes to become commercially successful. Over the years, many different writers have credited many different disc jockeys with playing the first record by Johnny Cash and the Tennessee Two. Here's how I remember it:

One day in the middle of June 1955, as I was going to work, I was listening to a radio program hosted by Sleepy Eyed John, a local disc jockey whose show ran from 6 to 7 a.m. weekdays. At the time, none of the stations in the area offered full-time country music, with the exception of KWEM across the river in West Memphis, Arkansas. All of the major stations in Memphis only had about an hour of country programming in the morning and sometimes an hour in the afternoon.

That morning, Sleepy Eyed John came on the air and in his distinctive Southern drawl said, "W-e-e-l-l-l, Sam brought me up a new record yesterday, and I want to play it for y'all out there. I'd like you to give me a call and let me know what you think about it. I'm gonna give it a spin right now. Let her go!" And then, lo and behold, he played "Hey Porter"!

I got so nervous, I had to pull my car to the side of the road. Coincidentally, I was almost in sight of the Sun studio, which was just a block and half away, around a bend. As I listened to the song John, Luther, and I had recorded, Sleepy Eyed John came on the air and said, "W-e-l-l-l, I'd like to know what y'all think about that. I think these guys, Johnny Cash and the Tennessee Two, are gonna be around for a long, long, l-o-o-o-n-g time."

My heart was racing and I was shaking so hard all over that I had to sit there for a few minutes to calm my nerves. I cranked up my old car and drove on to work, but as I pulled through the service door I noticed a large group of people inside. Mechanics, salespeople, folks from the parts department, and several others were standing around and talking. As I pulled up, they all began asking, "Did you hear it? Did you hear it?"

I parked my car and raced inside to call John. When he answered, I shouted, "Sleepy Eyed John just played 'Hey Porter'!" John said, "You got to be kidding me!" I said, "No, man, he played it! And not only that, he said, 'I think Johnny Cash and the Tennessee Two are gonna be around for a long time'!" John chuckled, "Boy, oh boy, that's special!"

Many disc jockeys have claimed they were the first to play the initial recording by Johnny Cash and Tennessee Two, but here's what happened: I'm sure Sam Phillips shipped copies of "Hey Porter" to other deejays around the country about the same time he took the record over to Sleepy Eyed John. But I don't think any of those folks had received their copies yet; they were still in the mail.

So, as far as I'm concerned, Sleepy Eyed John was the first to play our initial recording on the radio. Later that day, another disc jockey at the same station played "Cry, Cry, Cry."

That was so exciting, and everybody kept talking about it. It was almost overwhelming. The next morning I was again listening to Sleepy Eyed John on my way to work, and he played "Cry, Cry,

Cry." Later in his show, he played "Hey Porter." So not only were Luther, John, and I on the radio, but we were getting airplay on both sides of the record on its second day out. We heard "Cry, Cry, Cry" several times that day as we spun the radio dial between all the stations in Memphis and the surrounding area.

The three of us kept getting together and rehearsing and learning new songs we'd heard on the radio. We were perfecting what we had, but we had a long way to go.

Soon our record was being played quite heavily all over Memphis, and people were beginning to get interested in us. A woman contacted us through Sun Records and wanted us to perform for a group of ladies at a church on the corner of Cooper and Young. We jumped at the chance.

When the day arrived, we drove to the church and entered the building through a door on the southwest side that led to a sort of basement that contained half a dozen small rooms, each about the size of a bedroom. Behind the third door on the right we heard some people talking, so we knocked and stuck our heads in and told them who we were. "Oh, yeah, we're waiting on you," one of the women said. "Come right on in. We're anxious to hear ya!"

We went in and Luther plugged in his little amplifier. We didn't have a microphone or a public address system or any other equipment. There were about eight or ten women in the room, and by the time we three crowded in there, it was completely full. We played for about twenty minutes, starting out by singing a couple of gospel songs before playing "Hey Porter" and "Cry, Cry, Cry." The ladies were very nice, and we talked to them for a little while and then left. It was just a small church group, that's all it was, but that was the very first public appearance by Johnny Cash and the Tennessee Two.

As time passed, the record got stronger and we started getting reports (or at least Sam started getting reports) from other cities and states where it was getting good airplay. Despite that strong showing, however, there still wasn't a demand for us to go out and play concerts or anything like that.

About that time, a boat club I was a member of staged a benefit for a friend of mine who had been hurt in a boat-racing accident.

The event was being held at a barbecue place on Summer Avenue in Memphis, and the organizers invited us to perform. It was our second public appearance, and in a manner of speaking it was our first paid concert—we got to eat all the free barbecue we wanted! We did about a fifteen-minute set, performing the same songs we had for the church group. The crowd's response was fantastic, and everyone kept applauding, which gave the three of us a really good feeling.

Our third personal appearance was the first one for which we were paid in cash, and the date itself was quite unusual. Located next door to Automobile Sales was a car dealership called Herff Ford, which, of all things in the world, wanted us to perform on the bed of a flatbed truck while it was driven slowly up and down Union Avenue. It was a two-hour gig that paid $50, and we took it.

There were some problems—no microphone, no PA system, no electricity for the amplifier—but it didn't really matter that much. Luther just got another rhythm guitar and I played my old upright bass and John played his old guitar. Since we were moving along the street and no one watching could hear much more than a few bars of what we were playing, we just sang "Cry, Cry, Cry" and "Hey Porter" over and over as the flatbed rolled along. We did that for two hours and collected fifty bucks, the first money we ever made as a band.

Now, $50 divided by three comes out to a little over $16 dollars apiece—but we were being paid to do something that we dearly loved. That $16 was very important to John, though, because he had so little money coming in that anything he made over and above what he got from his regular job at Home Equipment was a big bonus. We were all appreciative of the cash.

Radio station KWEM moved over to the Memphis side of the Mississippi and became KWAM, and Home Equipment Company sponsored a fifteen-minute show on the station. Every Saturday at 4 p.m. we'd go down to their studio and perform a fifteen-minute show, and boy, was that exciting! Everyone kept coming up to us afterward, saying, "Heard you on the radio." "Heard the record." "You must be doing fantastic." And for all practical purposes, we were doing phenomenally well.

We started looking for places to play around Memphis and in Arkansas and Mississippi. We'd go into a town and find out what kind of entertainment facility they had, and then we'd find the operator and tell him, "Hey, we're Johnny Cash and the Tennessee Two and we'd like to do a show here." Sometimes we'd work out a deal to perform, sometimes we wouldn't. Some of those old buildings were so primitive, the owners would let us play there without charge.

I remember one night in Parkin, Arkansas, we did a date in what the locals called a theater. The building had a dirt floor, and seating consisted of two-by-eight boards nailed to stumps. I don't think more than thirty-five people showed up for the show, but at least we played that night and made a few bucks.

Money was very important to us at the time, since none of us had much. While we were on the road, we'd often stop at a truck stop, pool our cash, and hope we had enough to buy a hamburger for everyone. John, in particular, was really struggling, but he had a lot of pride and wouldn't ask to borrow money from anyone to tide him over.

Most times our wives would travel with us, especially when Vivian could find a babysitter for Rosanne, and that was usually Pat Isom. The only time John borrowed money from me was when Vivian was pregnant and wanted to go back to Texas to see her family. That hurt his pride, too, and he didn't come to me himself. His brother Roy came to me and said, "Marshall, would you loan him fifty dollars? I'm going to loan him my car so he can take Vivian home to see her parents." Fifty bucks was about all I had at that time, but I loaned it to John anyway, and he paid me back.

Eventually, when John got his mustering-out pay from the military, he bought a car of his own. We helped him negotiate with the dealership's owner, Alvert Schmidt, who sold John a green four-door Plymouth at cost. Although he had a little money left over, it wasn't a lot, and John was still struggling to make ends meet.

We set up a show one night in a little steel building in Magnolia, Mississippi, about forty-five miles south of Memphis. There was no such thing as advance ticket sales at the time; they were sold only at the door. I remember Magnolia so well because Etta and Vivian set up a little table out front and were selling tickets and making change out of a shoebox. I guess they sold maybe a hundred tickets that night, which meant there were a few more people there than we'd had at our earlier dates. The tickets were just a quarter apiece, but we at least made enough money to stop at a truck stop and buy sandwiches for the trip back home.

While we were traveling around the area playing shows, we were still getting together at our homes, playing music, learning new songs, and trying to perfect our sound. There was no drinking of any kind, but John and Luther both smoked like freight trains. It was a good bunch of people, and we had so much in common that it was a great feeling when we all got together.

During that first year, we learned quite a bit about performing, and we learned a *little* bit about the music business. We continued to practice our instruments, which we were determined to master, one way or another. We still tried to copy other people's styles, but we just couldn't do it. Finally, we decided that instead of trying to play and sing like those guys, we'd just do our own thing and see how that worked out.

"Hey Porter" and "Cry, Cry, Cry" had been out for a few weeks when Sam Phillips called and said, "Guys, you did pretty well with that one; it got to number fourteen in the nation. Let's think about doing another record." Having a song reach number fourteen nationally wasn't bad at all, since Sun was basically a regional label. The company had sent promotional copies of our record only to disc jockeys in the South, Southwest, and portions of the Southeast, and those were about the only areas where you could buy the thing. So, with no more than 25 percent of the nation serviced, having our record go to number fourteen was pretty amazing. The record's popularity was growing, Sam was expanding, and that was all good.

We started talking about cutting another record, but we really didn't have any new material. There was an older song, "Crescent City Blues," that John liked an awful lot. It was sort of a bluesy song, and he always liked that, so we started playing around with it and John finally rewrote it. We worked hard and eventually got the song the way we wanted.

Sam liked what we'd done, but we really didn't quite have the song completed, so we started getting together again on Friday and

Saturday nights to finish it. Luther had problems at first, but he again learned his part note by note. After he got that down, we worked on the song for a month until it sounded the way we wanted, including a phenomenal guitar break by Luther that was almost impossible to duplicate.

At that point, we went back in to Sam, and on July 30, 1955, we cut the original version of "Folsom Prison Blues." We still needed another song for the flip side of the record, though. After about a month or so, John wrote "So Doggone Lonesome," which we worked up and went back into the studio to record. Sun released "Folsom Prison Blues" and "So Doggone Lonesome" in December 1955, and a few more doors started opening for us.

B ob Neal, a disc jockey on WMPS, and Sam Phillips were partnered in a booking agency called Stars Incorporated, located at 1616 Sterick Building in Memphis. Bob had been Elvis Presley's first professional manager, before Elvis signed with Colonel Tom Parker the previous August. It was his job was to book shows for artists on the Sun label, which at the time included Elvis, Carl Perkins, Jerry Lee Lewis, Roy Orbison, Warren Smith, and Johnny Cash and the Tennessee Two.

In January 1956, we joined the *Louisiana Hayride*, a popular radio show that was broadcast from the Municipal Auditorium in Shreveport on Saturday nights. The show's listening area included the Mid-South—Texas, Louisiana, Arkansas, Tennessee—and even parts of New Mexico, and as a result of our appearances on the *Hayride*, we played a lot of shows in those states. We also started doing package tours with country artists from the *Grand Ole Opry* as well, among them, Webb Pierce, Faron Young, Ferlin Husky, Ernest Tubb, and Hank Snow. Elvis also appeared on a lot of those shows, since he was essentially considered a country performer at the time. We worked tons of dates with all those folks.

One night we were coming out of West Texas after opening a show for Elvis that had also included Warren Smith and someone else on the bill. John, Luther, and I often traveled to tour dates in a caravan of vehicles with other acts, and on that particular trip, we pulled into a truck stop in Amarillo with Elvis and his guitarist, Scotty Moore, and bass player, Bill Black. We'd been there many times before, and since it was three o'clock in the morning, there were only about half a dozen people inside. Nobody knew Johnny Cash, and very few people at that time knew Elvis Presley, especially by sight, because he hadn't been on television yet. As far as they were concerned, we were just regular travelers taking a break from the road.

We had breakfast, and when John, Elvis, and I went to pay our bills, the cashier was doing something back in the kitchen. There was a pie display on the counter, a round case that rotated so you could turn it around, open the door, and take out a piece of pie. Inside was a slice of pumpkin pie that didn't have any whipped cream on it. This gave me an idea, since we often took our toiletry articles with us into restaurants so that we could go into the bathroom and freshen up, and I had mine with me.

Nobody was around except Elvis, myself, and John, so I decided I'd take my shaving foam and put a little "whipped cream" on that pumpkin pie. It looked pretty realistic when I got through, and we all had a good laugh. Elvis thought it was one of the funniest things he'd ever seen. The cashier came out directly, and we paid our bill and got ready to leave. "Nope," Elvis said, "y'all go on. I'm not going to leave this place until somebody buys that piece of pie."

The rest of us headed out, and when we saw Elvis the next day in Dallas, where we were scheduled to play that evening, I said, "What about it, Elvis? Did anybody ever buy that pie?" He said, "Would you believe it? I stood there for two hours and nobody bought that piece of pie, and it got to where I had to leave."

⁂

A few months earlier, we'd played a tour date in Nebraska, and Carl Perkins and his band were the night's opening act. We always had a lot of fun when Carl was around. His older brother Jay played gui-tar, his younger brother Clayton played bass, W. S. Holland was the drummer, and Carl played lead guitar. They were a real swinging little group, and if we stayed in town after a show and didn't head on down the road, we'd all get together and have a great time.

On that particular night, the hotel in which we were staying had a large waiting area near the elevator landing on each floor. The area looked a lot like our room, except that it was bigger. We decided to take the furniture out of Clayton's room and set it up in the elevator lobby. Then we called downstairs and ordered room service.

When the elevator doors opened, the bellboy with our dinner stepped halfway out, stopped, and began to look around. Clayton and W. S. were in the bed pretending to be sound asleep. We'd set up all the furniture—even the night light—so the area looked like a real room. The bellboy took all this in, and when he noticed W. S. and Clayton "sleeping," he sort of stepped back into the elevator, pushed the button, and went back downstairs. We knew that he would probably come back with the manager, so we quickly yanked the furniture back up, threw it into Clayton's room, and shut the door.

Sure enough, about fifteen minutes later, the bellboy showed up with the night manager in tow. They got off the elevator, and after looking around, the manager said, "What are you talking about? There's no furniture here." The bellboy stammered, "W-w-well, there was! Th-th-there were two people asleep right here. They had the lights all set up and the bed set up. It was like walking into a room."

When the manager said, "I think you must have walked into one of their rooms," the bellboy shot back, "No sir, I didn't! There was a bedroom set up right here." The manager was shaking his head as they went back downstairs.

As soon as they left, we got the furniture back out and set it up again. Then we called the desk and said, "We ordered some Cokes a while ago, but they never did arrive. Can you send them up?" The clerk said he'd take care of it immediately. Clayton and W. S. climbed back into the bed and again pretended to be asleep. The ele-vator doors opened, and out stepped the same bellboy.

He looked around, and there was the same room he'd seen before, down to the two men sleeping in bed. He just backed into the elevator again and punched the down button, looking very confused as the doors closed. We quickly tossed the furniture back into Clayton's room, and then we all went to bed. We never saw the bellboy or the manager again.

⋅⊷≺≡≻⊶⋅

Over the years, there have been countless stories about how and where Carl Perkins wrote his signature hit "Blue Suede Shoes," and most of them are just plain wrong. I've read articles that claimed Carl wrote the song in a bathroom, that he wrote it on an airplane, or in a restaurant, or somewhere else. None of that's right. Here's what really happened:

We were all on a Sun tour in 1955 and were talking backstage at the auditorium in Bono, Arkansas. John said, "You know, Carl, I had a buddy in the service who liked to dance. While we were in Germany, he'd go to dances everywhere and he was always telling people not to step on his fancy shoes. He'd say, 'Don't step on my blue suede shoes.' I always thought that had kind of a ring to it. You need to write a song about them blue suede shoes." Carl thought that over for a second and said, "Good idea!"

A little bit later, while another act was onstage, Carl went into the dressing room and jotted down some lyrics and a few chords. When it came time for his set, Carl walked out onstage with his great little rockabilly band and performed "Blue Suede Shoes" just exactly the way it sounds on the record. They didn't even rehearse it—they just came out and nailed it. Afterward, Carl called Sam Phillips and told him he had a song he wanted to record, and not too long after that, he went into the studio and laid down tracks that made musical history.

John loved Carl so much, and there was a tremendous bond between them. They respected each other, personally and professionally, and they always had fun pulling practical jokes. The idea that inspired Carl to write "Blue Suede Shoes" was essentially a gift from John to his good friend.

Shortly after its release in early January 1956, "Blue Suede Shoes" began climbing the national charts, despite Sun's limited, regional distribution of the recording. In early March, as the song was really catching on, Carl was on his way to New York to appear on *The Perry Como Show* when the car in which he was riding smashed into a poultry truck near Dover, Delaware. Carl and his brother Jay were seriously injured, and the wreck pretty much derailed Carl's career.

Elvis Presley had recently signed with RCA, and shortly after hearing Carl's version of "Blue Suede Shoes," he "covered" the song, which quickly—in part due to RCA's national distribution—began to take off. While Carl was recuperating in the hospital, he saw Elvis perform the song on national television, on *The Dorsey Brothers Stage Show*. With that performance, "Blue Suede Shoes" soon became a huge hit for Elvis, and Carl saw his moment of fame and glory essentially disappear. He dissolved his band but, after recovering from his injuries, returned to the studio and began putting out a string of records, although none sold as well as "Blue Suede Shoes."

By February 1956, Johnny Cash and the Tennessee Two had two records and four songs out—"Folsom Prison Blues," "So Doggone Lonesome," "Hey Porter," and "Cry, Cry, Cry"—and they were doing really will. We were off and running in a good way.

John's second daughter, Kathy, was born on April 16 that year. He was a very happy camper since he was beginning to make a good living in the music business and everything was looking up. The only problem was that he had to leave Vivian at home alone with two babies while he was touring. That was very tough on Vivian, and every time we'd leave town, whether for a couple of days or a week or more, Etta would bring Vivian and Rosanne and Kathy over to our house where they would all live together while we were on the road.

Sam told us we needed to do another recording session before too long, so we needed to come up with another couple of songs. We started working on that and practiced our instruments constantly, because we could see that our career was outpacing our musical ability.

As far as Luther and I were concerned, it was pretty iffy whether we were going to pursue music as a career or go back to the shop at Automobile Sales. Being mechanics didn't sound all that great because we were really starting to make waves in the music business. But the countless hours of rehearsal and days spent traveling were a great hardship on our families, especially Vivian. Without Etta's help, I really don't know what would have happened, since it was very difficult for Vivian to handle the two babies with John gone all the time.

Etta and I had a son, Randy, and Luther and Bertie had a daughter, Linda, but both were old enough that caring for them when we were on the road wasn't as tough for our wives as it was for Vivian. And as time passed and circumstances changed, that would become a serious problem.

<hr>

Johnny Cash and the Tennessee Two were booked to play a show in Longview, Texas, in the spring of 1956. We came in from Odessa, and instead of checking into a hotel we went straight to the building where we were to perform, arriving early, as we often did. We set up our equipment and began practicing our instruments, just fiddling around, really, especially me with my bass and Luther with his guitar. Luther was starting to gain quite a reputation as a guitarist, and our sound was becoming the talk of the music industry.

John was standing on the side of the stage, so I carried my big ol' bass over and started working on a series of lead runs from one chord to another, from A to D. *Boom, boom, boom, boom—boom, boom, boom, boom.* I'd been practicing the runs for quite some time when John asked what I was doing. "Well, to tell you the truth," I said, "I'm trying to learn to play this big SOB." He said, "No, I'm not talkin' about that. Those little runs, those little lead-ins—do that again." So I played:

Boom, boom, boom, boom—boom, boom (E to A)
Boom, boom, boom, boom (A down to D)—*boom, boom*
Boom, boom, boom, boom (D up to E)—*boom, boom*

Boom, boom, boom, boom (E up to B)—*boom, boom*
Boom, boom, boom, boom (B up to E)—*boom, boom*

"That's what I'm talking about," he said. "Now do those things one more time, and when you get through doing them, come back to the chord of E and keep a rhythm going, and I'm going to come in with you." So I did, and he leaned in close to me and quietly began to sing: *"Hmmmm, I keep a close watch on this heart of mine . . ."* Then he stopped and said, "Now don't forget those little things, because tonight we're going to write a song. We're gonna write our next record."

We played that night's show, which also featured Roy Orbison and Elvis Presley, and then loaded up and headed down the highway. We were in my car, and I was driving while John sat in the back and Luther occupied the passenger seat. John said, "Marshall, do you remember those little runs you were doing?" I told him, "Yeah, I do, but the bass is strapped on top of the car." We all laughed, and then I said, "I'll teach 'em to Luther, and that way he can play 'em on the rhythm guitar."

Luther grabbed the rhythm guitar out of the back, and I began to teach him the runs. "It's just simply going from one chord to another," I told him, "starting in E and going to A, from A down to D, from D back up to E, from E up to B, and then go from B back to E. That's what I was doing; that's what he wants to hear." Luther started working on those runs, and John started singing the first verse of a new song he was writing. Over the next hour or so, with all three of us pitching in everything we could as we motored down that dark Texas highway, "I Walk the Line" began to take shape.

By the time we got to the next town, we had the arrangement worked out and John was signing the whole song. John sang it as a ballad, and it didn't sound a whole lot like the version we would later record. We got back home the next week and called Sam to tell him that we'd written the next song we wanted to cut, and when we went into the studio and played it for him, he liked it a great deal.

After we'd done about three takes on "I Walk the Line" as a v-e-r-y slow ballad, Sam said, "Boys, we got it. That's good. It's a great song; I love it to death! But do me a favor. Just do one more take for me, and let's move the tempo up quite a bit." John said, "Sam, we don't want to make a rock 'n' roll song out of this. I wrote this song for my wife, and I want to keep it as a real slow ballad." Sam said, "I don't have no problem with that, John, I just want to hear it one time for my own personal view. Just move the tempo up to a good flow and record it for me just one time." We did.

———✺———

Luther was still laboring with his guitar, and because of the state of recording technology at the time, that was sometimes a problem. He had a unique style, but it was mainly single-note stuff, and in those days if you missed a note, there was no way to correct it on tape. You just had to do the whole song over. Today, recording engineers can fix anything. If someone hits a flat note or blows a riff, the sound engineer in the booth can digitally fix the track. Everything today is repairable, but in those days, nothing was. You had to get it right the first time, because whatever you heard during playback was what would go on the record.

I would never put down Luther Perkins for struggling with his guitar, because he was trying to improve. It's my belief that Luther's guitar work was just as important to our sound as anything else—including John's voice. The chemistry of all three instruments was what created the boom-chicka-boom sound, and most of that, as I said before, was the result of our *inability* to play them. We were just doing the only thing we could do.

———✺———

A couple of months later, in May, we were in Shreveport playing on the *Louisiana Hayride*. While we were in town we always tuned the car radio to KWKH because we liked to listen to Horace Logan and Frank Page, one of whom always seemed to be on the air. It was about one o'clock in the morning and we were driving home after the show, and Horace, I think, was working the late shift. "Well, well, well," he said, "we got a new record here by Johnny Cash and the Tennessee Two. We'll give it a spin and see what we think about it."

That got our attention, and we perked up our ears as "I Walk the Line" began to blare from the radio—the fast, up-tempo version. We were so upset we had to pull off on the side of the highway to listen to it. We were furious because we thought we had an understanding with Sam that the song was to be released as a slow ballad. That's the way we wanted it, but Sam went ahead and released the up-tempo version instead. We discussed the situation all the way home and decided that we'd pay a visit to Sam the first thing Monday morning.

When we got to the studio, Sam was already in and saw us coming. He met us holding up both of his hands and said, "Wait, guys, wait! I know what you're thinking! But give me two weeks. If it don't do what I think it's going to do, I promise you right here, I'll pull the record and we'll release the slow ballad." We agreed to that—of course, there wasn't anything we could have done about it anyhow, since the record had already been released. We just had to live with it.

Two weeks later, we were back on the *Hayride* and performed "I Walk the Line"—the up-tempo version, just like the record—and it went over with a bang. People just loved it! Afterward, while driving home, we kept twisting the radio dial back and forth, hoping to hear our new song, and in a two-hour stretch we heard "I Walk the Line" thirteen times on thirteen different radio stations.

There's no doubt that "I Walk the Line" was the turning point in our career. As the popularity of the record grew, so did the demand for Johnny Cash and the Tennessee Two. While we were thrilled that success seemed to be coming our way, playing all those shows was beginning to wear on Luther and me, since we were still working at Automobile Sales. We were touring a lot, playing dates throughout the week that were mostly within driving distance of Memphis, but we often wouldn't get home until four or five in the morning. There were a few occasions when we got home about 6 a.m. and only had time to take a quick shower, grab a bite of breakfast, and go right to work.

Etta and I sat down one day and had a long talk about things. I said, "Hon, you know we gotta give up one of these things. I can't go on in the music business and continue to be a mechanic at the same time, because it's really getting to me. I'm not getting any rest. I'm not at my best at either of my jobs. We've got to make a decision on what we're going to do. Do I stay with this music business or give it up and go back to being a mechanic?"

We wrestled with that decision for the better part of a week and finally decided that because so many people were involved—John's family, Luther's family, my family—giving up steady employment to jump into the music business with all six of our feet might not be the best thing to do. Etta and I decided that I would go to Automobile Sales and talk to Mr. Schmidt, the owner, and try to get a leave of absence. I didn't want to give up my job as a mechanic because we still didn't know if we were going to be successful entertainers. What we did know was that we had three records out and that all three were hits. In fact, "I Walk the Line" looked like it was just going to be a monster record for us.

When I explained the situation to Mr. Schmidt, he said, "Grant, I'll tell you what you do. Take a leave of absence, and anytime you want to come back, you don't even have to call me, just come on back. If you want, you can leave your toolbox here and come back at any time you want. Your stall will be here waiting on you, and you can just go back to work." Then he said, "And I think you'll be back. This is a very shaky thing you're getting into, but I can understand why you'd like to try it."

Luther also got a leave of absence, and soon the three of us started hitting the road pretty hard. We learned a lot, and we learned it fast.

We were still alternating cars, taking my car on one tour, Luther's car on the next, and John's little Plymouth on the tour after that. This created a bit of a hardship for our families because neither Luther nor John had a second car. I did have a second car, an old Plymouth that Etta could use whenever we went on tour in my better car. She would go over and pick up Vivian and the girls and ride around, and they'd usually wind up at my house and stay the night or perhaps two or three days, depending on how long we expected to be gone.

At first, we'd swap off the driving chores, but since John wasn't a very good driver and neither Luther nor I felt safe riding with him, we ended up doing almost all of the driving. We'd let

John rest because we knew he was having a tough time keeping up with the grind of being on the road. He was a strong bull of a man, but he needed a lot of rest every day, usually a two- or three-hour nap in the afternoon, to be in top form that evening. If he couldn't take a nap, he'd have an awfully tough time staying awake that night, so whenever possible, we'd try to get to a town early enough that he could grab a nap at the hotel before we played that evening's show.

Our performance schedule was becoming very hectic, and traveling by car was strenuous, to say the least, because in those days there were no interstate highways. In fact, there were only a handful of four-lane divided highways in the entire United States, and a trip of three hundred or four hundred miles made for a very long, very hard drive. Touring was beginning to take a noticeable toll on all three of us.

———————

One night a little later that year, we were in Georgia playing on a show with Faron Young, whose band included a fiddle player by the name of Gordon Terry. John was complaining about how tired he was, that he didn't know if he could perform, when Gordon told him, "Wait, I got something that will fix you right up." He reached into his pocket and pulled out a handful of little pills. I found out later that those whitish, creamy-looking pills were a powerful drug called amphetamines, commonly known as "speed" or "uppers."

John looked at the pills and asked, "What's this?" Gordon said, "Well, take this and you won't be tired for long, and you'll get through the night with no problem whatsoever." John swallowed one of the pills, and sure enough, his fatigue soon disappeared and he made it through the night with no problem.

From that night on, John always had those pills with him. He didn't abuse them at first; they were just a crutch, something he could lean on to get him through the night.

But had I known then what I know now, John never would have taken that first upper. What happened in the years that followed as a result of his amphetamine abuse was unbelievable. Even if I were to exaggerate the story in every way possible, it still wouldn't come close to explaining what it was like to live through.

After we'd been playing on the *Louisiana Hayride* for about six months, we received an invitation to perform on the *Grand Ole Opry* in Nashville. Our first appearance on that legendary radio show was in July 1956, and I remember it well. It was the first time we'd ever been inside the Ryman Auditorium—"the Mother Church of Country Music" that had been the home of the *Opry* since 1943—and we were so excited! We sang "Get Rhythm" during the first segment of the show and did "So Doggone Lonesome" and "I Walk the Line" during the later segment.

"I Walk the Line" was so hot at the time that we got an amazing reception from the audience. People stood and hollered and screamed and shouted until we went back out and played it again. It was very exciting to receive such an incredible response from the audience at our very first *Opry* appearance.

Backstage that night, John met an attractive young woman named June Carter, whose aunt, uncle, and mother had made American musical history as the Carter Family, performing country, gospel, and southeastern mountain tunes. After the trio's breakup, Mother Maybelle Carter and daughters June, Anita, and Helen continued the family tradition and had become quite successful performing as Mother Maybelle and the Carter Sisters.

June was a marvelous entertainer who not only sang and danced but was also a gifted comedienne. She'd had a Top 10 hit in the early 1950s with a novelty version of "Baby It's Cold Outside" that she recorded with country comedy duo Homer & Jethro. She was married at the time to country superstar Carl Smith and the previous year had given birth to a daughter, Rebecca Carlene (later known as Carlene Carter).

John was quite taken by June, and he later told me—and I had no reason not to believe him—that he had told her while backstage at the Ryman, "Someday I'm going to marry you." He said she just looked at him with a grin and said, "Do you think so?" And he replied, "Yeah, someday I'm going to marry you, June."

By January 1957, everything was rolling along smoothly for us. "I Walk the Line" had become an enormous hit record, and demand for Johnny Cash and the Tennessee Two was growing by leaps and bounds. *The Jackie Gleason Show* called and wanted us to make an appearance, and naturally we accepted the invitation.

We had quit alternating cars and were now traveling in a brand-new, 1957 black Cadillac. We jumped in it and drove all the way to New York City to appear on the show.

That was something out of the ordinary for us because we'd never been in a television studio before. The people at the *Gleason* show were very helpful and supportive. They realized that we hadn't been in show business very long and that we had a lot to learn.

The first rehearsal was a nerve-racking experience! We three were frightened to death, but as hard as we tried not to show it, it was pretty obvious to everyone else. A female member of the *Gleason* staff, a Girl Friday type, walked up to John and said, "Let me tell you something. There's no need to be excited, no need to be frightened. What I want you to do is look directly into that camera right there, just the same as if you were looking straight into my face, and you sing 'I Walk the Line' to that camera. I don't want you to worry about the people in the audience or on the stage. You sing to that camera and act like that camera is a human being and you'll be all right, because you can sing to a human being. You might have a little problem singing to a camera, but just picture it as a human being."

We ran through the song again, and that's exactly what John did—and what a difference that lady's coaching made!

In those days, everything on TV was live. We did get a rehearsal in the afternoon before the show, but everything was live that night. We did "I Walk the Line," and it knocked the socks off everyone in the audience as well as everyone else in the building. It was just a tremendous night, to say the least—our very first national TV appearance, January 19, 1957.

We did other television shows in New York during that time. Not long after we appeared on *Jackie Gleason* we did *The George Gobel Show*, and shortly after that we were invited to do *The Ed Sullivan Show*. Being in the same building for most of a day with Ed Sullivan and his staff was a treat in itself. They were tremendously nice people.

Later that year, we became regular members of the *Grand Ole Opry*. We got to join the *Opry* cast with the help of Ernest Tubb and Ferlin Husky, who both went to bat for us. We were always introduced as Johnny Cash and the Tennessee Two, and we'd go onstage together and come off the stage together, just like a vocal trio.

Most times when we played the *Opry*, we'd get together backstage beforehand and discuss which songs we were going to play, but as John's condition worsened, he would often forget the lineup and go out and start to play something else entirely. Joining the *Opry* was a real feather in our cap, but as our touring schedule grew, it got tougher and tougher to make it back to Nashville to fulfill our obligation to the radio show.

We had made our first appearance on *Town Hall Party* in Long Beach, California, in 1956 and spent quite a bit of time there over the years, meeting some extremely important people. Tex Ritter, one of my all-time heroes, was a regular on *Town Hall Party*, and I'll never forget the night in 1957 that I met him. Tex became an instant friend, and we later hired him as the opening act for many of our shows. He was a gentleman and a scholar in every sense of the words.

On the night I met Tex, Columbia Records' director of artists and repertoire, Don Law, saw us perform. Our contract with Sun was set to expire at the end of July 1957, and we'd been talking with several record companies in hopes of signing with one that could provide the national distribution of our recordings that Sun couldn't. Those conversations hadn't gotten very far. We knew that Don had a great roster of artists at Columbia, and we knew that was where we probably needed to be. He'd heard our records and liked John's voice and our sound—in fact, he liked the whole package.

Don watched our shows (we did two that night), and when we met him backstage, he said he wanted us to sign with Columbia. That conversation started a series of discussions that would soon take our career to a much higher level, and in November 1957 we signed with Columbia.

Don also gave use some good advice: "Don't try to change anything when you go in to record. Just hang on to what you've got, and I think you'll be tremendously successful." That sounded good to us.

We'd never gone into a recording session at Sun without knowing exactly what we were going to do. When we got into the studio, there were no changes made. In fact, we were hardly capable of making a change because, even though we were improving, we were still struggling with our instruments. Sam Phillips knew that, too, so he never tried to "produce" us, that is, shape our sound to fit whatever the label execs thought was popular at the time. We always produced ourselves. We played to the extent of our abilities, and that's why it was so important for all three of us to know exactly what we were going to do when we got into the studio: so we wouldn't have to change anything. All Sam would do was turn on the tape machine, adjust the mikes, and say, "OK, boys, let's try it."

As our popularity grew, John began lobbying Sam for a larger share of royalties on his songs, but Sam refused, which was one of the reasons we began shopping around for a new label. We were pretty upfront with Sam, and when John stopped bringing in new songs to record, he realized we would soon be joining other top Sun artists, like Elvis and Jerry Lee Lewis, who had left for greener pastures with other labels.

Because our deal with Sun called for us to do a certain number of songs, Sam had us come in and record several old country music standards by artists such as Ernest Tubb, Hank Williams, and several others. Our last single for Sun was "The Ways of a Woman in Love," which was written by Charlie Rich.

Sam assigned Jack Clement to produce our sessions, and while we were skeptical of the additional background vocals and other instruments he added to our tracks, we did some good work together. The first thing we recorded with Jack was "Big River," which became a big hit, as did "Ballad of a Teenage Queen," both of which would be released in 1958. Things turned out very well from that association, and Jack became a good friend of ours.

John started leaning on amphetamines more and more as time passed. At first, he wouldn't take a big dose, just enough to get through the night, but soon we began to notice a change in his behavior. When he'd take one of those pills, he'd become irritable and arrogant and difficult to get along with, but he performed well onstage—he'd always do a good show if you could get him onstage. Those side effects eventually wore off, and after he'd been taking the pills a few months, he got them pretty well under control and they often made him playful. But sometimes he liked to play a little more than the rest of us wanted to.

Whenever we'd stop for the night while touring, Luther, John, and I would share one room. We'd get a room with two beds, and so we always ended up sleeping with one another. It was a chore to sleep with John. Even before John started using uppers, he was never a sound sleeper and squirmed and moved around a lot. More than a few times, he pushed me off the bed, and I'd have to get up, walk around, and crawl back in on the other side. He was also liable to whup you upside the head or throw his big ol' arm across you. It was a real challenge to sleep with him. When I would say to Luther, "Tonight's your turn," he would roll his eyes and say, "Ugh, not again."

We never made reservations; we'd just pull into town and get a room at the first decent place we saw. As I was getting out of the car to get a room at a hotel in South Carolina one day, John said, "Hey, Marshall, if they don't have a room with three beds, let's splurge tonight and get two different rooms so we can all have a bed apiece." I told him I'd do that, and he hollered, "Try to get a room with a connecting door!" When I came back outside, I said, "OK, guys, I don't have rooms with a connecting door, but I got two rooms side by side, and, John, you can have the one room and Luther and I'll take the other."

It was early afternoon and we were tired since we'd been driving all night, so we decided to lie down and rest a bit. About the time I lay down and got half asleep, I heard the damnedest noise right above my head. I was so scared I literally jumped out of the bed. Then I heard the noise again—a terrific banging that kept going on and on and on. A minute or so later, the blade of an ax crashed through the wall above the headboard of my bed.

What in the world is going on here? I thought as the blade continued to slam through the wall. I hustled into the hallway and headed for John's room next door. When I opened the door, there he stood, ax in hand, cutting a hole between his room and ours! He'd gone down the hall, grabbed a fire ax, and was busily chopping his way through the wall. As John stood there and whacked away at the wall, we couldn't help but laugh, even though we knew we were going to have to pay for the damage. I went back to the room and moved my bed aside, and John proudly announced, "Now we have a room with a connecting door!"

John just wanted to come over and chat with us a bit. Luther and I were bone tired and trying to sleep, but John had been taking uppers and couldn't wind down. He no longer needed to take those afternoon naps he'd once been so fond of. The pills got him through the night, every night, and they often kept him up during the days, too.

With John awake more of the time now, we actually started having more fun and began to pull practical jokes and devilish little pranks for which we were becoming notorious. They were the kind of pranks that, if you tried to do them today, you'd probably get thrown in jail before you could turn around. We pulled a lot of crazy stunts, but I have to admit, many of them were very funny—and they also kept John occupied and out of worse mischief.

———

I can honestly say that if it hadn't been for my ability as a mechanic, we would have had to stop touring. We couldn't afford to get our cars repaired at a garage, and sometimes we couldn't afford the parts. But if I could get my hands on the necessary parts, it didn't matter what was wrong with the vehicle, I was able and willing to do whatever it took to fix it.

Almost every tour, when we'd get back home, there'd be something wrong with the car. We didn't treat our vehicles very well—actually, we drove the hell out of them. John didn't care, and neither did Luther. They just seemed to think that everything somehow would be all right. But if we were home for ten days, I'd spend at least half that time working on one of our cars getting it ready to go back on the road.

At one point we were carrying so much stuff in and on top of the car that we had to do something. Since we couldn't afford to buy a trailer, I went out to a buddy's shop on the north side of Memphis and built us a little solid-steel trailer that we could tow behind the car. It sure helped, because up to that point we'd been carrying John's guitar, Luther's guitar, the amplifiers, and all our luggage inside with us or in the trunk. We tied the bass on top of the car, but if it was raining, we'd have to bring it inside, which really scrunched up the luggage and didn't leave much room for us. But when we got that little trailer, we were able to put everything in there, and life on the road got a lot more comfortable.

———

Over the decades, countless people have asked me how we developed the stage presence that Johnny Cash and the Tennessee Two displayed. John just stood there sort of flat-footed, singing his songs and strumming his guitar. Luther, on John's left, stood in one spot all the time, never moving anything but his eyes and his fingers. I was on John's right, playing the old slap bass, jumping up and down, and chewing my gum. All that made for an odd-looking trio onstage. It was somewhat comical, too.

We didn't sit down and plot out what to do, or try to come up with some flashy choreography. Whatever we did onstage was natural—it just happened. And it happened strictly because, when we first started playing shows, that was how we acted onstage.

Early on, Luther was scared to death and had a lot of pressure on him musically. He wasn't a polished guitar player, and he had a lot of problems with his breaks in songs and even with the kickoffs. Onstage, he was basically frozen in his tracks, like a deer in the headlights, and every once in a while he'd manage to cut his eyes over to John and me and then look back straight ahead.

That became quite an attraction for the audience. Very seldom could you get Luther to grin onstage, but John would try, and when he did get him to crack a smile, the audience would go wild. They'd finally see a crack in Luther's stone face and laugh, but Luther wasn't trying to make them laugh—that's just the way he was.

I think audiences were amused by me because I was so active, jumping up and down. What I was trying to do was set the rhythm of the song. We didn't have a drummer at the time, and when I was playing the slap bass, it was almost like playing bass and drums at the same time, so I was moving around a lot. I wasn't trying to show off or act like a rock 'n' roller—that was just the way I moved when I played the slap bass. It was all natural.

And John. Well, John had a mystique about him—there was no one else like him. His stage presence was just so powerful that the people in the audience couldn't take their eyes off him. When he performed, he held the crowd in the palm of his hand.

The combination of the three of us onstage, each with his own unique "style," really got to a lot of people in a very positive way.

⟨⟨⟨ ♪ ⟩⟩⟩

We arranged to put out a Johnny Cash songbook, which in addition to containing lyrics and sheet music for several of our songs, also had a lot of pictures. It offered a good opportunity for us to make some additional income by selling the songbooks at our shows. I'd order the books from Hill & Raines, store them in my garage, and then we'd take them to our tour dates.

Our car and trailer were crammed so full of stuff that we couldn't carry more than a box or two, because they were so big and heavy. Because of that, I'd usually drop-ship them to places we were going, and if we ran out, I'd call Etta, and she and Randy would send more to me. I'd ship the boxes on a Greyhound bus, so when we'd get into a town, I'd go down to the Greyhound station and pick them up. I think the songbooks cost us twenty-five cents apiece, and we'd sell them for a dollar (the regular retail price was a dollar and a half). The money we got from selling merchandise like those songbooks helped pay our automobile expenses.

I deposited all the income from the songbook sales into an account I opened at the First Tennessee Bank in Memphis. That gave us something we could rely on. There wasn't a lot of money there, but it was enough to buy a tire, some parts, or an oil change. Boy, did that account ever help! In some cases, it made the difference between us being able to go out on the road or having to stay home, because by that time I was almost broke. I had put up a lot of money for our expenses, and it was awfully hard to get it back—most times I did, but sometimes I didn't. During those long periods when Luther and I didn't receive any money at all because John was missing shows, cash was scarce, and the proceeds from the merchandise sales really helped keep us afloat financially.

The account was kept totally separate from everything else we had. John, of course, knew about it and could draw on the account, but I hoped he'd forget it existed. A few years later, however, after he'd blown through all of his cash and needed more to buy pills, he remembered that account.

"Yeah, I still have it, John," I told him when he asked. "It's in the First Tennessee Bank, and that's how I'm paying all the automobile expenses. I buy the gas, the tires, parts—it comes in real handy." He said he had to have the money, but I told him, "I need it, too, for the car. So, you know, we got a problem here." But he insisted, "Well, I gotta have it. I gotta have that money."

There wasn't all that much in the account, maybe twelve hundred dollars at that point. So I said, "OK, buddy, if that's what you want, then I'll send it to you." So I had the bank cut a cashier's check for the whole amount and sent it to him. That left us back at square one as far as having any money for transportation expenses.

⸺◆⸺

John's drug problems were getting worse as we headed to New York in early 1958 to appear on Steve Lawrence and Eydie Gorme's television show. The rehearsal on the first day went fine, and we weren't due back at the studio until the telecast the next night. I think our "call," the time we were supposed to arrive, was 6 p.m. for makeup, with the show to start at 7:00 or 7:30. Luther and I got ready to leave our hotel, but John wasn't around. I thought he was out on the town and would meet us at the studio, but when we arrived, John wasn't there. I started making calls to people who might know where he was, but no one had a clue.

About ten minutes before airtime, John showed up—in the worst shape you could possibly imagine. He hadn't shaved, his clothes were filthy, he hadn't eaten anything, and he was totally out of control. The show's producer saw that John was in no condition to perform, and he got pretty hacked off at him because he'd been looking for John all afternoon. "Get him out of here!" the producer yelled. "And don't ever bring him back."

That was a very embarrassing situation. We gathered up all of our stuff and went back to the hotel and spent the night there. I wouldn't let John go out and stayed right there with him trying to get him calmed down enough so we could leave town the next day. He finally "crashed" and went to bed. I knew from past experience that once he lay down, he'd sleep for fourteen to sixteen hours and then wake up feeling fine. And that's exactly what happened. When he awoke feeling OK after fifteen hours in the sack, we grabbed our bags, headed to La Guardia, and caught a plane for home.

Our booking agent, Bob Neal, had been working quite a bit with a West Coast promoter named Stew Carnell. We worked a lot with Stew, playing mostly club dates up and down the coast, which was the big thing those days in California. Stew and Bob got together and dreamed up this crazy idea that we should move to California and pursue movie careers. That didn't sound so great to Luther and me, but John loved the idea and really wanted to do it. We all sat down with our families and talked about heading west to give things a try, and in late summer 1958 we all packed up and moved to California.

I wouldn't say the move was a life-changing experience, but things were sure different. My son, Randy, was in third grade, so Etta and I had to enroll him in a school he'd never seen and where he knew no one at all. That was very sad, because we had been so protective of him. Etta was doing a fantastic job raising him while I was on the road, and he was just a great kid. One of the saddest times of my life was when I took him to the first day of class at his new school in Los Angeles and watched him go in the front door, knowing that he didn't know a soul there.

We'd had a wonderful home in Memphis, and now we were living in an upstairs apartment until we could find a house to rent. Prices were so high, we sure weren't going to buy anything out there! After several months, we moved into a furnished house on Babcock in North Hollywood, which was a nice enough place. Luther and Bertie got an apartment near where we lived in North Hollywood, and John moved into a magnificent house on Havenhurst that Johnny Carson had once owned.

Bertie hated California. All of her people were back in Memphis, and she just didn't like California. Even though she saw Etta and Vivian a lot, especially when we guys were on the road, she didn't allow herself to get too close to them. She and Luther had two beautiful children, Linda and Claudia, who took up a lot of her time.

As time passed, the move to California proved to be terrible for Luther and me. For instance, one tour we did ended at the Mid-South Coliseum in Memphis, which was about three miles from where Etta and I used to live, but we still had to drive about 1,800 miles to get back to our homes in California—a very tiresome drive since there were no interstates. On another occasion, we ended a tour in Chattanooga, Tennessee, drove some 350 miles to Memphis, and then just kept right on going all the way to North Hollywood.

The travel started taking its toll after a while, particularly since all of our dates seemed to be back east. When we were living in Memphis, we had done a lot of work on the West Coast with Stew Carnell, but now that our popularity was growing, we were touring all over the country and our itinerary was becoming a real problem.

John was leaning pretty heavily on the pills, and he didn't want to crawl into the car anymore and drive very far. Luther and I talked at great length and finally decided that we'd try to get him to fly to the first concert date and then fly back home after the last one, and we'd just handle the car ourselves. John began flying to the opening date and then would travel by car with us to the remainder of the shows, and at the end of the tour, we'd put him on a plane and send him back to California. That worked out well for Luther and me, because John was becoming a little difficult to get along with, and driving a couple of thousand miles across the country with him wasn't a terribly pleasant thought.

———

You never could tell when John was going to be straight or when he wasn't, because he could change at the drop of a hat. But his substance abuse wasn't constant, and sometimes he'd straighten up for quite some time. When he did, it was great, because he'd be the same ol' John we used to know and the three of us would have a great time doing the things we used to do and talking about the early days. We felt like we were sitting on top of the world—or if we weren't on top yet, we were sure climbing up there pretty dog-gone fast!

When John was in good shape, all of us would be in high spirits, and that often meant we'd amuse ourselves by pulling little pranks and such, to break up the grind of being on the road. We were driving through Michigan on a tour when we saw a hatchery and decided that we just had to buy some baby chicks. The tour was about two weeks long, so we got some chicken feed, some water bowls, and a dozen chicks that we figured we could raise while we were on the road. We'd take them into our hotel rooms and put them in a dresser drawer with their food and water while we went to the show. When we'd come back to the hotel, they'd usually be curled up in a corner of the drawer, sound asleep.

Those chicks grew pretty fast, and when the tour was over and it was time to go back home, I asked what we were going to do with them. John said, "I'm gonna take 'em home with me. I got a fenced-in backyard there, and I'm gonna turn 'em loose and raise 'em." I laughed and said, "Well, OK."

We'd all flown back east to start that tour, and when we got to the Detroit airport for the return trip to Los Angeles, the counter agent noticed we had some live poultry with us. "What are you guys going to do with these chickens?" he asked. "Well, we're gonna take them home," John said. "You can't do that," the agent told him. "They're not allowed on the plane unless the captain gives you permission." John looked at the agent and said, "You know, these are expensive chickens. They're imported, and we've had them checked out and vaccinated. They're perfectly healthy, no diseases. And we've gone to a lot of trouble to get them. We like to never got them here from France, and we've got to take them home."

The clerk basically told us that rules were rules, and if we wanted to take the chickens on the plane, we'd have to get the captain's OK. And then he called the pilot and had him come to the ticket counter! John stood there with a straight face and gave the airline captain this big story about how those chickens were a special breed and were very expensive (I think we paid about ten cents apiece for them), and he finally talked him into letting us take them on the plane.

The pilot made it very clear that we would have to keep the chickens contained. "You have to keep them in this box, and you need to sit and hold them in your lap," he said. "And do not let them get away!"

Well, as soon as we reached cruising altitude, John turned those chickens loose in the cabin. There were some women sitting nearby, and when the chickens started crawling around their feet, they must have thought it was a mouse or something. They started screaming and pulling their feet up into their seats. John got down on the floor and started scrambling between seats trying to catch the chickens, while the women kept hollering and screaming.

They raised so much ruckus that the captain came back to see what was going on, and he just got all over us. He threatened to land the plane, but John said, "No, we'll catch 'em; we'll get 'em back in the box. It was just a mistake; I dropped the box and they jumped out." We finally caught them all and got them back into the box and kept them there until we landed in Los Angeles after almost a whole day in the air. And sure enough, John took them home and raised them in his backyard. As it turned out, there were a couple of roosters among those chickens, and they would jump up on John's fence and crow like they were in a barnyard, which disturbed all of his neighbors.

After ten days off, we flew back to Detroit and started another tour.

<hr />

Toward the latter part of 1958, John began to lose interest in recording. Part of that was due to the fact that he couldn't seem to get straight enough to make it into the studio and do anything meaningful. Another reason was that, when he did get reasonably straight, he felt so bad about what he'd done and who he'd hurt while he was high that he lost his self-esteem and quit writing.

The whole time we were at Sun, we'd worked hard and dedicated ourselves to making better music almost twenty-four hours a day. As we drove down the highway to tour dates, we'd talk about recording, we'd talk about songs, we'd work up arrangements—we just couldn't get enough of it. But now John was starting to miss a lot of recording sessions, and at that point in our career, recording was critical to our continued success. We soon found ourselves struggling to come up with hit records.

John started dropping out of sight between tours and not returning home to stay with Vivian and their children. This caused a lot of concern for everyone who knew him, especially Vivian. There were so many times she called and begged me to find John and send him home because she hadn't seen him for so long. John would sometimes work three or four tours without going back to Los Angeles, and it might be a month or sometimes two before he'd return home. I knew he was doing that, but I never knew where he was going instead.

With John gone so much of the time, Vivian was trying to raise their children pretty much by herself. Vivian was a wonderful person, but John's long spells on the road and his growing dependence on drugs was really hurting their relationship.

We once finished a tour in Duluth, Minnesota, and Vivian called and said she wanted John to come home, the babies were crying for him. I told her, "I promise you I'll stay over here until tomorrow, and

I'll put him on a plane. I'll buy his tickets, and I'll put him on a plane, and I'll tell you when he's supposed to arrive there."

There weren't many flights out of Duluth, so I took John to the airport in the middle of the morning, put him on the plane, and stayed there until it took off. I called Vivian from the airport, told her that he was on the plane and would be changing planes in Dallas, and then gave her the flight number and time that he would be getting to Los Angeles. But when Vivian went down to pick him up, he wasn't on the flight.

She called me, and all I could tell her was: "I have no earthly idea where he is. I put his luggage on the plane. I put him on the plane. He had his connecting ticket, and I have no idea where he is. No idea." I started trying to track him down by phone, calling friends and anyone else I could think of who might know where John was.

When he dropped out of sight like that, John would usually go to a certain place or a certain town, and many times he'd go to Mexico, where he could get some of those little pills. At that time, John was just popping pills; he wasn't using cocaine, or crack, or marijuana, or heroin. It was just those stupid pills, those "Speckled Birds," those "Bennies," those "L.A. Turnarounds." At times it seemed like that was all John was living for.

Money meant nothing to him. It didn't make a difference how much cash he had in his luggage, in his pocket, in his briefcase, or whatever, if he found what he wanted, he'd spend it all on those pills.

John and Vivian weren't the only ones having problems—trouble was brewing between Luther and Bertie, and that was very sad. Bertie was a good person, but as I said before, she was a little different. She never liked show business—it made her extremely uncomfortable—and she didn't like Luther being gone for so long so often.

After we'd been living in California for about six months, she gave Luther a choice: either move back to Memphis or she would leave him and go back by herself. That was very tough on Luther because he loved Bertie and his kids. But he also loved show business, and he loved John and me and my family. Bertie left Luther and moved back to Memphis, and Luther moved in with Etta and me at our house in North Hollywood.

Driving all over the country to play tour dates was getting to be just too much for us. Luther and I talked about it on several different occasions and decided that we would move back to Memphis. So in the middle of 1959, we packed up everything and headed back to the Bluff City. Etta and I moved back into our old house on Nakomis, and since Luther was now alone, he got an apartment of his own, although he stayed over at our house an awful lot.

Through it all, Etta was like the Rock of Gibraltar. She never ceased to amaze me. She never complained; she just did what she felt she had to do, and she hung in there and helped everybody. When Luther lived with us, she washed his clothes and took care of everything else for him, just like he was a child. An amazing woman indeed.

It's difficult to explain the difference in John when he was straight and when he wasn't. When he was straight, he couldn't do enough for you; he was just a terrific person. But if he showed up high, or if he got ninety seconds alone behind a closed door to take some pills, his behavior would turn around 180 degrees and the "other John" would appear. And that's when the trouble would start—especially when he began to chase the amphetamines with vodka, which could really make him wild.

There were never any problems between John and me, that is, unless he was blown out of his mind. Then he seemed to resent everything that I did, especially the things I was doing to try to get us from date to date, and in some instances to keep him alive. I think that, on some level, John understood what was going on, because when he straightened up, he would come and say something like, "Marshall, I appreciate [whatever I'd done], and I'm forever in debt to you." But if he showed up the next day and was wiped out, it was a completely different story, and not a particularly pretty one. This created ripples in the organization, and things started to get very serious as he began to miss more and more dates.

The shows John was missing were usually the first date on a tour or maybe a single date somewhere in the schedule. For instance, during the summer of 1959, when Luther and I were living in Memphis and John was still in California, we were booked for two days at the Calgary Stampede in Alberta, Canada. Luther and I drove from Memphis to Calgary, which is a little over 2,200 miles. We arrived about eight o'clock in the morning on the first day of our engagement and were to play two shows, one at two o'clock in the afternoon and another at eight that evening.

When we got to our hotel, John hadn't checked in yet. I started calling around, but nobody knew where he was. A couple of hours later, Stew Carnell called me and said, "He won't come. He will not be there." That really put us in an awkward position. It was almost one o'clock in the afternoon, we were scheduled to go on in an hour, and John was a no-show. I was never one for making excuses, so the only thing for me to do was to go over to the huge arena where they held the rodeo—it probably seated about 12,000 people—and try to explain things to the people in the front office.

Situations like that were very tough, and sometimes the local show promoters or building managers would threaten me, but I just had to tell them what was happening. It wasn't right not to show up for a date. In this particular case, John wasn't there and he wasn't going to be, so what could Luther and I do? After driving halfway across the continent, we had to pack our bags, turn around, and drive all the way back to Memphis, a round-trip of nearly 4,500 miles—and that was just one date.

By the time Luther and I got back home, five days had gone by. That's five days with no income, a lot of expenses, and a lot of wear and tear on our bodies and the car, not to mention the humiliation we'd suffered. It got to the point that it seemed we were just packing our bags and going home without playing the shows for which we'd been booked.

W ith John missing so many shows and us not getting paid
for those dates, we were still struggling financially in the
late fifties. We weren't spending money foolishly, though.
If a young artist today had the success that we had, he'd be running
up and down the road with two or three tour buses and a truck full
of sound and lighting equipment. Not us! We strapped the bass on
top of the car and shoved everything else inside.

We'd often go into buildings where we were scheduled to play,
wondering if there would be microphones or a PA system or even
lights. Unless we'd been there before and could remember it, we
always wondered. A lot of places didn't have show lighting; they just
shined some regular lights on the stage. People in the audience
couldn't see very well, but then again, sometimes we didn't have
very many people in the audience.

We used whatever a building had for our PA system, and a few
times we played places that didn't have a PA. We learned real quick

that we needed to carry a microphone and a cord that we could plug into Luther's amplifier. On more than one occasion, our PA system was the same little amp that Luther was also playing through.

There were a couple of buildings we played that didn't even have a stand that we could put a microphone on. We had to come up with some sort of makeshift rig to hold the mike in front of John so he could sing into it. And if Luther and I were singing harmony with him on some of the gospel songs, we'd just have to do the best we could to crowd around it.

John's behavior was really puzzling. He was a tremendous person, one of the finest people I've ever known in my life. But when he was taking those pills, it was almost as if he had a split personality. He'd be fine one day, when he was straight, but if he popped some of those pills, the next day he'd be just the opposite. It seemed that all of his enemies would become his best friends, and all of his friends would become his worst enemies. That was very difficult to deal with, especially on the road when we were trying to do our best.

As well as I knew John, I was never able to figure out what kept driving him back to drugs. He would get straight and stay that way for a month or two or three, and on a couple of occasions for as long as six months. But then some little thing—and you never knew what it would be—would set him off, and he'd start popping pills again. When he'd straighten up after one of those amphetamine binges, we'd have to be very careful about discussing drugs with him, because he knew he'd dug himself a deep hole and had done some bad things. You pretty much had to treat him with kid gloves and make things as easy for him as possible, because you didn't want that little thing to happen that would push him to start taking drugs again.

When John was right, everybody was right. But when he was wrong, everybody was wrong. Sometimes when John was wiped out, he would go completely blank onstage. There were many nights during the late fifties that I stood beside him onstage when he couldn't even remember the words to "Hey Porter," "Cry, Cry, Cry," or "Folsom Prison Blues." I'd keep a close watch, and if I saw him start to stumble, I'd lean real close and whisper the lyrics to him, and he'd start singing them into the microphone. When John was straight, however, he never missed a word, never missed a beat.

John might be wasted on one tour and create a lot of havoc, but on the next trip out, he'd be straight as an arrow and things would be wonderful. You'd be so proud to see him straight, to see him come back to life and become that dynamic stage presence, that you just had to forgive his shenanigans; you couldn't hold his bad behavior against him. And every time, you'd hope and pray that the "good John" would stay and the "bad John" would never return.

⬦

Unfortunately, the "bad John" kept returning, and as he began missing more dates, concert promoters and fans began to call him Johnny "No Show" Cash. Luther and I were able to salvage some of the dates—and the gate receipts—by entertaining the crowd with a short set of instrumental versions of our songs.

We'd walk out on the stage, and I'd go to the microphone and say, "Ladies and gentlemen, Luther and I are here, but John's not, so we'd like to play instrumentals of some of the songs we've recorded. If you'll just keep your seats, we'll be onstage about twenty or thirty minutes, and then when you leave you can go by the box office and get a refund. We certainly appreciate you coming. We wish he was here, but unfortunately, he's not."

Sometimes we'd play nonstop for fifteen minutes or longer, and the audience would just love it. We never tried to sing any of our songs, because that would have been disastrous and we knew it. However, our unique sound—Johnny Cash's sound—would pacify almost everyone who had turned out for the show. There were very few times that we had to refund any of the ticket money, even if the tour lasted three days, four days, or whatever. I'd collect all of the money, have the local bank cut a cashier's check, and then send the check to our office in an effort to keep the business afloat financially. This kept the wolves away from the door, so to speak, but we needed to do more.

I soon was able to work out a deal with Roger Miller, a dear friend of ours who was a successful songwriter and would soon be nationally known for a string of hit novelty songs. If John didn't show up for a date, and there was enough time, I'd call Roger to come and sit in. This happened many times.

I'd be honest with the people in the audience and tell them, "John's not here; however, Roger Miller was able to get here. So we'll give you fifteen minutes—anybody that wants a refund, you've got fifteen minutes. We thank you for coming. Since you're here, there's no reason to leave . . . you're gonna see a great show. You're gonna have Roger Miller and the Tennessee Two, and we're gonna do our best to entertain you."

Having Roger sit in solved some of our problems, because the people usually would stay, so we didn't lose many ticket sales. We'd give Roger half of the gate, whatever it was, and take the rest for expenses, and when those were paid, I'd send the balance to the bookkeeper.

When John, Luther, and I first got together, we formed a three-way partnership and split everything we made equally. Like nearly everything else at the time, it was a handshake deal, since we were friends and never saw the need to put anything in writing.

That worked for a while, but as John's drug problems worsened and he needed money for pills, our partnership started falling apart right before our eyes, and there was nothing Luther and I could do about it. The band was called Johnny Cash and the Tennessee Two, not Luther Perkins or Marshall Grant and the Tennessee Two, so if John asked a show promoter or a record label executive for something, he tended to have more clout than we did and he usually got what he asked for, especially if it involved money.

In those days, the concert business operated on a cash basis, and we would often settle up at the box office after a show. Since I was handling our travel arrangements and other chores, I was the one designated to get the money from the promoters and ensure that it made its way into our bank account back home.

When we first started touring, I'd usually settle up at the first date for the rest of the tour. As time passed and John started using drugs, however, I discovered that as long as I could keep him from getting his hands on the money, there usually wouldn't be any problems.

That worked for a while, but as his drug habit worsened, he began to make off with our show receipts. I'd get our cut, put the cash in my briefcase, then lock it and hide it in the hotel room for safekeeping. Somewhere close to the end of the tour, if John needed money to buy pills, he'd go to the hotel room or our vehicle or wherever, find my briefcase, break into it (usually destroying it in the process), and then take all the money and disappear. Money had lost all meaning to John, and he would simply blow it all on whatever caught his fancy at the time, and that was usually drugs.

There were several highlights in our personal and professional lives during 1959. One was the birth of John's third daughter, Cindy, on July 29. Another was that we finally got to record our first gospel album, which is what we had wanted to do all along.

John showed tremendous interest in doing that album, which Columbia released as *Hymns by Johnny Cash*, and he worked feverishly to get everything just the way we wanted. It included so many great songs, like "It Was Jesus," "I Saw a Man," "Are All the Children In," "Old Account," "Lead Me Gently Home Father," "Swing Low Sweet Chariot," "Snow In His Hair," "Lead Me Father," "I Called Him," "These Things Shall Pass," and "He'll Be a Friend." I still love listening to it today.

Many people have asked where they can find it and whether it will be re-released. Unfortunately, I don't think it will be, but stranger things have happened and it could surface again. *Hymns by Johnny Cash* wasn't the only gospel album we did, but it was our first and most precious one.

After all those years, getting to do a gospel album was a high point in John's life, and it had a tremendous effect on him. After we recorded it, he sort of turned in a different direction. He was a God-loving, Christian man at heart, and he tried to walk that path—he just had problems doing it sometimes. But he did try.

Later that year, we were asked to perform the theme song for the popular weekly television show *The Rebel*, starring Nick Adams. John made a couple of guest appearances on the show as time went along—and that was a thrill for us. I mean, we had finally done something in Hollywood! Our earlier move to the West Coast in hopes of getting into the movie business hadn't panned out—it was a little premature. But now things were starting to happen. So every week, when *The Rebel* came on, John, Luther, and I would sit back and listen to ourselves perform the theme song for a hit TV show.

John also made guest appearances that year on the Westerns *Shotgun Sledge* and the very popular *Wagon Train*.

On November 19, 1959, we made our first trip overseas, just John, Luther, and I. We flew to Germany and played a ten-day tour of Army bases, sometimes doing two, three, or four shows a night. We'd play two or three little clubs on the same base and finally wind up at the officers' club where we'd play another show. It was pretty doggone tiring, but John was in excellent shape on that trip. I remember it well because there were no problems of any kind and he did great shows.

Since John had been stationed in Germany for a long time while he was in the Air Force, he was able to show us a lot of interesting things that we otherwise would never have been able to see. He even spoke a little German, which was a big help whenever we'd go into a restaurant because John could translate for us and the waiter.

Columbia and Sun were both releasing records by Johnny Cash and the Tennessee Two in 1959. The Sun recordings weren't the greatest things in the world; they were mostly covers of old standards, but they had that distinct, stripped-down, tape-echo sound and got more play on country radio stations around the nation than the Columbia releases did.

There were two things we had going for us early in our career: the Sun sound and our unique style. The sound was one thing, and the style was something else. When we moved to Columbia, we lost that Sun sound with the echo, but the style of Johnny Cash and the Tennessee Two remained the same. It seemed that the fans and the radio disc jockeys and program directors preferred the earlier combination, so for a long while, even though we made some career-building records at Columbia, our Sun recordings were actually getting more airplay.

The good thing was that we were getting twice as much exposure. Columbia would release one of our records, and the radio stations would play it. Then Sun would release one of our records, and they'd play it, too. It got to the point that anytime you turned on a radio and tuned across the dial, you'd hear Johnny Cash and the Tennessee Two several times.

Today, as I look back at what we did, I realize that it really didn't matter whether John had written a particular song—or whether it was Bob Dylan, Peter La Farge, Shel Silverstein, or Harlan Howard—he made it his own. Very few artists had the talent John did, or could sing with the same kind of feeling. He could go from one end of the musical spectrum to the other, from a simple gospel song to an off-the-wall novelty tune that no other performer would attempt for fear of hurting his or her career.

We were releasing so many records by the late 1950s that we were recording a little bit of everything, and that was making John a more complete artist. And I think it's fair to say that he wound up being the most complete artist in the history of country music.

Again, I think it was our *inability* that made the difference, because we were still doing what we *could* do and not what we *would like to do* in most cases. Maybe this helped us along, because we might have gotten off track if we'd had the ability to do the songs we wanted, songs that might have been too polished or didn't fit the mold. But, looking back, whatever we did worked, and the number of our songs that were released in the five years after we signed with Columbia was absolutely mind-boggling. I think that Johnny Cash and the Tennessee Two (and later the Tennessee Three) probably recorded and released more records in that time span than any other artist, not only in the history of country music but in the history of music. Period.

PART TWO
The Sixties

In August 1960, we were booked for a four-day stand at the big Three Rivers Club right outside Syracuse, New York, then we were to go down to Atlantic City to play three days on the Boardwalk. Since the buildings were bigger than those we'd been playing, John thought we might do something a little different. "You know," he said, "for these two places we may need a little more noise. Maybe we should take a drummer along, with just a snare drum and some brushes."

Luther suggested a drummer friend of his who was working with Jerry Lee Lewis at the time, but his style just wasn't compatible with ours. I also had a drummer friend, W. S. Holland, who had been Carl Perkins's drummer before Carl's 1956 highway accident. W. S. and I had a lot in common and had done a lot of things together. Whenever we'd been on the road together, W. S. and I spent a lot of time together and we'd become good friends.

I called W. S. and told him what we wanted him for, and he said, "Gramps [my nickname], I'm going back to work this coming

Monday at S. M. Lawrence Heating and Air Conditioning. I got my old job back, and I told them I'd come back to work Monday morning." I said, "Could you call them and maybe put it off a week, and go up there with us and do this thing?" He said, "Well, I'll check it out." He called me back a little later and said, "Yep, they said whenever I get back to just come on in, so I'll go with you."

On August 5 we took W. S. up to the Three Rivers Club, and he fell right in with us. He duplicated that slap I was doing on the bass, and it just worked real well. John was in excellent shape, and we had a lot of fun at the shows. We had a blast at the shows on the Boardwalk at Atlantic City, too. The crowds were very enthusiastic, John was in good shape, and everything rolled along in high gear.

W. S. worked out perfectly and added a lot. Luther and I didn't have to play so hard to try to be heard. We had some rhythmic support, and even if it was just a snare drum, it made a big difference.

In the car on the way back home, we hired W. S. full time. At first, John would introduce us onstage as the "Tennessee Two Plus One," but slowly, after about a year, our name evolved into the Tennessee Three, and Luther and I had absolutely no problem with that. After all, in the very beginning, John, Luther, and I were going to call ourselves the Tennessee Three, so we thought it was really cool that things had worked out to where we were now Johnny Cash and the Tennessee Three.

⤙⬥⤚

That same year, Luther and I signed a recording contract with Columbia Records for instrumentals. We cut a couple of albums, and had a couple of singles released off of those.

One of them had to do with singer Johnny Horton, who was a really good friend of all of us; we toured a lot together. He and John were the closest of friends, and Horton would talk a lot to John about his drug problem. Of course, John would never listen; he wouldn't listen to anybody about his drug problem. I don't think he was addicted, but John sure treasured those drugs—they were something he could use to erase all the memories of the bad things that may or may not have happened.

After Johnny Horton's death in November 1960, Luther and I recorded a song called "Jerry and Nina's Melody." Jerry and Nina were Johnny's two young children, and it just seemed fitting that we write an instrumental and name it after them. It was released in January 1961.

—————

We played a lot of dates in Canada in the late 1950s and early sixties. In fact, we played just about everywhere that a vehicle could go. We worked for a promoter out of London, Ontario, named Saul Holiff, who was a good promoter and did a great job for us. He was very thorough and easy to get along with, and after John, Luther, and I talked about it for some time, we approached him to see if he would be interested in handling our bookings.

In 1961, at the end of another Canadian tour we had worked for Saul, he accepted the position as booking agent for Johnny Cash and the Tennessee Three, which took us to another level.

—————

We made it a point to have a lot of fun on the road, hoping that would encourage John to stay straight, enjoy life, and move forward with our career. We always tried to keep him occupied with something, to keep him from leaving the hotel, because he had a knack for disappearing and getting into trouble. If he'd been straight for a few days, you could depend on him coming right back if he left the hotel, but other times you could tell that if he got away from you, things were going to get out of control.

We did a lot of silly things to keep John occupied, but looking back, I've become rather proud of some of the pranks we pulled. We never harmed anyone; we just killed a lot of time making mischief. We didn't dare try to pull any sort of shenanigans when John was high, because he could get very destructive. And there's a difference between being destructive and pulling the harmless pranks we did to have fun.

For instance, while playing a four-day stand at a club in Minneapolis, we decided that we didn't like the color of our hotel room, even though it was a nice room in a nice hotel. We went out and bought three paintbrushes and some orange, green, red, and black paint, and went back to the hotel, where we took everything off the walls and painted our room. We laughed a lot while doing it, trying to imagine the looks on the faces of the hotel staff when they saw our handiwork.

We called for room service, as we did a lot of times when we had pulled a prank in our room. The room service guy showed up and set the trays down, then started looking at the room. He whirled round and round looking at the room and must have stood there for four or five minutes, he was so puzzled. Well, after he left, it wasn't more than fifteen minutes before he was back with some of the housekeeping staff and a supervisor. We just acted as if the room had looked that way when we checked in.

Probably five or six different people came to look at the room before someone pretty high up in the hotel's management showed up. We told him, "Hey, man, we really like the room. We think it's great. We're colorful people, and we like the color of this room. Don't worry about it—it's just fine." When the management guy offered to put us in another room while ours was repainted, we told him, "No, we love this room. We appreciate you getting it all colorful for us."

Another time, we were in Des Moines, Iowa, and we decided to take several rolls of toilet paper and turn Luther into a mummy. We wrapped him in roll after roll until all you could see were his eyes and nose. We called downstairs and ordered some Cokes, and when the bellman brought them up to the room, there sat Luther right in front of the door looking like a mummy! He was squirming around, acting like he was trying to get away, and John and I were hollering at him.

When it looked like Luther was going to lunge out of the chair, John picked up a muzzle-loading pistol we used in a skit onstage, filled it with black powder and paper wadding (no bullet), and shot it at Luther. The smoke boiled out of the barrel, and the sound was almost deafening. The bellman's eyes bugged out, and we just howled when he threw down the tray and cut out for the elevator!

We sat and laughed about that for a couple of hours, and it killed some time and kept John straight and in the mood to do a good show that night. And if we could keep him occupied with those little pranks, that's exactly what he would do.

John was always a phenomenal entertainer. While most country music artists at the time would just go out onstage and sing their hit songs, John believed in giving the audience something more. He did things onstage that no one else had ever done—and probably never will.

We developed a comedy routine and did imitations of several artists, like Red Foley and Kitty Wells, but the highlight was John's impersonation of Elvis Presley. He'd shake and moan, his hair would fall down in his face, and then he'd turn to me and ask to borrow my comb. I'd pull my comb out of my back pocket, hand it to him, and he'd get his hair all straightened up, then hand the comb back to me.

I'd start looking at that comb and would act like there was a cootie on it, then throw it to the floor. At that point, I'd pull the old muzzle-loading pistol out from under my coat, or wherever I'd kept it hidden throughout the show, and shoot the comb. Man, was that gun loud! And smoke would just billow across the stage. It would really startle people at first—they didn't know what to think. But then John would stand there and look at them without saying a word, and pretty soon the applause would start and everybody would start laughing and hollering. We got quite a few standing ovations with that routine. John loved to do things like that, things that were different. He liked to do more than just stand at the mike and sing his songs.

John was very unpredictable onstage, so each show we did was different; they were never cut and dried. In fact, I can't remember us ever doing exactly the same show every night on a tour. We had so much chemistry between us that many times, without John even saying a word, Luther would just kick off a song—and it would be exactly the song John was thinking about. That was the kind of chemistry the three of us had initially, and that the four of us shared after W. S. Holland joined the group.

Because each show was different, we never got bored and actually looked forward to going onstage. Afterward, we'd all go back to the dressing room and have a good laugh talking about something we'd done, or some changes that had or hadn't worked, or something strange that had happened.

We kept things fresh, which was important, because if you go out and do the same show night after night, week after week, month after month, you'll eventually get bored and the people will notice. We never knew what we were going to do onstage other than the first song. From there on, it was every man for himself.

We didn't end our shows with the same song, either, like a lot of artists do. John would walk off the stage when he felt it was right to do so. He'd always come back for an encore, and we never knew what he was going to do. Sometimes, before John could get back to the microphone, Luther would just kick off something that was appropriate, and we'd all take it from there.

Our shows just happened. We didn't choreograph our skits and routines; we never rehearsed them, never talked about them. We just did what felt natural at the time. And we did it for years: Luther standing there just moving his eyes and fingers; John growling out songs with that big, deep voice and playing fantastic rhythm guitar; and me jumping up and down, slapping the bass, and chewing my gum. When I look at the films taken of us forty years ago and listen to Luther, I begin to realize just how great we were.

There can never be enough credit given to Luther Perkins. He was a plain and simple man with a heart of gold. He didn't say much generally, and he never said anything onstage—he was one of a kind, and his playing style was unique. By the early 1960s, everyone was trying to copy Luther—but nobody could. It was like trying to copy Chet Atkins or Merle Travis. Luther knew who he was and what he was born to do, and he did it well. His guitar playing was so powerful that he shocked people. They'd watch Luther standing there so still, barely moving, yet pulling those powerful sounds from his guitar—it was an unbelievable sight.

John's problems were growing at home. With the birth of their fourth daughter, Tara, on August 24, 1961, Vivian found herself trying to raise four children almost completely on her own. She was a great mother, doing the best she could, and still John occasionally wouldn't go home between tours. It was really tough on her when he just wouldn't show up.

Vivian continued to call me at times, and I'd put John on a plane for California wherever a tour ended. But he very seldom arrived when I told her he would. If I could put him on a nonstop flight, he'd make it to Los Angeles, but if he had to change planes anywhere, you could bet that he wasn't going to get home on schedule. He'd get off the plane at a stopover and go do his thing for days at a time. Nobody really knew where he was, and he never called anyone.

Whenever John did get home, Reverend Floyd Gressett, his pastor and a magnificent man, would do every thing he could to help him. He spent a lot of time with John, and sometimes they'd go into the mountains together or go hunting or do whatever John wanted to do. Reverend Gressett really tried to help, but his efforts didn't do much good. They would sit down and talk, and sometimes John would attend services at Reverend Gressett's church. But after church, you never knew if he was going to go home or go back to the mountains or wherever. I think John was a terribly unhappy man at that point in his life.

Even as John's drug abuse was getting worse, there were times when everyone was happy. I remember very well a New Year's Eve 1961 date we played in Camden, New Jersey. It was a package show that consisted of Lester Flatt and Earl Scruggs, Marty Robbins, June Carter, and Johnny Cash and the Tennessee Two. It was about 10 p.m., and Marty was onstage. Everyone shared one big dressing room, a huge thing that looked like something a basketball team might use.

There were urinals on the wall in the men's restroom, but they seemed to be stopped up and didn't flush very well. We'd been shooting firecrackers and had bought a bunch of M-80s, which are powerful firecrackers that will explode underwater. We were putting two and sometimes three of them together, and they made a pretty good little blast! Somebody suggested that we ought to flush a firecracker down one of the urinals to help open it up a little. I said, "I can do that!"

So, I lit an M-80, flushed it down the urinal, and waited a few seconds. Suddenly, without a sound, the urinal just crumbled off the wall and fell to the floor! Everybody started laughing—at that point, it was awfully funny—but then water started shooting out of the pipe into the dressing room. About that time, Marty Robbins came off stage, and when he saw what was going on, I think he pretty much knew who had done it, and hollered, "Where's that damn Grant?"

I ran upstairs to a public dressing room that was on the floor directly above ours, and when I walked in, there was sewage all over the room, and people were standing there brushing off their wet clothes, wondering what in the world had happened. No one had a clue!

We called the police, mainly to get ahead of everything because we knew somebody would call them. When they arrived, fifteen or twenty minutes later, we told them that someone had been in our dressing room and had broken the urinal on the wall and done a lot of damage, ruining our clothes and other belongings.

When they asked if anyone had seen who did it, John said, "Yeah, I saw him. He looked like a logger—a great big guy and he had an ax on his shoulder." Warming to the tale, John continued: "He come in here with that ax and started swinging, busted this urinal up—the water was running all over the floor and every-thing—and then he leaves." When the police asked which way the "logger" had gone, John pointed to an emergency exit and said, "He went out that door right there. Last time I saw him, he was headed for that little patch of woods over there." The last time we saw the police, they were headed for the woods John had pointed to, search-ing for that logger.

Everyone thought it was terrifically funny, and we laughed about it for the rest of the night. It was probably something we shouldn't have done, but we did.

⁓◁▥▥◊▥▥▷⁓

A few months later, in March, we traveled to Korea to entertain the troops. While we were there, a sergeant knocked on my door at about two o'clock in the morning and said, "Hey, I need you to come over here. We got a little problem." As it turned out, John and some sol-dier had gotten into a tank, started it up, and were driving it all over the base, poking the barrel of the main gun through windows. They even rolled over to the officers' quarters, stuck that gun through a window into a room with bunk beds, and shook it back and forth.

John could have gotten into serious trouble for "borrowing" that tank and tearing things up—what he called having fun—but the military didn't bring any charges. We all got together and talked things out, and John promised that he wouldn't get into any more mischief. We stayed on the base for a week or so, flying in and out to do shows all over Korea. After a while, the schedule got so tough that John didn't have the stamina to pull any more pranks, so I didn't worry about him so much. That was just vintage J. R.

⁓◁▥▥◊▥▥▷⁓

In May that year, we played to a completely sold-out Carnegie Hall in New York City, which generated a lot of publicity for us. John gave a marvelous performance, which boosted our popularity greatly, since there were people from all walks of life at the show, including a lot of music industry people from New York. The show was just so well received, and everyone got to see the real Johnny Cash onstage that night. His performance was probably the best he'd ever done up to that point.

At some point in the early sixties, John started becoming known as the "Man in Black." In later years, everyone thought that was because he'd always worn black at our shows, particularly during our first appearance on the *Grand Ole Opry*, when his black outfit really stood out from the other entertainers' gaudy costumes. When he appeared on the *Larry King Live* cable-television show in the 1990s, John told Larry just that. But he just wasn't thinking straight when he said that, because early in our career, we dressed any way we wanted onstage. We didn't dress alike, didn't even try to, but things just sort of slowly drifted around to where we wore mostly black onstage, especially John. Luther and I would often wear whatever we had, but never dungarees or polo shirts or anything that didn't fit our image.

To be honest, the Man in Black mystique came about by accident. We had decided to have Nudie Cohn—the well-known rodeo tailor in Hollywood who was responsible for all those rhinestone outfits worn by the western and country & western stars—make some stage clothes for us. We were in California, and we had Nudie come to our hotel and measure us. I had never worn black before, although John occasionally had. After he'd taken our measurements, Nudie asked, "What color are we going to make these clothes?" I think Luther and I had each gotten suits in burgundy, blue, and black, but John said, "Just make all of mine black." And that's when he started wearing black onstage at every show.

The Man in Black nickname didn't catch on right away, although it did sort of fit the songs we were doing, such as "Dark as a Dungeon" and "Folsom Prison Blues." It just sort of grew up over time as more people saw him perform. And, like our shows, nothing about it was planned, nothing was thought out—John's powerful onstage image just slowly evolved from a spontaneous remark he once made: "Just make all of mine black."

———

Rumors also began to circulate that John had been in prison, which was untrue. He never spent a day in prison, although he did go to jail a couple of times over the years. Maybe the rumors started because we'd been playing shows at prisons since the mid-1950s. As I recall, the very first penitentiary we ever played was the Texas State Prison in Huntsville, in 1956, which brought us in as a special attraction for their big annual rodeo. We played in the rodeo arena, which was sort of like an outdoor ballpark. The inmates sat on bleachers, and there were guards in towers, guards everywhere, watching everything that was going on.

Suddenly, just as we were about to take the stage, a downpour hit. The prison authorities threw some plywood out in the mud for us to stand on while we played, a piece for me, one for Luther, and one for John. We went out onstage, and when Luther—the only one of us playing an electric instrument at the time—plugged in his amplifier and touched his guitar strings, he got shocked big time! We worked on that a little while and finally got the amp set up where it wouldn't electrocute him, and then we started playing.

I don't know how long we stood in the rain playing "Folsom Prison Blues," which the prisoners requested over and over again. There were reports that John played that show by himself, but that's not true. We all played the show, and we somehow made it through by the skin of our teeth.

Eventually we played prisons all over the country, including San Quentin and Folsom in California, the Tennessee State Prison in Nashville, and many others.

John really had a soft spot in his heart for people who were down and out. He was always for the underdog—homeless people, drunks, the sick and elderly, the Indians. John always felt very sorry for the Indians because of how they were treated as America expanded west. That led us to record the album *Bitter Tears* in the mid-sixties, which featured "The Ballad of Ira Hayes," about the American Indian soldier who helped raise the flag at Iwo Jima.

But no matter who or from what walk of life a person was, if he was the underdog, John was for helping him out. Many times I saw John open his heart to someone who was having a rough time and give him money or anything he could to help out. He just really felt sorry for the person who couldn't make a go of it.

There were many times on tours when we'd stop at a grocery store to buy food and supplies, and John would see an elderly man or woman or someone who seemed to be struggling. He'd say, "Marshall, see that woman right down there? Would you make sure her groceries are paid for? I'd like to pay for her groceries." When we'd get to the checkout line, he and Luther would go on out, and I'd wait until the cashier had rung up the woman's total and say, "I'd like to take care of this lady's groceries, please." John didn't want his name mentioned. He didn't want me to say, "Johnny Cash wants to pay for this lady's groceries."

He started doing those little acts of kindness back in the fifties, and as far as I know, he never stopped. He always had a big heart for people who had been struck by misfortune, and he tried to take care of them the best way he knew how.

John also had a soft spot for our fans, many of whom we'd get to know as friends over the years. I remember we were playing a date in Cheyenne, Wyoming, and there were several fans who had followed us out there. We'd seen them at our shows before and knew they were from somewhere in the Midwest, maybe Ohio. John and I were sitting in a restaurant one day, and he asked me about some of the folks who were following us to our shows. After I told him all I knew about them, he said, "It costs them a lot of money to come out here and do this, doesn't it?" I said, "Well, yeah, their transportation, their food, lodging—it takes a lot of money. They're really devoted fans."

He thought for a second and said, "I tell you what I want you to do. First of all, I want you to go get their check and pay for their food today. Then, make arrangements with the hotel, and we'll pay for their rooms. And if you would, go to the people [there were six or eight of them] and tell them that whenever they come to the restaurant [we were in town for a week] to just sign their check. And if you would, Marshall, make sure this is all taken care of." I told him I'd be glad to handle things. John sure made those fans feel good! That was just ol' J. R. He'd give you the shirt off his back, and if he was straight, everything else he had in his possession.

Many of the pranks we pulled to keep John entertained and in a good mood involved a brass starter cannon that I acquired somewhere along the line when I used to race boats. It fired blank 10-gauge shotgun shells, and man, was that sucker ever LOUD! John loved that cannon, and he wanted me to bring it on every tour.

Just before each night's show, I would always give a one-minute countdown to make sure all of the performers, tech people, and building staff were ready to go on time. I'd be offstage and would look at my watch and say, "Four, three, two, ONE MINUTE TO SHOW TIME!" And at that point, if John was in the building, he'd shoot that cannon! Man, smoke would boil across the stage and out into the seats, and people in the audience would start hollering. We all got a big kick out of that, but the commotion usually meant we weren't able to start the show on time—it took ten minutes or so to get everybody calmed down and for me to go out and explain what had happened.

I remember we were heading for a date somewhere in Minnesota, and John had us stop at a farm on the outskirts of town and buy some horse manure and hay. He was just bubbling over as he explained what he was planning to do.

Gordon Terry did a song called "Johnson's Old Grey Mule" during his opening set, and he'd bray exactly like a mule, which made everyone laugh. That night after the show, we went back to the hotel, and about 2 a.m. John got the horse manure and hay and spread them up and down the hallway outside our room. Then Gordon began braying like a mule—and he just kept going and going, hoping that some of the other guests would stick their heads out and see the barnyard scene John had created in the hall. No one did, which deprived John of his fun, so he told Gordon, "Do it one more time."

When Gordon let loose with a big hee-haw, *BAM!* John fired that starter cannon. Smoke rolled down the hallway, and all the doors on both sides began opening as people—some in pajamas, some in their underwear, and some half-dressed—leaned out to see what in the world was going on. John played it to the hilt. "I saw him!" he yelled as he headed toward the elevator. "He was a great big tall guy, about six foot six! Musta weighed two hundred pounds, and he had the biggest gun on his shoulder you've ever seen! He was headed downstairs, I don't know where. I saw him! He shot a mule, and he was trying to get it on the elevator and go down to the lobby!"

About fifteen minutes later, after things had calmed down, housekeeping came up and started cleaning up the hay and manure. And just as if we were good Samaritans, we all pitched in and helped them.

—————

John just loved that cannon, and he'd often sit in the backseat of the car and mess with it. We always had a box or two of 10-gauge shotgun shells with us, and one day he put one in the cannon and accidentally set it off. The noise was deafening, and there was so much smoke inside the car that we had to stop on the side of the road until it cleared. None of us could hear anything except a ringing in our ears. Luther said, "You know, my head is ringing so bad, I don't think we'll ever be in tune again onstage!" And for a while there we weren't, because that high-pitched ringing lasted for days.

The starter cannon had wheels and looked just like a miniature Civil War cannon. It had a long string attached to it, and when we'd check into a hotel, John would pull the cannon along behind him, right through the lobby, onto the elevator, and down the hallway right to our rooms. The people in the hotel—guests and management alike—had no idea what was in store for them later, because John just loved to go out into the hall in the wee hours of the morning and shoot that sucker.

When he was in that fun-loving, mischievous mood, we did everything and anything we could to keep him that way. That's why we started pulling all of those little pranks that we sort of became known for throughout the fifties and early sixties. They were just light-hearted things we did to keep John happy, to keep him laughing, and to keep him looking forward to the next day and not looking forward to getting that next shipment of pills or whatever else he could get his hands on.

———

Sometime during the early sixties, Vivian bought John a camper, a pickup truck with a metal enclosure over the bed, that he just loved. We took it on tour sometimes and had a lot of fun in it, often taking our shotguns and going out into the desert and shooting cactus and things like that. John would cook in the camper while we were motoring down the highway.

I remember one morning John and I were in the back and he was cooking breakfast for Luther, who was in front driving. The camper had a sliding window, and we could pass stuff through it to whoever was in the cab. John had fried some bacon, scrambled a couple of eggs, and made toast, but when he set the plate on the edge of the table, Luther went around a curve and the plate landed upside down on the floor.

"Oh Lord, John, now we gotta cook Luther's breakfast again." I said. But John got the spatula and scooped up the food, put it all back on the plate, and blew on it a couple of times. "Ah, he'll never know," he said to me before he passed the plate through the window and said, "Here, Luther, here's your breakfast." You know, Luther ate every bite as he drove down the road, and he never knew his food had been upside down on the floor.

That camper made for a lot of good memories, but there were some not so good ones, too. One day the camper's brakes overheated and started a fire in California's Los Padres National Forest. The federal government sued John and was awarded $125,000 in damages, but he finally was able to settle for $82,000. Shortly after the fire, he was driving through downtown Ventura, California, in the middle of the night and either fell asleep or lost control and ran the camper into a telephone pole. And that was the end of John's camper.

⚬⚬⚬

John faced death several times as a result of mishaps with his automobiles, campers, and trucks. One day he refilled the propane tank for his camper and tossed it into the trunk of his car and headed home. As he was driving through Beverly Hills, the tank somehow exploded and set the car on fire. John was driving probably forty or fifty miles per hour, and the car became engulfed in flames. He jumped out, and the car continued down the street, jumped a curb, and smashed into a tree in somebody's yard, where it continued to burn. The fire department was called and put out the blaze, and a wrecker hauled the burned-out vehicle to John's place.

Shortly after that, Luther and I were in California, and John asked me to take the car back to Memphis to see if I could get it repaired. We bought a tow bar and hauled the car all the way back to Memphis, but it was beyond repair; I couldn't do anything with it. A lady came by the shop one day and for some unknown reason wanted to buy it, so we sold it to her.

Another time, John and Curly Lewis, the contractor who built his house in Casitas Springs, were up in the mountains running around doing things they shouldn't have been doing, and they let John's truck get away from them. As the out-of-control vehicle headed for a ravine that must have been five hundred feet deep, they both jumped out just before the truck plunged over the edge. John later took us up there to show us where the accident had occurred. We stood at the edge of the drop-off and looked into the ravine, and way down at the bottom we could just barely see the remains of the truck. It was so far down the slope that I don't think anybody had ever gone down to check on it; they'd just left it there.

Whenever we were in the area, we'd make it a point to play the *Big D Jamboree* in Dallas, a weekly radio program that we first worked in 1955 and played four or five times a year. There were a lot of local acts on the show, and each week they'd bring in a couple of name artists. The Sportatorium, the building where the *Jamboree* was held, had originally been built for boxing and wrestling events and featured "in-the-round" seating, with the stage in the center surrounded by rows of seats on all sides. The shows were always on Saturday night and were very popular.

One night in 1962 when we came in, June Carter was onstage, so I stood and watched her for a couple of minutes. She was doing her comedy routine and had a pair of staff musicians backing her. She sang and danced a little, and I thought she was really good. At that point, I had never officially met her, although John had met her when we played the *Grand Ole Opry* for the first time a couple of years earlier.

There were two shows that evening, and as I was sitting alone in the dressing room between performances, June stuck her head in the door and said, "Hey, big buddy, somebody told me I needed to talk to you about a little problem I've got." I introduced myself and said, "Well, lady, what's your problem?" She said, "Well, I'm in Oklahoma City tomorrow afternoon with y'all, and I need a ride. I ain't got no ride up there, and I was wondering if I could ride up with you."

"Well, June, I'm not sure," I told her. By that time, we'd added a couple of regulars to our road show—Johnny Western, who was a great emcee, and fiddle player Gordon Terry, who opened the show. Since they were traveling with John, W. S., Luther, and myself, things were pretty crowded already. I said, "Lady, our car is crammed so full, I don't think we can get another person in it." She said, "Well, I'll sit in somebody's lap." I told her, "Let me check with my cohorts here and see what they say. If it's all right with them, then we'll see if we can fit you in."

I walked across the hall to where John was talking with some other people. I called him over and said, "John, June Carter is on the show with us in Oklahoma City tomorrow, and she wants to know if she can ride up with us. I told her we were completely full, and she said she'd sit in somebody's lap." He very abruptly said, "She can sit in my lap." I sort of laughed and asked if he was kidding.

"No," he said, "if she wants to go—we're full, I understand that—but let her sit in my lap." When I went back across the hall and told June that John had agreed to the special seating arrangement, she grinned and said, "Well, if I gotta sit in somebody's lap, it may as well be his!"

We finished our stand in Dallas and headed for Oklahoma City the next morning. Unfortunately, we ran into sleet and snow, and the farther north we drove, the worse it got. When we finally pulled into Oklahoma City, everything was a solid sheet of ice. The show was canceled, and since it was the last date of the tour, we spent the night there and headed for home the next morning.

———

Later that year, June Carter became a regular member of our troupe and probably went with us on 95 percent of our dates. Occasionally, Mother Maybelle Carter and June's sisters, Helen and Anita, would come along, and in 1967 they would begin touring full time with the Johnny Cash Show as the Carter Family.

June had divorced Carl Smith in 1957 and gone on tour with Elvis before marrying Edwin "Rip" Nix, a police officer. The following year, she gave birth to a daughter, Rozanna Lee (Rosie), then went to New York to study at The Actors Studio, where her classmates included Joel Grey, Jack Lord, and Julie Newmar. She appeared in the movie *Country Music Holiday* and also on several TV Westerns and soap operas before leaving the Big Apple and joining the Johnny Cash road show.

The first time I met Mother Maybelle was one of the highlights of my life. As I was growing up back in North Carolina, our whole family would gather around the radio (whenever it would play) and listen to the Carter Family. We heard the Carters do live performances in Knoxville, Tennessee, and on the *Grand Ole Opry*, and I never thought, even in my wildest dreams, that I would ever have the chance to meet one of those musical legends. I was very excited when I first met June, but when I met Mother Maybelle, I thought I'd reached the end of the line. I felt like I did when I met Tex Ritter at the *Town Hall Party*.

Mother Maybelle was one of the most gracious people I've ever known, and I just can't say enough good things about her. When we were on the road, she took care of her daughters like they were teenagers. She combed their hair, helped them put on their clothes and makeup, and was always there for them.

If we stayed in town after a show, we'd often go to the local bowling alley or somewhere else nearby to have fun, and Mother Maybelle was always ready to go out with the boys. We all just had a great time with her—especially Luther. She loved Luther and Luther loved her. A lot of times they'd grab a cab and go out bowling all night, and then come in the next morning just dragging. But Mother Maybelle was a trouper!

Mother Maybelle Carter came as close to being a perfect person as anyone I've ever known. She absolutely knew no wrong and was opposed to anybody doing anything wrong. She noticed John's problems early on, and she did everything she possibly could to help him, even nursing him time and again through the bad times. She had a great deal of influence over him, but not enough—no one and nothing could influence John enough to stay away from drugs.

I n March 1963, we went in to do a recording session that most
of us were dreading. John's condition was such that Luther,
W. S., and I didn't know what was going to happen, and we
were very concerned that the session might not come off at all, or
if it did, we'd just be wasting our time. However, John had made
up his mind to record another hit, and he was focused on that
when he arrived at the studio. "Guys," he said, "just listen to me,
and we're going to put this thing together right here and cut a hit
record."

W. S., Luther, and I started working on the rhythm parts, and
when we were ready, John brought in two Mexican trumpet players
and started explaining what he wanted them to do. John did his
own arrangement, all his own way, and since none of us read music,
nothing was written down. The trumpet players, however, were
expecting written charts, so they had a bit of a problem when John
told them to "just jump in . . ." He explained to them, note by note,

what he wanted them to play, and finally, after about thirty minutes, we recorded "Ring of Fire," which, as John had predicted, turned out to be a hit for us.

———◁◦◦◦◦◦▷———

The trumpets on "Ring of Fire," which was co-written by June Carter and Merle Kilgore, were something new in the country music world—no one had ever heard anything like them before. A lot of people listened in disbelief when they played back the tape, but that fresh sound was something John believed in and wanted to do. He was very unpredictable when it came to exploring new musical territory. While some of us wanted to hang on to the style of the Tennessee Two that we'd started with, he was willing to try almost anything different, and he was usually very successful when he did so.

A good example is "The Legend of John Henry's Hammer," a song we recorded that was based on the legend of steel-driving man John Henry. When we were in the studio, John asked me where he could come up with something he could bang together to sound like a big hammer driving a metal spike. I found a place that sold steel and got two fourteen-inch pieces of cold-rolled steel that made exactly the sound he wanted.

John wasn't in very good shape when we recorded "John Henry's Hammer," and I can still see him getting down on his hands and knees on the floor with his microphone, clanging those two pieces of steel together as he growled out the lyrics to the song. The record didn't get a lot of airplay, but when we played it onstage, John would give an absolutely marvelous performance.

The lights would come down low, and John would kneel there banging together those two pieces of steel. A lot of times you could see sparks flying from them, and every once in a while there would be no sound—and we'd know that John had missed and hit his hand instead! There were times when his hand would be swollen pretty badly, but he'd still go out and perform. That song was popular with audiences around the world and made for a truly dramatic performance onstage.

———◁◦◦◦◦◦▷———

In late June 1963, we played the Hollywood Bowl—and much to our surprise, we sold it out. Just like at Carnegie Hall, a lot of important people from the entertainment industry attended that show, and it was very well received. It was a beautiful night, and all of our families were there. It was really great to be onstage at the Hollywood Bowl with your entire family watching you from the front row. It was a night I'll never forget, and I'm sure that no one else associated with the Johnny Cash Show will ever forget it either.

Even though drugs were dominating John's life—and the lives of almost everyone around him—he'd come around and act like his old sweet self when he wanted to, or when he felt like he should. He was clean and sober during our first appearances at Carnegie Hall and the Hollywood Bowl, and while he didn't look his best and his voice hadn't returned to top form, his performances at both dates were just stunning.

When John would get wiped out and stay that way for a long time, it would take quite a bit of time for his voice to regain its power. It was like he had laryngitis or had something hung in his throat. But even after his voice cleared up, particularly in later years when our performances would run an hour and a half, it would begin to weaken and crack toward the latter part of the show.

John mistreated his voice something terrible, and although he was a very strong person, his voice would go almost completely away at times. If he gave his voice an opportunity to rest, however, that clean, crisp, clear baritone would return. It was just amazing how it could bounce back.

In mid-August 1963, we were booked to play at Watermelon Park, a primitive little campground outside Richmond, Virginia, where country and bluegrass shows were held. There were two shows scheduled that day, one at three o'clock and one at seven. We got there a little late, as we often did, and as we started unloading the car, the announcer introduced a group of four gentlemen who took the stage and began to perform.

There must have been a thousand people at the park, not a huge crowd, sitting on wooden benches in a clearing surrounded by trees. There weren't any dressing rooms, just a couple of tiny rooms, about eight feet square, behind the stage. We put our instruments in one room and John in the other so he could change clothes. We were to go onstage next, so after I tuned my bass, I went outside, leaned against a tree, and watched those four young guys perform.

Two things really stood out about them: they were neatly dressed in gold coats and black pants, and they sang great harmony. They also did a good show. I had no idea who they were, which wasn't unusual since we often played shows that had local groups on them. Sometimes we'd meet the local guys and talk to them, and sometimes we wouldn't.

When the group finished their set, Luther went onstage and set up his amplifier, we tuned a little bit, and then I went in to see if John was ready to go on. We managed to make it through the first show and then hung around, killing time, until it was time for the second to start.

Since it was the middle of summer, it was still quite light out when the second show began. The announcer again introduced those four guys, who were to play for about forty-five minutes. We couldn't all fit in that tiny dressing room, and I didn't want to sit in the car, so I went back out and leaned against the same tree and listened to their set. After a while, W. S. came out and joined me. We both agreed that those guys were pretty good for a local group. They had everything down to the nth degree—they were professional in every sense of the word, even though they weren't professionals per se because they were still just working whatever dates they could get in Virginia.

When they left the stage, we went on and played our show. I don't remember if we talked to those four guys or not that day, although in the months to come, I thought about the sharp way they dressed and played.

About six months later, while driving between tour dates in Mobile and Montgomery, Alabama, we got to talking and decided that we needed to take a male backup group on the road with us so when we performed our songs onstage they would sound like the recordings. Songs like "Ballad of a Teenage Queen" and "Guess Things Happen That Way" had backup voices on them, and at that point in time, Elvis was using the Jordanaires, Marty Robbins was using Tompall Glaser and the Glaser Brothers, and other country artists had begun to use backup groups. We felt that we needed one, too.

But who to get? We were focused on Nashville and the *Louisiana Hayride*, but no one came to mind. After about an hour, I recalled the four gentlemen we'd seen the previous summer. I asked John if he remembered the shows at Watermelon Park, and surprisingly he did. I said, "There was a group onstage—you probably didn't see them—but there was a group of young guys on the stage. I remember them because they had on gold coats and black pants and they were really good. I bet they'd jump at the chance to get on the road."

Saul Holiff, our booking agent, was in the car with us, and I asked him who had promoted that show. He said the promoter was Carlton Haney, who had promoted a lot of shows for us. I suggested that we get in touch with Carlton and see who they were and work up a contact with them. Saul got the contact information from Carlton and made arrangements for them to come to our show in Canton, Ohio, on March 9, 1964, to talk with us.

—————

Just inside the back door of the little auditorium we were playing in Canton were a lot of steps that led to the stage, and right under the stage was a boiler room, which I'd been using as a dressing room since there weren't any of those available. The four guys were there when we arrived, and they came backstage and talked to me a little bit before I introduced them to John. Luther and W. S. were also there, so we asked the four if they wanted to go down to the boiler room and run over a couple of songs with us. They jumped at the chance.

Luther took his guitar, and we ran through a few songs like "Ballad of a Teenage Queen" and "Guess Things Happen That Way," and those guys sounded just exactly like the record—they were absolutely perfect. We were all extremely impressed, and John asked, "Y'all going onstage with us?" And they said, "Yeah!" We ran through another couple of songs and then went upstairs and went onstage. About halfway through our set, John introduced the four fellows, who came out and sang backup like they'd been with us all their lives. They sounded fantastic, better in fact than the original recordings.

We never met the people who sang backup on our records. When we cut "Ballad of a Teenage Queen," for instance, we did our parts and then Jack Clement brought in the backup singers and pickers and laid down their tracks (this was after Sun had updated its equipment to allow multi-track recording). But the sound we achieved that night in Canton was even better than the original record. That little quartet stayed onstage with us for quite a while and did all of our songs that had backup vocals on them. Afterward, John thanked them and they left, and we went on and played another twenty or thirty minutes and closed the show.

Later, we had a little talk on the side of the stage and asked the four if they wanted to join the tour as our backup singers. They told us they were looking for work and were "packed and ready to go." Sure enough, when we looked out into the parking area, there was their car with a small trailer behind it all packed and ready to go.

Our next date was the following night in Rockford, Illinois, and after we had packed up our gear and were getting into the car to head down the road, one of the four hollered, "Hey, Mister Grant, which way is Rockford, Illinois?" I said, "It's a little hard to explain. Why don't you just follow us, and we'll lead you right there." They followed us to the date and once again did an absolutely beautiful job backing us onstage.

By the time the tour ended a couple of dates later, they'd worked up a little segment of their own that ran about fifteen minutes, with Luther, W. S., and me playing for them, and then they'd come back out and back us on all those old Sun recordings. They were a fantastic group of guys: Don Reid, Harold Reid, Phil Balsley, and Lew DeWitt—The Statler Brothers.

There have been many tales about how the Statlers were "discovered." I didn't discover the Statler Brothers; the Johnny Cash Show did, and it happened because they were in the right place at the right time. And that's what I've told countless people who have asked me over the years how to get into show business: it's a matter of being at the right place at the right time. It always works out that way.

───※───

We were in Nashville at the old Owen Bradley studio they used to call the "Quonset Hut," killing time while waiting for John to show up for a session, when Don Law laughingly asked from the control booth, "Well, does anybody out there want to do something?" Harold Reid held up his hand and said, "Yes! We do." Don said, "Let's do it!" And with that, the Tennessee Three and the Statler Brothers began laying down tracks for what would become the Statlers' signature song, "Flowers on the Wall."

That recording was really the beginning of the Statler Brothers as a presence in country music. Touring with the Johnny Cash Show gave them exposure that nobody else could buy, especially since crowds at our shows were growing, John seemed to be improving, and things were looking up. Every night, the Statlers would go out and do their act, and the crowds just loved them. Their popularity was starting to soar, and it would continue to increase as time went on.

John's condition sometimes could go from good to bad very quickly. For instance, in 1964, we were scheduled to play three days at Spring Lake Park in Oklahoma City and decided that we would take our cars and families along and make a vacation out of it. Etta, Randy, and I were almost done packing the car when John called. "Marshall, when are you going to leave to go to Oklahoma City?" he asked. "June and I and Rosie and Carlene are on the way to Memphis, and we need to stay all night somewhere because we can't drive all the way through. I was wondering if we could stay at your house tonight, if you don't mind?"

He seemed to be sober and in good shape, so I said, "Of course that will be just fine." I was honored to have them stay in the house; we had plenty of room, and it seemed silly for them to have to check into a hotel, so I told John and the others to come on over and make themselves at home. Since he was about three hours outside of Memphis when he called, I hid a key for him outside and told him I'd get it back when he got to Oklahoma City.

The next day, while we were getting everything ready for the first show at Spring Lake Park, I could see there was something bothering June. She sort of had her head down, but I didn't ask her about it because I thought she might be a bit out of sorts because the kids were there and she wasn't in the same frame of mind she normally would have been in.

———

The shows that weekend went great, even though John wasn't in the best shape when he got there and didn't improve much over the three days. But he had sounded fine when he called and asked if he, June, and the girls could stay at my house.

When Etta and I got home the day after the final show in Oklahoma City, I discovered what June had been all cowed down about. I guess after June and the girls had gone to sleep, John had ransacked my house. He'd gone through all of the drawers, turning everything upside down. You could tell he'd been all over the place, even though he'd sort of tried to put things back in order. I have no earthly idea what he was looking for. He knew there were no illegal drugs of any kind in the house, because I was totally against them, and no prescription medications either.

Nothing ever turned up missing, so I don't think he took anything, but he sure turned everything inside out, and it took Etta a long time to put everything back the way it had been. Trashing my house was the last thing on earth that John would have done if he were drug free. But when he got strung out a little bit, he'd do almost anything.

There again, that was the difference between J. R. and Johnny. When John was drug free, it didn't matter what you were doing or where you were, he was simply one of the guys. He didn't want people to look up to him or cater to him in any way. He just wanted to mix in with the group and be part of whatever was going on, no matter what it was.

But when he was taking drugs, he demanded attention. He called all the shots, and when he made up his mind to do something, you had to go along with him—there was no getting around it. This was especially true when it came to the music business, because he couldn't go one way and let everyone else go the other—

everyone had to go *his* way. That was very difficult, because when he was strung out, he loved it when people bowed and scraped to him, and he loved to keep everybody guessing about what he was going to do next.

You could predict what John was going to do when he was drug free; you could talk to him like a brother, a father, a friend, and he wouldn't lie to you in any shape, form, or fashion. As the old saying goes, whatever he told you, you could take it to the bank. However, when he was strung out, it was very difficult even to carry on a conversation with him; you had no confidence at all in what he said.

Whenever John straightened up after doing something particularly bad, he often couldn't recall if or why he had done it. He never acknowledged the fact that he ransacked my house, and on a couple of occasions, just to let him know that I knew he had, I said something to him about it. I asked him once when he was straight, "John, when you went through my house, what where you looking for?" He just sort of grinned and said, "Ahhh, I don't know." I believed him. I really don't think he had any earthly idea what he was looking for.

One of my favorite memories of the road involves a date we played in Grand Rapids, Michigan. The building where we performed was directly across the street from our hotel, which was very nice. We were headed back to the hotel after the show that night, and as we approached the front door, we saw a bell-man trying to pull a huge black and white dog, possibly a St. Bernard, outside.

"Hey, wait, man," W. S. Holland told the bellman. "Where you going with my dog?" The bellman replied that he didn't know the dog belonged to one of the hotel's guests. W. S. said, "Yeah, that's my prize dog, I don't know how he got down here." The bellman turned the dog loose, and W. S. looked at that big ball of fur and said, "Come on, James Lewis, let's go to the room." And the dog turned right around and followed us to the elevator. On the way up to our floor, everybody was petting the dog and laughing, and we started calling him James Lewis. When we got off the elevator, W. S. said,

"Come on, James Lewis, let's go down to the room." And the dog followed us once again.

W. S., Luther, and I were staying together in a very large room with three beds, and James Lewis just trotted right in behind us and seemed to be awfully happy. We decided to order something for him to eat and called room service and told them we wanted eighteen hamburgers, all of the side orders, and a great big bowl of slaw. After about thirty minutes, the bellman knocked on the door and brought in the food.

You've never seen so many hamburgers in your life! We took everything off the burgers and tossed it into the slaw bowl and then fed James Lewis all of the meat. We'd toss the patties into the air, and he would grab them and wolf them down without chewing—he gobbled down all eighteen of them that way.

After a while, we started wondering what we were going to do with all the slaw and the leftover trimmings from the burgers. I said, "Let's just stir it all up in this big bowl, and I'll dispose of it." Then I picked up the muzzle-loading gun I used in our skits onstage, filled the barrel about half full of powder, stuck the barrel down into the slaw bowl, and pulled the trigger—and all of that stuff just disappeared! Actually, everything just flew all over the room, covering everybody in bits of slaw and lettuce and who knows what else. We laughed until we could hardly stand up, but my magic trick had worked—I'd made that whole bowl full of food disappear.

———

After that, we concentrated on James Lewis, who was absolutely filthy and smelled like a Billy goat. John said, "If we're going to keep this dog overnight, we need to give him a bath." Luther had gone downstairs to the coffee shop, so the rest of us led James Lewis to the bathtub, and he jumped right in. We then got all the shampoo we had and gave that sucker a bath that took thirty minutes. He was covered with filthy, black coal smut, and when he shook himself off, he made a horrendous mess all over the bathroom.

After we'd gotten him pretty clean and took him out of the tub, James Lewis walked into the room and sat down beside Luther's bed. He started nodding off a bit, and John said, "Well, let's put him to bed." Luther still hadn't gotten back yet, so we put James Lewis into his bed, covered him up, and put his head on the pillow—he looked just like a human being lying there, and the sight made us all laugh really hard.

Luther came in directly, and when he looked over toward his bed, there was James Lewis, snoozing away. Luther didn't say a word to anyone; he just turned around, shut the door real easy, and walked away. We laughed a long time about that and then decided that if Luther came back upstairs, he could just sleep with James Lewis, and so we left that big dog in his bed. After about three hours, Luther still hadn't returned, so we all decided to turn in. John went to his room, W. S. and I crawled into our respective beds, and James Lewis continued to sleep in Luther's bed.

Luther finally came back to the room, but when he saw James Lewis sleeping in his bed, he left again. W. S. and I started laughing about the look on Luther's face, and we laughed until almost dawn.

About sunrise, James Lewis started getting real antsy, I told W. S., "You know, I believe he needs to go to the bathroom. I think we ought to take him downstairs and walk him." We got dressed and said, "Come on, James Lewis," and he jumped out of bed and followed us all the way into the elevator.

The lobby of the hotel had a highly polished slate floor that extended all the way out to the curb where the guests could be loaded and unloaded. When the elevator door opened, James Lewis cut out across the lobby as fast as his legs would go, but he could barely get a toehold on the slick floor. His legs must have been churning a hundred miles an hour, but he was barely moving because his paws kept slipping on the shiny floor.

He finally made it across the lobby to the revolving door and pushed his way outside. Standing on the curb were three pieces of luggage and a lady who was waiting for someone to pick her up. James Lewis made a beeline for the largest suitcase, hiked his leg, and proceeded to wet on that bag for what seemed like five minutes. We stepped back inside and started laughing so hard that we could barely stand. Finally, we pulled ourselves together and went back out.

We didn't really want to claim James Lewis right then, because the lady was screaming and hollering and carrying on pretty good, and we weren't sure what she might do. So we just stood there, milling around until the dog had finished his business, and then turned to him and said, "Come on, James Lewis, let's go back upstairs." He trotted over to us, and as the lady stood staring, we cut out across the lobby as fast as we could, got on the elevator, and went back up to the room. Everybody rolled with laughter when we told them what had happened.

When it came time to check out, everyone gathered in my room, and we talked about what we were going to do with James Lewis. We couldn't take him with us, since we were still traveling in the car and there just wasn't room for him. And so, when we had loaded up and were ready to leave, everyone patted him on the head and said goodbye, then got into the car and started to drive away. It was very sad, because James Lewis followed us for about three blocks as we kept looking out the back window at him, and then he finally sat down on a street corner and watched until we were out of sight.

I still think about James Lewis an awful lot. He was one of the greatest dogs I've ever known.

Although we were playing a lot of dates, money was still tight, since John was blowing through most of our concert proceeds. I was paying most of our travel expenses out of my own pocket and often had to wait a long time to be reimbursed, so I thought that a credit card might help to solve that problem and keep us on the road. In 1964, I applied for and received an American Express credit card and started charging all of our expenses—hotel bills, food, gas, everything, from the time we left home until we got back—to that card, which was my personal credit card. I knew I was taking a chance and might not get that money back, but thanks to a lot of bookkeeping work on Etta's part, I usually managed to get reimbursed, although sometimes it still took a long time.

I used that American Express card for years to pay all of the expenses for the Johnny Cash Show. No matter what the tab came to, it was all charged to that one card—and I never again had to worry about settling up at the box office after our first date to get enough money to let us move on down the road to the next show.

By this time, traveling by car was getting to be quite a problem. Not only did Johnny Cash and the Tennessee Three travel to dates in the car, but we also carried Carl Perkins and sometimes booking agent Stew Carnell. I kept seeing these vehicles, the first motor homes built by Dodge. They were manufactured in Traverse City, Michigan, and looked like nice units. I went to Chuck Hutton's dealership on Union Avenue in Memphis and got a brochure, which I showed to Luther and John. We talked about it and decided to buy a Dodge motor home.

The new vehicle would serve a lot of purposes. Not only would it get us all out of the car, but it had a bed that John could use whenever he needed to sleep. I felt that if I could get us into the motor home, things would work better for everybody, especially John. I also believed the motor home would keep John from missing so many opening tour dates, provided we could get him to ride in it.

As it turned out, the "bus," as we called the Dodge, worked out real well for John. It made a tremendous difference and brought new life to the organization.

June also began traveling with us in the motor home, and guys being guys, sometimes we'd say something off-color, which she didn't particularly appreciate, being a good Christian woman and all. To help break us of that habit, she came up with what she called a "Cuss Box," and if you said a bad word or something naughty, you had to put a quarter in the box. When she'd collected a good bit of cash, she'd use it to buy groceries.

We weren't a bunch of rank folks, and we never said really terrible four-letter words in front of her, but if one of us said damn or hell or something like that, we'd have to put a quarter in the Cuss Box. If June heard you, there was no way around it; she'd make you do it one way or another. If you tried to renege even a little bit, she'd jam her hand into your pocket and start pulling out coins until she'd gotten twenty-five cents to put into that dang box.

She did it in a joking way, but on the other hand, it was June's way of controlling what we said on the bus so things didn't get too raunchy. And it worked, too. After you'd put two or three quarters a day into that box, you began to watch what you said. It got to be that going up and down the road in that motor home was sort of like sitting in church, because you had to behave yourself or pay the price! I still smile when I see that Cuss Box, which Etta and I still have.

We found out real quick, however, after about ten thousand miles or so, that the motor home was made for leisure camping, not to go over the road at seventy miles per hour day after day after day. It just didn't hold up.

We were driving from Memphis to Lansing, Michigan, to open a tour later that year when I noticed the engine was getting weaker and weaker. Being a mechanic, I figured the valves were burning out—on more than one cylinder—so I nursed it into Lansing, arriving in the middle of the next afternoon.

Since the motor home was built upstate, in Traverse City, I called the service manager there, Bubba Smith, and told him my problem, explaining that we had a long tour ahead of us. He said, "The only thing I can do is send you two complete cylinder heads, with valves and the whole ball of wax, and you see if you can get somebody to put them on." I told him to send them on down, and he shipped them by Greyhound bus.

We played the show that night, and I got a friend from town to take me to the Greyhound station to pick up the cylinder heads. I couldn't find anybody to install them, so I did it myself, starting at about 11:30 p.m. It was a tough job, but I worked and worked and finally finished about the time the sun came up. I started the engine and it ran real well, so I got everything squared away, went to the room, cleaned up, packed, and loaded my stuff in the motor home.

I'd been up all night and was really tired, and I wanted to go to bed so bad, but the schedule called for us to leave at 7 a.m. for Toronto, which was a pretty good jump. Tired or not, I got a bite to eat in the hotel restaurant, and everyone else came down and ate, and then we were ready to go. I didn't say anything to anybody about the all-nighter I'd pulled to fix the motor home.

W e crossed the border into Canada and made it to Toronto without any problems. We played two shows that night at Massey Hall, and both were sold out. Afterward, we went to our hotel, and I was really looking forward to finally going to bed and getting a good night's sleep. At the time, John was just fine; the problem was that he had some contacts in Toronto, people I didn't associate with, who owned clubs and other things. One fellow, Ronnie Hawkins, was also an entertainer, and he had a band and owned a club not too far from the hotel where we were staying.

I'd been asleep just a little while when, at about two o'clock in the morning, June called. "Marshall," she said, "I certainly hate to wake you up, but John left with Ronnie Hawkins and a bunch of people, and I'm just so afraid that he's not going to be here for leave time at 7 a.m." We had a show in Watertown, New York, the next day, so I told her, "Well, let me see what I can do about finding him, June. But I don't know where in the world to start."

I went downstairs and asked the guy at the front desk if he'd seen John. "Yeah," he said, he left here about an hour or so ago with a guy I know, Ronnie Hawkins." I asked, "Do you know where he went?" He said, "They've probably gone up to the Hawk's Nest [Ronnie Hawkins's club]. Just go out the front door, go right about three blocks, and it will be up there on the corner."

It was pouring down rain as I walked over there. When I tried to open the front door, it was locked, so I walked around the building to all of the doors, but they were locked, too. I knew people were inside, because I could hear sounds coming from the second floor. I walked around to the back alley and hollered, and somebody finally stuck his head out of a window. I told him who I was and that I needed to talk with John. "Just a minute," he told me as his head disappeared back into the building. He came back in a minute and said, "He's not here; he's gone over to the Chinese restaurant."

The restaurant was in the next block, not more than a hundred yards away, but when I got there I found it was closed, not surprising since it was now 3 a.m. I walked back to the club and hollered and screamed until somebody stuck his head out the window. I told them who I was and said, "Look, I gotta talk to John, because he's got problems at home and he needs to know about it."

The fellow disappeared, and not long after that John stuck his head out the window. I said, "John, you need to come and call Vivian, because you got a problem with the kids." He said, "I'll be there in a little bit." I said, "You need to come on. We need to do this because it's three o'clock now, and you know we gotta leave at seven to go to Watertown." He said, "I'll be there, don't worry about it."

I went back to the hotel and got back into bed. I had been sleeping about an hour when the phone rang. "What's wrong with the kids?" John said when I picked up the receiver. I said, "John, there's nothing wrong with the kids. We got a show in Watertown tomorrow. We leave town at seven o'clock, and you just need to get in bed and get a little rest, and I need to know where you are so we can get loaded up and get out of here because it's going to be a hard drive, and it's going to be very, very close, and we gotta leave on time."

He didn't like that a whole lot, but he said, very abruptly, "Well, I'll be there." I told him, "That's good; that's all I ask. Seven o'clock, we'll leave."

I got up at 6 a.m., which meant that I didn't get much sleep that night, on top of not getting any sleep the night before. I went down to the coffee shop to grab a bite to eat, then got my suitcase from upstairs and went to put it in the motor home, but the door was locked from the inside. My key wouldn't open it. I carried the suitcase back to the lobby, then went up to John's room to see if he was up and moving. He wasn't in, and his room was a total disaster, with clothes thrown everywhere. I picked up all of his clothes, put them in his old suitcases, and carried them out to the motor home, which was still locked.

I knocked on the door several times, but no one answered. I thought, *Well, the only thing to do is take out the side window right by the steering wheel and crawl through the opening.* I got my tools out of the storage compartment, and with a little help from some friends, was able to remove the side window and slide right into the driver's compartment.

Once inside, I saw John in the little dinette area, just about ten feet from where I had crawled through the window. His head was on the floor, but his butt was still in the dinette seat and he was holding a knife in one hand. I said, "Oh my gosh!" and pulled him up into sort of a sitting position. He'd been peeling a potato and was apparently going to cook himself some potatoes and onions, a dish he dearly loved.

I couldn't tell if he was breathing, so I laid him down on his back on the floor, and when I couldn't see any signs of life, I started to get a little panicky. I didn't think I had time to go back inside for help, but I knew something had to be done, so I started blowing air into his lungs. I didn't know much about CPR, but I'd take a big breath and just blow it into his mouth and then I would push on his stomach.

I kept doing this for what seemed like five minutes, and then John went, "Uhhhh," so I kept on for several seconds, blowing the air in and then pushing on his stomach to force it out. I kept that up for what seemed like forever, but was probably no more than thirty or forty seconds, and then I noticed one of John's eyes had opened just a little bit and there was a faint breath. I blew some more air into his lungs, and when it was obvious that he was breathing on his own, I ran back inside the hotel for help.

I got some of the band members and told them what had happened. "You guys come out here and help me put him in the bed," I told them. A couple of them followed me out to the motor home, and we picked John up, carried him to the back, and put him to bed. He was breathing fine, and he looked like he was going to be all right.

I called June and told her that we needed to decide what to do with John. We talked at great length, and she finally said, "Marshall, I think that he's going to be all right now, and maybe we should just go on." I said that was fine and went to find the other members of our troupe and get them checked out of the hotel and on the road to Watertown.

June came up and sat by me as I was driving and said, "What are we going to do about getting him across the border?" I told her the only thing I knew to do was to cover him up with coats and guitar cases and take our chances that he wouldn't be discovered by the border guards. "If we get caught, we're just caught," I said. "If they see him, or we tell them he's back there and the shape he's in, they're probably going to detain us and we'll miss the show."

June went into the back and covered John up real well, leaving room for him to breathe, as I drove toward the States. We got to the border, the fact that it was a Sunday helped a lot, since it wasn't very busy. The border official stepped inside the motor home and jokingly said, "Well, what have we got here?" I replied, "This is the Johnny Cash Show. We played Massey Hall last night, and we're headed over to Watertown, and we're a little late, but we'll make it." He looked around a little and then signed our documents, handed them back to me, and said, "OK, have a good trip." We all breathed a huge sigh of relief, and I drove just as hard as I could to Watertown.

The drive to Watertown was long and hard, and by the time we got there the show had already started. There were several acts on the bill, and Faron Young was onstage. I ran in to see exactly where they were in the show and found there was an intermission scheduled as soon as Faron finished his set. We were to be the closing act.

I told the band and the others in our troupe, "You guys go in and get a dressing room and get ready. We're going to get John up, and we're going to do the show." June said, "Do you think we can do it?" I said, "We can do it. He'll be just fine." I told some folks standing around outside to bring me as much coffee as they could, and then I pulled John out of bed. While June washed his face with cold water, I tried to get him dressed. I took off his shirt and managed to put another on him, and I was just about ready to swap his pants when the people showed up with the coffee.

"Here, John, let's just drink all of this," I told him. "Let's just drink all of this coffee because we have a show to do." He hadn't said a word yet, but at least he was conscious and sitting up on his own. I had told some of our people to let me know when it was time for intermission, and about thirty or forty minutes after the coffee arrived, somebody came in and said, "They're starting intermission for twenty minutes."

I told John, "I want you to stand up here now. We're going to put your clothes on. June and I are going to help you, and in about twenty minutes we're going to go in there and we're going to knock 'em dead." John still didn't say anything, but he seemed to understand what we were talking about and cooperated as we put his clothes on.

For all practical purposes, a few hours earlier the guy had been dead. Now, he was very, very weak, but he was sitting up and drinking coffee. I tried to give him a sandwich, but he wouldn't eat anything; he just kept drinking coffee and began to come around. I told the band, "You all go and get in place. I'll be there in a few minutes, and we're going to do the show." I got John up, and June and I sort of walked him through the back door of the building, up six or eight steps, and then to the edge of the stage, where we sat him down in a chair.

We still had about ten minutes or so before the show started, and I asked him, "Can you stand up, son?" John stood and said, "Yeah." I said, "I'm gonna tell you, I'm going out on the stage right now, and we're going to kick off 'Folsom Prison Blues.' When we get into it real good, you walk out on the stage, and you're going to be just fine."

I went out, and we kicked off "Folsom Prison Blues." John stood off to the side watching for eight or ten bars, then walked onstage.

You couldn't see anything but flashbulbs popping, and you couldn't hear anything but people hollering and screaming. The building was packed, and John stood there, bowed a time or two, then walked up to the microphone and delivered one of the best performances he'd ever done in his life. And nobody knew what had happened except for those of us who were in the motor home.

As John's problems at home kept mounting, June tried every way in the world to get him to go home after concert tours. She tried to get him to call home, tried to get him to communicate somehow with Vivian and the children, and I think she would have succeeded if we just could have kept him straight for longer periods of time. But just when things would start to look pretty good, his drug problem would surface again—maybe not always to the extent that it had in Toronto, but it was something we had to contend with continually.

John actually did more damage to himself than he did to anyone else. He was destroying himself little by little, and June and I worried about that a lot. We did everything we could to help him, to keep him straight, to get him from town to town, and to get him to go home—but that was something he just would not do. John would very seldom go home after a tour, but even when he did, he wouldn't go immediately after the tour ended; he'd just show up sometime later.

I asked him countless times at the end of a tour, when he would be in pretty good shape, "John, why don't you go home? Why don't you go home and see the kids and spend some time with Vivian? That's where we're all going. We're gonna relax a little bit and have a little fun. John, just go home!" Most times, however, he wouldn't, but even when he did go home, he seldom stayed long. He might stay overnight or for a day or two, but then he'd jump into whatever vehicle was available and head into the desert, sometimes for three or four days at a stretch.

It really worried me and everyone else when John disappeared like that. It was tough not knowing where he was, what he was doing, whether he was hurt, or if he'd hooked up with some of the undesirable people he sometimes ran with and was lying dead in the gutter somewhere. We couldn't help him if we couldn't find him, and when he'd drop out of sight like that, we wouldn't have a clue what state he was in, much less what town.

The wives and families of entertainers and the people who travel on the road with them get a raw deal because their loved ones are gone so often. Vivian had a hard time dealing with that, especially since she was trying to raise four children and John wasn't giving her much support.

He would have been a *great* father, if we could have kept him straight. But it just didn't work out that way, because his family wasn't his first priority. His top priority at that point in his life was drugs, and that constantly created problems at home. I would literally beg him to go home after we'd been out on the road, but he'd say, "No, I'm not going. When I set my foot in the front door, she won't start doing nothing but hollering and screaming. I'm just not up to it."

I'd say, "But John, did you ever think that maybe if you were to go home straight and sober and be the old John R. Cash and apologize and see if you could sit down and talk things out, and just *stop* this crap, that Vivian might turn into a different person? Your children would love you, and you would love your children, and that's where your priorities should be." But he'd say, "I can't do that. It won't last, it just won't last, because she hollers and screams at me all the time."

I'd tell him, "John, there's a reason for it. She's raising four children, and you're out here doing what you want to do, and you won't even go home and see them! So I can't blame her. You know our wives are getting the short end of this deal. They keep the home fires burning for us, and it's tough. It's very tough, especially for Vivian, with four kids."

He didn't want to look at it that way, though; he was going to keep on doing what he wanted to do. And that was the way it was going to be, no matter what anyone said.

John should have learned a lesson from Luther and Bertie, who just hadn't been cut out to be an entertainer's wife. She'd hated show business, pure and simple, and hadn't wanted any part of it, which is why she and Luther separated before we moved back to Memphis from California.

We appeared on *The Jimmy Dean Show* in the early sixties, and while we were in Washington, D.C., where the show originated, Luther met a woman named Margie Higgins, a very likable person who had a job at the Pentagon. As time went along, Luther and Margie spent more time together and got closer and closer until they eventually got married. Luther moved her to Memphis for a little while before deciding that he wanted to live in Nashville. He and Margie would make the move to Music City in the middle of 1966.

The two hundred or so dates a year that we were working could be a very depressing situation for the wives, who knew we were out there in the spotlight every night while they were sitting at home. It takes a great woman—and I mean a *great* woman—to be able to deal with it, live through it, and to help.

Thank God Etta was able to put up with all the hassle. And she did everything she could do to help Vivian, too, but after we moved back to Memphis from California, that became impossible.

Etta always contributed, not just to keeping everything stable on the home front, but also to helping the organization along in everything we were doing. It was a big job for her all the time, and she did it well. Those times when John would blow all our money on his habit, she'd pitch in and help me overhaul motors, brake systems, transmissions, whatever—she helped me do it all.

The Dodge had quite a few miles on it by this time, and it was very difficult to keep it running. Whenever we got off the road, Etta would clean the inside of the motor home and then help me fix whatever mechanical problems we were having—and there were *always* mechanical problems! If the Johnny Cash Show was off the road for ten days, we'd spend at least five of them working on the motor home to get it ready to go back out again.

On October 2, 1965, we closed a very successful tour in Dallas. John had been in really good shape for the whole outing, and like everyone else, he'd had a lot of fun. When the tour ended, he said he'd take the tour receipts and deposit them in our bank account when he flew home to California the next day. Since he'd been in such good spirits and appeared to be straight, I gave him the money, all of it.

When I got up the next morning, John was nowhere to be found. Most of his stuff was still in his room, so I packed it all up in his suitcases and then made some calls to people who might have an idea where he could be. No one had seen him, but I wasn't as worried as I normally would have been since we weren't going to be late for a date and John had been in good shape the last time I'd seen him.

The rest of us piled into the motor home and drove back to Memphis, pulling in on Sunday afternoon. I called Vivian to check on John, but she said he hadn't made it home. I went to bed that night still wondering where he was. The next morning, Etta and I were sitting at our little dinette table drinking coffee, like we did every morning when I was home, and when I picked up the paper, there was a picture of John in handcuffs. He'd been arrested in El Paso, Texas.

I had given him thousands of dollars in cash, but instead of flying home to see his family and deposit our money in the bank, John had flown to El Paso. There, he'd hired a taxi to take him across the border into Mexico, where he spent all of that money on amphetamines.

U.S. authorities at the time often paid taxi drivers to tip them off to passengers who had gone into Mexico to one of the places where illegal drugs were sold. John had gone south and bought a lot of amphetamines—about half a gallon of them—and an old, cheap guitar and case. He poured the pills inside that guitar and stuffed paper around them so they wouldn't rattle. When he came back across the border and went to the El Paso airport to catch a flight for home, the taxi driver reported him. John had just sat down in his seat on the plane when the authorities came on board and arrested him, confiscated his guitar, and took him to jail.

I mulled things over for several hours and didn't know what to do—but I knew that I had to do something. I had been on the road so much over the years that I knew someone in just about every town around, so I started making phone calls to see if I could find someone down there who could help—an attorney or a judge or whatever. I finally got in touch with an attorney named Woodrow Bean, who I hoped could get John out of jail and back home so we could try to sort things out.

I knew that since The Associated Press had picked up the story, it was sure to be in the Memphis paper, and probably in papers all over the world, and we needed to do something to keep a lot of people from getting hurt by the bad publicity John's problem was sure to stir up. All I could think of was his family—Vivian and the girls, his mother, his dad, his brothers and his sisters—not to mention his close friends (this was particularly hard on Etta and me) and his fans. It was almost unbelievable that this could have happened—but it did.

John recalled the episode in his autobiography, *Man In Black*:

> I could see my family crying. I could hear them ask, "Why, daddy?" "Why, John?" "Why, son?"
>
> And I cried. I wanted to pray, but I could only cry.
>
> "You have a phone call, Cash," the man said again.
>
> "Leave me alone," I said. And he left.
>
> A few minutes later he was back, opening the door, tapping me on the shoulder.
>
> "Come on," he said.
>
> At the front desk, a lawyer, Woodrow Bean, and two policemen stood waiting.
>
> "Marshall Grant called me," said the lawyer. "Know him?"
>
> "Yes," I said.
>
> "Bond is being posted, and we have to go over to the courthouse to get you released," he stated. "Put on these sunglasses."
>
> "Why?" I asked.
>
> "Because you have to wear *these*," said one of the policemen, as he put handcuffs on me. "Sorry, but it's the law."

After he was released, John caught a plane and flew home. I called and called to see how he was doing, but I didn't hear from him, not one word, until about two weeks later, when the next tour started and he showed up straight as an arrow and ten pounds heavier. I think his brush with the federal authorities scared the fire out of him.

I thought to myself, *This might be the greatest thing that ever happened to him and to us and to the people that love him. This might shake him up enough to where he'll get off these things.* That was the strangest part of it: John could stop taking those pills anytime he wanted, and he did it so many times over the years. He'd stay straight sometimes for a couple of months, so I don't think he was so much physically addicted to amphetamines as he was psychologically dependent on them.

I always thought that there was some little something, whatever it might be, that set him off. And after he'd go on a binge for a month or so, when he got straight it was very difficult for him to face the people he was associated with, the people who loved him, so his escape from that was . . . to take another pill. I think that's part of the reason he took them, because when he got high, it was like this other man surfaced and he (John) didn't have to face anyone or deal with anything.

However, after his brush with the law in El Paso, I thought John's problems—at least with drugs—were finally over.

———

That proved not to be the case, however, and one night that fall, John showed up for an appearance on the *Grand Ole Opry* drugged out of his mind and in really bad shape. Everybody stared at him, trying to figure out what was wrong. No one understood what was really going on. While doing his first song, John took the microphone stand and broke all the footlights.

The *Opry* manager hurried backstage and literally shut down the show for a while. He stormed over to where we were all milling around and I was trying to protect John from the media people who were there. "Marshall," he fumed, "get him out of here. And don't bring him back!"

———

Gordon Terry still brags that he gave Johnny Cash his first amphetamine, and the sad thing is, I think he thought he was doing John a favor. Gordon admits to having taken a lot of pills while he was touring with us, but they didn't affect him like they did John.

Luther was also beginning to take a fair amount of pills, but, like Gordon, they didn't affect him to the extent they did John. Luther never messed up onstage; he was very prompt; he was a great driver and did his share of the driving; and he never got completely blown out of his mind like John did. He and Gordon were quite jolly when the two of them were high.

Things were different for John, however. We were staying in a high-rise hotel in Indianapolis once when I got a phone call from Gordon about three o'clock in the morning. "Marshall," he yelled, "you got to get down here right quick! He's out on the balcony, and he's going to jump off!" I ran down the hall to John's room and found him dangling from the balcony railing about five or six stories above the ground.

"I've tried to get him in, but I just can't," a worried Gordon told me. The two of us were able to get hold of him so that he wouldn't fall, and finally pulled him over the railing and into the room. We locked the door leading out onto the balcony, then sat down and stayed with John the rest of the night to keep him from getting into any more trouble.

John always made sure he was in good shape when we went overseas. That helped a lot. He would make sure that he was basically straight. I always hoped that when we got back to the States it would carry over and maybe he'd be encouraged to give up his bad habits. Sometimes that was the case, but then the drugs would slowly sneak back in. I could never figure out why, because we had the world by the tail and John was an extremely intelligent man. I could never understand why he did that to himself, why was he so self-destructive.

His drug problems affected so many people's lives. I was very concerned about what would happen to Vivian and the girls if something were to happen to John. And for that matter, I worried about what would happen to me and my family, Luther and W. S. and their families, and all the people around the country who were employed by our organization.

But there really was nothing we could do about John's drug problem except live with it day to day and hope for the best. We did the best that we could in order to survive and to keep our career moving forward without taking too many steps back.

John's dad and mother were still living in Casitas Springs, and Vivian and "Mama" Cash, as we all called Carrie, were very close. Mama and Ray tried to help Vivian through her problems with John, but to no avail. Nobody could do anything with him at that point; in fact, his mother and dad became almost nonexistent to him when he was abusing drugs.

"What you need to do is file for divorce," a well-meaning Mama told Vivian. "That'll shake him up, and he'll come back home." That approach might have worked with her loving son J. R., but Carrie didn't know the amphetamine-popping Johnny Cash very well. She believed that he surely would go back home before giving up the wife and children he loved so dearly. But she was wrong. Johnny Cash actually *wanted* Vivian to file for divorce—and on January 3, 1966, that's just what she did.

For a while after that, John truly didn't have a home, so to speak, and later that year he moved to Nashville and shared an apartment with fellow songwriter and singer Waylon Jennings for quite a while. But that wasn't a home, and the two of them were bad influences on each other drug-wise, and that made things extra tough.

We'd drive to Nashville to pick up John to start a tour, but very often we couldn't find him. We'd call around looking for him, but many times he was just nowhere to be found. There was no way we could cancel the tour and go back home, so we'd head for the first date alone and hope that he'd show up. Most of the time he would, but sometimes we wouldn't see him until later in the tour.

If he did show up, we'd get him on the motor home and June would pamper him and cook for him and do everything she could to comfort him. She'd make sure that he ate, because if there were a two- or three-week break between tours, John often wouldn't eat, a side effect of the amphetamines. I don't know how he managed to stay alive sometimes; he'd just keep losing weight and losing weight and losing weight. During the worst times, John's weight plunged from his normal 200 pounds to barely over 140.

June would always try her best to fatten him up, and as a rule, he would not only eat, but her attention and home cooking often gave him some incentive to straighten up a little bit. Sometimes, by the end of a tour, he would be back in pretty good shape.

Normally, I'd try to keep an eye on John when we were on the road and usually knew where he was. But when we ended a tour in Starkville, Mississippi, in 1966, I made the mistake of leaving him on his own, thinking he'd have no trouble finding a ride back to Nashville. Since it was the end of the tour, our families had come down for the show, and Etta and Randy were waiting for me to finish up so we could drive back home to Memphis.

About two o'clock the next morning, the sheriff of Starkville found John crawling around on his hands and knees in some woman's front yard picking flowers. He locked John up and called me later that morning. We arranged for a bond company to post John's bail and get him out of jail. A local attorney handled everything and got John off the hook; he didn't even have to make an appearance in court. I always used to say that John was like a cat that had used up eight of its nine lives. And I was very concerned that, with the things he was getting into, he would soon use up that final one.

Sometimes we'd pull into a town and John would disappear. Show time would roll around and we couldn't find him. We wouldn't tell the audience he wasn't there, and June would go onstage as an opening act and perform for twenty or twenty-five minutes, and sometimes by then, he'd show up and the show would go on as usual. There were nights when June entertained the audience for an hour or more—and there were lots of times she saved the day by just staying onstage until John finally arrived.

Sometimes we knew he just wasn't going to show up, and I'd introduce June as the opening act and she'd go onstage and start her first song. About midway through, she'd stop singing and start talking to people in the audience. She'd say, "John's not going to be here, but you're going to be entertained! We've got the Tennessee Three here, and we'll stay here until all of you are happy. We may just stay on this stage all night!"

June would get the people excited and on her side immediately, and sometimes she'd stay onstage for an hour and half and everybody would leave happy. We'd just hope that John would show up the next day, and as a rule, he would.

Whenever June saw John after he'd missed a date, she would come down on him hard. She'd tell him, "You know this is ridiculous, childish, unnecessary . . ." I mean, she would really rake him over the coals. He'd pay attention to what she said for a couple of months or so, and he'd be Johnny-on-the-spot and everyone would have a lot of fun. During those times, it seemed as if John had completely given up drugs, because everything would go so well. But then, for whatever reason, he'd slip back into his old bad habits.

And whenever that happened, June would always be there to try to stop him. I had a war buddy for all the battles.

——————

When John was on a drug binge, he'd sometimes stay up for four or five days at a time. Whenever June and I could get him to go to bed and sleep, the two of us would ransack his room looking for pills. When we'd find them, we'd flush them down the toilet.

One time in Waterloo, Iowa, we got into town in the middle of the afternoon and John was so wiped out that he just lay down on the bed and passed out. June knew he'd be out for quite some time, so she called me and said, "Marshall, let's go up to his room and see what we can find." I always had a key to his room and could go in anytime, but June and I found absolutely nothing when we searched it that day. We looked and looked, sat down and tried to figure where he possibly could have hidden his stash of drugs, and then looked some more.

As we were leaving the room, I noticed a mini-refrigerator right by the door. "June, we've looked everywhere but this refrigerator," I said, but she replied, "Oh, I looked in it." I said, "Well, did you look in the back of it?" She said she hadn't thought to do that, so I picked up that little fridge and shook it real good—and a double handful of pills rolled out of the back. We dug around inside to make sure we'd gotten all of them, then took the pills into the bathroom.

"You want to flush them, or you want me to?" June asked. "Let's both flush them," I told her. So I placed my hand on the handle of the toilet, she laid her little hand on top of mine, and together we pushed down, sending those pills on a one-way journey to nowhere.

"Now what do you think we ought to do?" she asked. "Should we get him up?" It was getting close to time to leave for the show, but I said, "You know, if we leave him here, he'll be sound asleep for about another twelve hours, and then he'll be all right when he gets up. He might be hacked off at us, but he'll be all right; he'll sleep it off. But if we take him to the show, we'll have hell to pay, so it's best to let him sleep it off." And that's what we did.

June and I joined the other cast members, and when opening time rolled around, she went onstage and told the crowd that John wasn't going to be there that night but they'd be royally entertained with a full-length performance. June's little spiel helped us salvage the show, as very few people left. When we went back to the hotel, John was still sound asleep.

The next morning at eight o'clock, I walked into John's room and found him sitting on the side of the bed. "How you doing, man?" I asked. "Well, what day is it?" he mumbled. I told him and then said, "We did the show last night, John. We wanted you to sleep it off, and it looks like you have. Now, if you want to get dressed, we'll go on to the next town and everything will be all right." He said, "OK," but he soon discovered that June and I had found all of his pills and flushed them away. He got a little upset at that, but June calmed him down real quick.

"Listen," she told him, "Marshall and me, every time we can get you to sleep, no matter where you got them pills hid, we're going to find them and we're going to flush them. So, if you ever go to sleep, we're going to get them—you went to sleep yesterday and we got them. You can't stay awake forever! You're going to pass out and fall off your feet once in a while, and every time you do, we're going to get them and we're going to dispose of them. So just keep that in mind, big boy!"

After that, John got better at hiding his pills, and he could hide those suckers in places we never would have thought to look. He'd tear a little hole in the bedspread and hide them there. He'd punch a tiny hole in a pillow and stick them down inside with the feathers. He'd hide those pills everywhere, and I'm sure there were a lot of them June and I never found.

I n 1967, John bought a home on Old Hickory Lake in Hendersonville, Tennessee, about twenty miles northeast of
Nashville. It was a beautiful house, built by Braxton Dixon, a
great architect who became a very close friend of all of us. It was a
spacious, rambling place, a beautiful mansion on the water. I spent
many nights there and enjoyed all of them.

Now that he had a lovely home and his divorce from Vivian was
final, John started hounding June to fulfill that prediction he'd
made backstage at the *Opry* more than a decade ago and marry
him. June, who had divorced Rip Nix a year earlier, would always
tell him, "Not until you get yourself straight, John. I can't live with
it. You got to get yourself straightened up, and then I'll consider it."

John got locked up in Lafayette, Georgia, in October of that year. I
don't know why he was in that part of the country, although he sometimes would go down there to look for caves and climb rock piles and

such. Apparently, John had gotten high and had caused enough trouble to wind up in jail. Here's the story I got later from John:

The next morning, Sheriff Ralph Jones came to the jail, unlocked the cell, took John up to the front desk, and told him, "You know, last night I went home and told my wife, 'I got Johnny Cash in jail,' and told her what happened. She started crying, and she cried all night long. John, my wife and myself have every record you have ever recorded. We've followed your career. We love everything that you do. But I didn't know that you were doing this. I'd heard things, but I didn't know that it could be so bad and so terrible. When you came in here last night, you where totally 100 percent out of control, and my wife is still having a hard time dealing with it."

The sheriff opened his desk drawer, pulled out a handful of pills that he'd taken from John, and gave them back to him. "Here," he said, " I want you to take all of this and go do whatever you want to do. If you want to go and kill yourself, that's just fine. You're going to disappoint a lot of people, including myself and my wife, your family, your friends. There are going to be a lot of disappointed people, but if what you want to do is kill yourself, here. Go do it."

I think Sheriff Jones's talk had a bigger impact on John than anything anyone else had ever said or done up to that point. He talked like he was John's father. Now, I loved Ray and Mama Cash, too—they were like my own mother and daddy—but Ray wouldn't talk to John like that, and neither of them would stand up to him. In fact, very few people would stand up to John, but Ralph Jones did that day, and it made a difference, because that day John again started to back away a bit from those pills.

Unfortunately, that didn't last. Not long after that, John borrowed June's car to go to Chattanooga to see some friends. Bob Johnson, a great banjo player, and Norman Blake, one of the greatest guitar players I've ever known, both lived in Chattanooga, and I think he liked to visit them—but usually only when he was blown out of his mind. On that particular trip, he had an accident and totaled June's car, but John, of course, didn't get so much as a scratch.

He stayed in Chattanooga for three or four days, and when he got back home he called me and said he'd "hurt June's car," that it just wouldn't run anymore, and that he needed to buy her a new one. I went to the local Cadillac dealership in Memphis where I knew all the salesmen very well and bought June a new car and had it delivered to her—and lo and behold, John paid for it. He straightened up for a little while after that, because I think the accident had scared him and he felt he ought to toe the mark a little better. Unfortunately, that didn't last long either.

⸻⚬⸻

Sometimes when John was in bad shape, June would have him stay at her house on Due West Avenue in Nashville and try to take care of him. John was after June to marry him, but she wouldn't let him move in with her. So, whenever June took John in, Mother Maybelle would move in and care for him like he was her own son. On some occasions, she'd nurse him back to pretty good health, but he often didn't stay that way for any length of time.

Later, after June had moved out of the house, which she had gotten in the divorce settlement with Carl Smith, Mother Maybelle moved in. On several occasions during the sixties, when John would get back to Nashville in the wee hours of the morning and be looking for drugs, he'd go over there and ransack the house, much as he had done to my home in Memphis earlier. He'd break a window, climb inside, and rummage all through the house, even at times when he knew Mother Maybelle was there sleeping.

If he was straight when he got back into town, though, he'd go home, go to bed, and then probably visit Mother Maybelle the next day or so, because, like all of us, he loved Mother Maybelle Carter; she was an extremely precious person. You would think that, as much respect as John had for Mother Maybelle and the Carter Family in general, that he would have straightened up and left drugs alone. But for a long time, he didn't; he gave them all fits, and it was a very pathetic situation.

⸻⚬⸻

Dr. Nat Winston was Tennessee's commissioner of mental health and a longtime friend of the Carter Family whom we all had become very close to when we played shows for him when he ran for governor of Tennessee in the early sixties. He was a great doctor and had tried from time to time to help John overcome his drug problem.

That was impossible, however, because you simply could not talk John into doing something he didn't want to do, especially when he was high. But after he got home from Georgia, he made contact with Dr. Winston and told him that he needed help.

Dr. Winston went to John's home in Hendersonville where he, June, and her daddy, Ezra "Pop" Carter, proposed that John stay home for thirty days and try to wean himself off the amphetamines. John agreed to give the plan a shot, and we canceled all of our dates for the next month. Dr. Winston and June kept everyone away from John during that time, because they knew that some of John's so-called friends—including a couple of band members—would bring him anything he wanted. All he had to do was call, and those folks would come running with their drugs, in part because they knew John would pay whatever they asked. He never counted the money; he'd just pick up a stack of cash and give it to them—which is how he blew a lot of what we'd earned.

Much has been written about that episode, but I can say for a fact that for thirty days John never left the house, and Dr. Winston, June, and her dad pretty much stayed there with him. At the end of that month, John was a new man. He must have put on two pounds a day, because he'd gained a lot of weight and looked like a different person than the man who'd shut himself away inside that house. His facial expressions and everything else had changed, and the man who stood before us was the guy we all loved and wanted to know again: our friend John R. Cash—not drug-crazed Johnny Cash, who was a completely different person.

We went out on a couple of tours after that, and everything was fantastic. Everyone connected with the show was elated that John had overcome his problem and had returned to the fold. The old John was indeed back, but knowing him as I did, I worried whether he would remain clean and sober—and I just held my breath, hoping that he would.

I knew that very often when John would finally go to bed after a drug binge, he'd lie there and start thinking about all the wrongs he had done to so many people when he was high. Sometimes that would be more than he could stand, and he was liable to turn right back to amphetamines as a way of escaping his emotional pain. Not too long after his thirty-day drying-out period at home, that happened and he starting popping pills again. Everybody thought his problems were over, but somehow I just knew they weren't.

There was a lot of publicity about John's "recovery," and I can remember several times afterward, when John was blown out of his gourd, that a reporter would ask about his amphetamine addiction and he would assure the person that he had never, ever taken another pill since the month he'd spent under the care of Dr. Winston and June and her dad. That went on for years, and people began to look at him and wonder how he could say that when it was obvious that he was not as clean and sober as he made out.

I think the time he spent getting straight with Dr. Winston and June and her dad was, in a sense, a waste of time. Again, I don't think John was truly physically addicted to amphetamines, because I'd seen him wean himself off them many times before and stay straight for a month, two months, or even six months at a time—and then just start taking them again. So, I had my doubts that a thirty-day cleanup would be the end of John's drug taking. But as time passed, he started pointing to that month at home as the turning point in his life. But it wasn't the turning point at all; it was just a short interlude before he began taking those pills again.

By the mid- to late sixties, Luther was also using amphetamines pretty heavily, although he never got out of control like John did. Luther just wanted to love you and be loved by you when he was under the influence. He was normally such a lovable guy, however, that his behavior didn't change all that much when he was high, and he never missed a beat onstage.

Luther was sort of overpowered by John. No matter what John wanted, Luther would see that he got it. John would sometimes give him bunches of money to go out and buy amphetamines or whatever else he could get his hands on. And as the months passed, they both seemed to be getting deeper into drugs.

s 1968 arrived, we were still having a lot of trouble getting
John into the studio to record, especially anything that
would be career building or could potentially be a hit. He
just didn't have his mind on it. Earlier, once he'd decided to do it, he
could go into the studio and lay down tracks that would result in a
chart-topping record, and he proved that time and time again. Now,
however, he just couldn't do it. As a result, we decided to do a live
album instead.

Our friend Reverend Floyd Gressett arranged for us to go to
California's Folsom Prison to play a concert. He'd been working
with several prisons on the West Coast and managed to convince
the warden at Folsom to allow the Johnny Cash Show to come in
and play a concert for the prisoners. Reverend Gressett got all the
details worked out, and the prison officials were very receptive to
our plans to perform there. About the same time, Reverend Gressett gave John a song that had been written by an inmate at Folsom
named Glen Sherley.

On January 12, we flew into San Francisco and were met by a group of corrections officials who led us to an old prison bus that took us to a motel in Folsom where we all got together and worked up Glen Sherley's song, "Greystone Chapel." We didn't do any rehearsals at the prison because we would be performing the same show we'd been doing onstage. John got permission to introduce Glen Sherley just before we played "Greystone Chapel," and maybe bring him up onstage with us.

When we arrived at the prison the next day, January 13, security was very tight. The authorities had made every effort to protect us, but as we knew from past experience, anytime you go into a maximum-security penitentiary filled with hardened criminals, there was always the potential for violence. Despite the precautions, it was pretty scary at Folsom, especially since June was with us, and she was pretty uptight about being there.

They officials escorted us into a big room where we'd played the last time we had been at Folsom. It was sort of like a canteen or a mess hall, just a big cold room that could seat about three thousand people. The acoustics weren't the best and the room echoed a lot, but all of the sound and recording equipment had been set up when we got there. We couldn't see the sound truck, just the cables from all of the microphones and amplifiers snaking outside and around the corner to where it was parked. We got set up, tuned, did a sound check in the empty hall, and then ran through a quick rehearsal that included "Greystone Chapel."

We took a break, and they led us to a dining area that was quite nice, more like a buffet, although we were separated from the people serving us by a thick glass partition. The food was fantastic, and we began to feel pretty comfortable because the place didn't look too much like a prison. After we finished eating, everybody got into their stage uniforms and prepared to go on.

The hall where we were to perform was now packed with prisoners. You could feel the electricity in the air, as they were looking to have a good time and we were looking forward to entertaining them. I think it was the warden who introduced the show, and for what seemed like five minutes after that, all you could hear were three thousand inmates hollering and screaming, stomping their feet, and clapping their hands. We could tell it was going to be a very exciting night and a good place to record a live album. No one had told the prisoners we were going to record an album, and there was nothing on the stage to indicate that.

We started the show, and the reaction from our captive audience was incredible. I think their reception inspired us to perform every song better than we had ever done it before, every last one of them. But I don't think I've ever seen as much excitement in a room as when we launched into "Folsom Prison Blues." When John turned around and said, "Kick it off, Luther!" and Luther, in his unique style, began to play the opening notes, the roof almost blew off that place!

I hope everyone who reads this book will take the time to listen to the version of "Folsom Prison Blues" that appears on the live album. As good as the old Sun single sounds, it can't hold a candle to the version we recorded that night at the prison surrounded by all those screaming inmates. If you listen to Luther's guitar work, you can understand why he was such a musical icon. He just stood there and played so incredibly well, never cracking a smile, moving only his fingers and his eyeballs. It was Luther at his best.

John finally got around to introducing "Greystone Chapel," which came as a complete surprise to Glen Sherley, who was sitting near the front row. John told the audience that he wanted to do a song written by an inmate at Folsom, and then he talked a bit about it and said, "It's called 'Greystone Chapel,' and the writer is sitting right here," pointing to Glen. When he stood up, Glen had the strangest look on his face, a cross between happiness and fright. I watched him the whole time we were playing "Greystone Chapel," and he was so thrilled that it seemed as if he almost turned into a different person. After the show was over, they allowed Glen to come onstage and meet John.

———

Later, John decided that he wanted to get Glen Sherley out of prison. I didn't think that was such a great idea because Glen definitely had the look of a hardened criminal, like someone who was comfortable in prison, and I didn't know if he'd be able to make it on the outside. I found out later that he'd spent most of his life in prison—not for murder or anything, mostly for armed robbery and things of that nature—and hadn't remained free very long between stretches behind bars.

We went through the proper channels, with the help of Reverend Gressett and the warden at Folsom, and had to go all the way to the governor to secure Glen's release. It took a year or so, but John got Glen Sherley out of prison, set him with a job and a place to live in Nashville, and eventually produced an album for him. Glen met one of the secretaries at the House of Cash, John's business office in Hendersonville, and lo and behold, they got married.

We started taking Glen on the road with us, and at first things went pretty well, as he was anxious to start a career in the music business, but it seemed there was something else more important to him. I think that because Glen had spent so much of his life in prison, he felt out of place and was very insecure on the outside. This eventually became a problem, as Glen was very difficult to control, and John started to sort of pull away from him. I think he realized that he'd made a mistake in getting Glen released from prison. That left it up to me to make sure that Glen made it from town to town, in and out of hotels, and in and out of airports.

You couldn't get Glen into bed at night, and you couldn't get him out of bed in the morning, which began to be a problem because of our busy travel schedule. I woke him up one morning and was having a little talk with him about this, and he seemed to be taking it very well. He said, "I understand," but then he sort of opened up and gave me a chilling insight into his personality.

"Marshall, let me tell you something," he said. "You know I love you like a brother; I really love you. I love everybody on this show, but do you know what I'd really like to do to you?" I said, "I got no idea." Glen said, "I'd like to take a knife and start right now and just cut you all to hell. It's not because I don't love you, because I do. But that's just the type of person I am. I'd rather kill you than talk to you."

That scared the hell out of me, I want to tell you. I said, "Glen, I'm sorry, I'm not going to give you the opportunity to do that because I'm going to go on down and get ready to leave, and we're all going to get on the bus and go to the airport." Later that day, I had a talk with John, and I told him, "John, we can't have this. He's going to hurt somebody, some member of our entourage or somebody else, and he really needs to be back in prison."

John asked him to leave the show, and Glen eventually worked his way back to California and got a job on a dairy farm. I think the pressure of living as a free man outside prison walls got to be too much for him, and in 1978 he put a gun to his head, pulled the trigger, and committed suicide.

———

Johnny Cash At Folsom Prison was one of the best-selling albums in country music history and even today remains among the top ten country albums of all time. It has been credited with setting the direction that country music took in the two decades following its release.

I don't know if I'm too proud of the direction that country took in those two decades—but *Johnny Cash At Folsom Prison* got credit for it anyhow. John was notorious for trying things that nobody else would even think of attempting, but after the *Folsom Prison* album, he started taking things a little more seriously than he had in several years. He started looking for better songs and doing better recording sessions. Everything seemed to be getting a little better, and while John wasn't completely straight, he was maintaining control, and that was good enough for us at the time.

28

John kept hounding June to marry him, but she repeatedly turned him down, saying there was no way they could be man and wife as long as he was using drugs. But John really wanted to marry her and came up with a plan to make June an offer she couldn't refuse. During a show in London, Ontario, in late February 1968, he walked out onstage and proposed to her right in front of the audience. And with all those people cheering for her to accept, June just couldn't say no.

A few days later, on March 1, John and June were wed at a little church in Franklin, Kentucky. It was a small ceremony, with Merle Kilgore serving as John's best man and Mickey Brooks as June's bridesmaid. The only others attending the wedding were the Tennessee Three and our wives. There was no honeymoon. Immediately after the service, the newlyweds went back to John's home in Hendersonville where they stayed a few days before going back out on the road.

John was pretty pleased with himself. Not only had he finally made June his wife, but he'd done so on his own terms. He'd gotten the woman he wanted, and he didn't have to give up drugs.

⟡

John would occasionally go back to Casitas Springs to see his kids and visit his mother and dad. I remember one of those trips vividly. It was May 17, 1968, and Mama Cash was flying back to Nashville with John. I was at home when an American Airlines service agent I knew very well phoned from Memphis International Airport.

"Marshall," he said, "you need to come over here real quick! We're at the Admiral Benbow Inn [the airport motel at the time; it's a parking garage now] "and you need to get over here in a hurry! I've got John and his mother here, and things are out of control. The plane was coming from L.A. to Nashville, and they had to land in Memphis because he was creating a big problem. I got him out of the airport, and I've got him over here at the Admiral Benbow. I'm asking you to come over here, please, as quick as you can."

I jumped in the car, and five or six minutes later my friend was rushing me to a room where I found John and Mama Cash. John looked to be in the worst shape he could possibly be in and still be alive. "What in the world is happening here?" I asked. "Nothing," John said, at which point Mama Cash stood up and said, "We got put off the plane. They won't let us on another American flight, and they tell me that no other carrier will take us either. And I just want to get to Nashville."

I tried to talk to John, but he wouldn't answer any questions and was just very sullen and sarcastic. I finally found that he'd been thrown off the plane because he was wound up on drugs and creating a disturbance. Since no commercial airline would let John on a flight, I told Mama I'd see what I could do about chartering a plane to take them to Nashville.

I called DeSoto Air Park and explained who I was and said that Johnny Cash was in town with his mother and was having some health problems, and that I needed to charter a plane to get them to Nashville. He told me to come over, so I loaded up my car with all of their luggage and took John and Mama Cash to the airpark, paid for the plane (I still have that receipt for $129), and put them on board.

I called Tommy, John's younger brother, who was living in Nashville, and explained the situation to him and told him he should meet them at the private airport where the plane would land. I said, "Tommy, he's in as bad a shape as you'll ever see him in your life, and he has your mother with him. I suggest that you get over to the airport as fast as you can, before the plane gets in, because he shouldn't be around your mother right now. He's being totally irresponsible, and you need to get over there and take him wherever he wants to go and take your mother to your house. Something bad is going to happen if you don't." Tommy said, "Don't you worry about it, I'll be there."

Tommy jumped into his car and drove to the private airfield near town where the charter flight landed. As soon as John got off the plane, Tom walked up to him and demanded, "What do you mean, you bastard, insulting my mother this way?" They got into a fistfight and flailed away at each other all over the parking lot. Tom was certainly within his rights by trying to pound some sense into his older brother for upsetting Mama so badly, but when John was in that kind of shape, wound up on uppers and out of control, he didn't have any respect for anybody.

Luther Perkins had been a smoker ever since I'd known him, and he was often very careless with his cigarettes. He'd frequently fall asleep with a cigarette in his hand—be it in a hotel bed or while riding in the car on our way to a tour date—and many times it would burn down all the way to his fingers. If I was driving, I'd just let that happen, hoping that he'd wake up when he felt the heat and maybe learn to quit that dangerous habit. Very often, though, he wouldn't wake up but would just drop the smoldering butt onto the car seat or the floorboard. Several times I had to pull to the side of the road and dig around to find a lit cigarette that could have set the car on fire.

In May 1968, Luther bought a house on Old Hickory Lake just a couple of miles from where John lived. He loved that place, and everything was going great for him. A couple of months later, on August 5, however, he was a little high and had a misunderstanding of some sort with his wife, Margie. She left the house and went over to the home of some friends, Mr. and Mrs. Gene Ferguson. Gene worked at Columbia Records.

That afternoon, Luther climbed up on the roof of his house to install a television antenna. When he finished, he came back inside, turned on the TV, lay down on the coach—and lit a cigarette. He dropped off to sleep, and the cigarette slipped from his fingers and rolled into the couch cushions, where it started a small fire.

Luther apparently woke up, realized what was happening, and tried to escape, but he was overcome by dense smoke and couldn't make it to a sliding-glass door leading outside. The house itself never caught fire, but there was terrible smoke damage, the likes of which I've never seen. They told us at the hospital that if Luther had lived, the doctors probably would have had to amputate his hands, and I don't think he could have lived with that.

On August 7, 1968, we all attended Luther's funeral. He was buried in what today is Hendersonville Memory Gardens, and his grave is very close to what would later become the final resting places for John and June, Mother Maybelle and Pop Carter, Mama and Papa Cash, Anita and Helen Carter, and John's sister Reba Cash Hancock.

⸺⸎⸻

After Luther's tragic death, Carl Perkins, who had joined the Johnny Cash Show in 1965, took over as our guitar player for a while. He still performed his segment early in the show and then would come out onstage and play guitar with John, W. S., and myself. Carl was a phenomenal musician and a great guitar player in his own right—which is evident in all of his recordings, including "Blue Suede Shoes"—but he was no Luther Perkins. Luther had a style that no one at the time could match, no one.

We made it through our shows, and the audiences—which were definitely getting larger after the *Folsom Prison* album—understood that we were struggling with the loss of Luther and were sympathetic, because they missed him, too. Carl did an incredibly good job of trying to fill an extremely large pair of shoes.

Especially after the *Folsom Prison* album, Luther truly became a musical icon, and his passing left a huge void onstage. I missed so much looking toward the side of the stage and seeing him standing there like a statue, just moving his fingers and his eyes. He was so awesome to watch, and such a fantastic person and a great ambassador for country music worldwide. Everyone loved Luther, and those of us who knew him intimately will never forget him. Not a day goes by that I don't think about Luther Perkins.

John got a little better after Luther's passing, which I think shook him up pretty good. While he wasn't totally straight, he had his drug use a little more under control. He knew that drugs were at the root of Luther's problems, and I think he also knew something like that could happen to him, too, although he didn't necessarily want to look at it that way.

He thought about it, though, at least enough so that he didn't get blown away as much or as often. He and June were slowly but surely building a new life together, and everybody was behind them. We all loved them and would have done everything possible to help them keep moving forward.

In late August, Johnny Cash and the Tennessee Three made a guest appearance on *The Summer Smothers Brothers Show*, the summer replacement for the duo's comedy/variety series on CBS. The series was hosted by Glen Campbell, and we were featured on the season finale, which also included country and bluegrass artists the Stoneman Family.

Luther's death was still fresh in everybody's minds, but we pulled together and did outstanding performances of "Folsom Prison Blues" and "Ballad of the Harp-Weaver." John in particular made a good impression on the television folks, which would pay big dividends for us not too far down the line.

We all knew that for the Johnny Cash Show to be successful, we had to get someone to fill Luther's spot. Carl Perkins was doing a great job filling in for our departed friend, but his playing style was different and our sound had lost its distinctive character.

In September 1968, Arkansas Governor Winthrop Rockefeller was campaigning for re-election and thought it might be a good idea to hire John to do some shows at his political rallies throughout the state. After playing a rally in Little Rock, we had two days off, and Carl and I decided that since we were just 135 miles from Memphis, we would just go home and then rejoin the group on September 17 for the last date of the tour. We'd been out for quite a while and were anxious to spend a couple of days at home, so we caught a plane in Little Rock and flew into Memphis, with Carl going on to Jackson, Tennessee.

On the morning of the seventeenth, Carl drove up from Jackson and we went to the Memphis airport to hop a flight back to Arkansas. After boarding the plane, the captain announced that there was some severe weather between Memphis and Little Rock and that we would remain on the ground until conditions improved. We'd been sitting on that plane for about an hour and a half when the captain announced the flight had been cancelled.

By then I was getting a little worried about making it to the show on time. When we got off the plane, Carl and I talked to the gate agent, who said American Airlines had a flight that was getting ready to leave and we could use our tickets to board it. We raced to the American gate, got on the plane, and sat down—just in time to hear that flight had also been canceled due to bad weather between Memphis and Little Rock.

Now I was really getting worried, so I called Governor Rockefeller's office and told them the problem. "Don't worry about it; we'll send a plane to get you," one of the governor's staff people told me. I said, "That's well and good, but there's some severe weather between here and there, and I don't feel great about being on a small plane in weather like that." The staffer said that wasn't a problem, the plane would just go around any storms. It was about 4:30 in the afternoon, and if they sent the plane quickly, we could still make the show, since the flight to Little Rock was no more than thirty minutes and it would take another hour to drive to the rally in Fayetteville.

We rushed over to the private terminal to wait for the plane, but it didn't show up. I made several calls to the governor's office, and every time the staff person said, "He's on his way! He's on his way!" After a while, I finally said, "There's not much need in his coming now, because the show has already started." The staffer apparently had trouble understanding that, so I told him, "Send the plane anyhow, because our motor home is over there and we have to get it back. So send the plane on."

We waited around that private terminal for a long time, and after it got dark, a plane finally taxied up to the terminal. We walked over and asked if it was Governor Rockefeller's plane, and when the pilot said yes, Carl and I jumped aboard and we immediately took off. I told the pilot, "I don't think there is any big hurry here, because I know the show is over." We went anyway, as there was no way to get in touch with John or June or W. S. at the concert to let them know what was happening.

When we finally got to the hotel where everyone was staying, I gave John a call and explained the situation, and he said he understood and that everything was fine. He added, "You know, Marshall, a strange thing happened here. We did two shows, and W. S. and I went out by ourselves and did the first one, and I brought June on and she did a little. It was all right. For the second show, a girl came out of the audience and said that her boyfriend played guitar exactly like Luther."

John told the girl to bring her boyfriend backstage between the shows, and when they arrived, he gave the guy Carl's guitar and ran through a couple of songs with him, like "Folsom Prison Blues" and "I Walk the Line." The young man had every note down to the nth degree, and he played just like Luther and even sounded like Luther. He played the entire second show that night, and John said he did a fantastic job. "I want you to talk to him," John told me. "His name is Bob Wootton, and he lives over in Tulsa, Oklahoma. I've got his number; give him a call. I'd like to get him to come out and see the show, the way we would normally do it, not necessarily the way we did this show, and see if he would fit in and could do the job."

<hr />

Our next date was in Memphis, about a week later, and it was a show I had promoted. I invited Bob to see the show and put him in the audience with Etta and some other family members. This wasn't a little campaign-rally show where we probably played to no more than a thousand people; this was the Mid-South Coliseum, which was completely packed with more than 11,000 screaming fans.

Bob got a little nervous and told Etta, "I didn't realize this is the way it was." He was about ready to get up and go home, but she told him, "Bob, you stay right here. Everything is going to be all right. You stay here and you talk to Marshall and John after this is over and then make up your mind what you want to do." So, Bob watched the show, and although he was very nervous when we brought him backstage afterward to talk, he said he thought he could handle playing lead guitar for us.

John and I talked it over and decided we'd try him out on our next date, which was set for Knoxville. Bob went onstage with us that night, and it was absolutely scary to look over and see a new face, but his guitar work was as close to Luther's as anybody could possibly dream. John, W. S., and I could tell the difference in their playing, but I don't think anyone in the audience could. Bob had everything down—every song, the keys, the kickoffs, the breaks, the endings—he had all of it down pat. It was absolutely amazing. Nobody, short of Luther, could have done the job that Bob did that night, and we hired him immediately.

Bob was a godsend. Most musical scholars say that it was the style, more than the sound, of the Tennessee Two and Tennessee Three that was crucial to John's career, contributing at least 50 percent to his overall success. But if you take Luther out of the mix, that falls well below 50 percent, so it was critical that we find somebody who could mimic Luther's style. But it turned out that somebody found us instead. It's funny how things work out sometimes. Had bad weather not grounded our plane that day, I don't think Bob's girlfriend would have come up to anybody and said, "I've got a boyfriend who plays guitar exactly like Luther."

We were the first country music artists to use video as part of our performance onstage, and we did so in the late 1960s, before VCRs and similar electronic equipment came on the scene. We set up a front-screen projector on the light board in the center of the hall and would project a video clip that we'd put together on freight trains on the wall behind the stage.

The segment ran about five minutes and ended very abruptly with two locomotives crashing into each other head on. It was very effective. In fact, there were many nights when the locomotives would collide, and the house lights would come all the way up, that the people in the audience would jump to their feet and cheer and clap for five minutes or more.

⚊⚋〰⚋⚊

We were enjoying phenomenal success with the *Folsom Prison* album as 1969 began, and all of our careers were starting to grow by leaps and bounds. We couldn't believe how well everything was going, and then things suddenly got even better.

Our appearance on *The Summer Smothers Brothers Show* apparently had opened a lot of eyes in Hollywood, and the executives over at ABC were considering John to host a summer musical variety show. That really excited John, enough to where he began getting his act together even more. Since cutting down on his drug use after Luther's death the previous summer, he was turning into a different man. The old J. R. was coming back, and everybody was glad because we hadn't seen him in quite some time.

The Johnny Cash Show was really blossoming, coming together the way it could have years earlier if John had been in the condition he appeared to be in now. If everyone had been giving 100 percent effort on our tours, I think John's improved physical and mental state, coupled with the success we were having with the *Folsom Prison* album, inspired everybody—including John—to start giving 115 percent.

We were doing fantastic concerts, and everywhere we went, the fans just loved us. I think it's fair to say we knocked the socks off everyone in the audience night after night after night. Things were going great—and they got even better when the ABC television network called and offered us a shot at our own national television show.

⟞⟝⟞⟝⟞⟝

Despite all the wonderful things that were happening, John still didn't have his heart in recording. So, rather than try to grind something out in the studio, we decided instead to cut another live album, and this time we would take the entire cast to California's San Quentin State Prison in February to do it. Not wanting to do the same show that we did on the *Folsom Prison* album, we changed things up a little and learned some new songs. However, it was a song we *didn't* learn that really helped to put that concert and the album on the musical map.

The show at the prison was going over really well—judging from the response of our captive audience, the guards, and everyone onstage—when, right in the middle of the concert, John stopped and asked someone to get his briefcase from the "dressing room," a tiny room behind the stage that was just big enough to change clothes in. When the briefcase was brought onstage, he got down on his hands and knees, opened it, and rifled through it until he found what he was looking for (if you listen to the unedited version of the album, you can hear all that).

Apparently, John had remembered there was a song June had wanted him to sing that night. It was written by Shel Silverstein, who I guess had been out to John's house a few days earlier and played the song. June had just loved it and thought it might go over well at the San Quentin show.

Knowing how unpredictable John could be, a nervous Carl Perkins, who was onstage with us, walked over to me and said, "What are we going to do?" "Man, I got no earthly idea," I told him. John kept talking, and in a little bit Carl came back over and said, "You don't have any idea what we're going to do?" I said I didn't but told him, "If he says, 'Kick it off,' just grab something and carry it around the horn [play a musical riff over and over], and when we see which direction he's going, we'll follow him." It wasn't long until John turned to Carl and said, "Kick it off, Carl," and Carl started a rhythm pattern that we all began to follow. When everything was moving along well, John stepped up to the mike and, for the first time ever, performed "Boy Named Sue" onstage.

That song tore the crowd—and us—apart, because it was the first time any of us had ever heard it. It was so funny, we laughed all the way through it and weren't very focused on what we were playing—and then we remembered they were recording the show! We kept right on going, and the song went over so well that the inmates jumped to their feet and hollered and screamed and laughed and cut up. And so did we.

When *Johnny Cash At San Quentin* was released a few weeks later, it didn't prove to be as commercially successful as the *Folsom Prison* album, but we really hadn't expected it to. However, "Boy Named Sue" soared to No. 1 right away and stayed there for a long time, becoming a major career-building song for us. It was a song that we just happened to run into, but we could tell by the chemistry it generated onstage and in the audience that "Boy Named Sue" was going to be a smash hit. It's a song I'll never forget recording and one that will always be one of my favorites.

Things were rolling along at such a breakneck pace that we were forced to make some changes in our organization. We'd been using Saul Holiff as our agent and promoter, but while he was a good guy and a decent promoter, he just wasn't equipped to do what we needed of him. Saul was a one-man operation, but with the way our career was exploding, we needed companies with staffs big enough to handle what lay in front of us.

As a result, we signed with Marty Klein and the Agency for the Performing Arts in Los Angeles for bookings, and we hired Alan Tinkley and Lou Robin of Artist Consultants Productions in Los Angeles to handle our management and promote our shows.

In June 1969, the television show became a reality. *The Johnny Cash Show* was taped before a live studio audience at Nashville's Ryman Auditorium and aired on Wednesday nights. We were surrounded by good people from ABC, all of whom were very professional, and the talent coordinator came up with several great supporting acts. We rehearsed for a day and then taped the show on Wednesday evening, which was very nerve-racking since stopping tape to go back and erase a mistake was very expensive and greatly frowned upon by the producers. But everybody pitched in together, and we didn't make any mistakes that needed to be erased.

John, who was straight as an arrow by then, was a tremendous host. His talent seemed to grow larger with each passing week, and since he wasn't popping amphetamines, he had gained fifty or sixty pounds, so his clothes fit him well and he looked absolutely handsome. He was so good on the show that the Johnny Cash mystique seemed to grow tenfold.

We had done a lot of TV by then, although nothing that John had hosted all the way through, but he was such a natural that he became a great TV host almost overnight. He had total control of everything that was going on with the show, and everybody—the audience, the cast, the network—was behind him 100 percent, and the finished product showed it.

We taped every show at the Ryman, which was really the only place to do a musical variety show like ours because of all of the great talent in the area. The show opened with the camera focused on John's back, and when he turned around and said, "Hello, I'm Johnny Cash," the roof would almost come off that historic old building.

The regular segments on the show, like "Ride This Train," were just extensions of John. In fact, everything was an extension of John. He had his head on straight, and it was absolutely an honor to be a part of the great things that were happening to us at that time.

It's ironic that Luther Perkins, who had been so instrumental in the development of our unique style and sound, wasn't around to see things really take off. We'd struggled since the early days, and now, less than a year after Luther's death, our careers were exploding but he wasn't there to take advantage of it. That was very heartbreaking, and it still hurts me today.

———

With Marty Klein at APA and Artist Consultants on board, everything went to the next level and we started playing the biggest buildings in the United States. We started flying everywhere because our schedule was so full we didn't have time to drive to dates the way we had earlier. We might play a show in Los Angeles one night and the next evening perform in Philadelphia or Pittsburgh or New York City, which meant flying was the only option. Everything became more complicated . . . better but more complicated.

I was still in charge of all our travel and lodging arrangements, and handling them had become quite a chore. About the only thing I did differently was to hire a travel agency to help with the airline and hotel bookings. There were no loose ends on anyone's part.

We had the greatest show on earth; the country music world had never seen or heard anything like the Johnny Cash Show. We carried a lot of people on our tours, and it cost a lot of money to do so, but that's what we wanted to do, especially John, who was determined to give the best shows possible to repay all the fans who had supported him through good times and bad. And pay them back we did! When Johnny Cash, the Tennessee Three, June Carter Cash, the Statler Brothers, the Carter Family, and Carl Perkins left the stage after a show, audiences knew they'd seen the greatest musical attraction that had ever been in that particular building.

Today, it's not unusual for a top act to sell out a huge arena in twenty minutes or less, thanks to agencies like Ticketmaster and sales over the Internet. Tickets go on sale almost instantly worldwide, and with the push of a few buttons big shows can sell out before many fans even know tickets are available. But when we were playing those same buildings, there weren't any electronic sales or twenty-minute sellouts. People had to buy their tickets at the box office, and in some cases lines could be almost a mile long. With each person buying one or two or maybe up to five tickets, and with perhaps a half-dozen ticket sellers, it could take a long time to sell out a show. But regardless of where we went or how long it took, all of our concerts were selling out.

Our shows appealed to people from all walks of life, all races, creeds, and colors. It didn't make any difference what type of music you liked, if you came to see the Johnny Cash Show, you were going to be entertained! No matter what your problems were, come to the Johnny Cash Show and you'd forget them for a couple of hours. I think that everyone who saw our concerts went home feeling better about themselves, their families, their jobs, and about life in general. We could see the positive effect our music had on people when we'd look out into the audience and see the joy on their faces. There were many newcomers, but the crowds included droves of our old fans who had stuck with us through thick and thin. We were so appreciative of them then, and I still am today.

⚓

Later that year, John moved his parents to Nashville from California and bought them a house that sat kind of catty-cornered across the street from his home in Hendersonville. Mama Cash and Ray were dear friends of Etta's and mine. Etta and Mama were like two peas in a pod, and when we'd all been living in California, Mama, Vivian, and Etta had been like the Three Musketeers, hanging around together all the time.

Even though Mama and Ray had sort of looked after Vivian and the girls before and after the divorce, they really didn't realize how bad off John was. I don't think either of them really understood what was wrong with him or why he wouldn't go home after tours. As John's condition worsened, the Cashes called me often. Mama would say, "Marshall, I just want to know what's wrong with my son." It was tough to tell her what was going on, and I'd often make excuses, but I never lied to her. I'd say, "Mama, I think he's going to be all right. He's just going through some bad times. He's going to come around. Everybody just hold their breath, and it'll be all right."

It got to the point that they were calling me two or three times a week, no matter where I was. I think John knew they were doing that, and he sort of resented it. I wouldn't say it created any problems, but it did put me in the middle. I wasn't going to lie to Mama and Ray, but on the other hand, I couldn't tell them the whole truth either.

⟞⟝⟞⟝

There was one very unpleasant surprise in store for us in 1969. *Johnny Cash At Folsom Prison* was well on its way to becoming the biggest-selling album in country music history and was earning us a lot of royalties from Columbia. When we first signed with the label, John, Luther, and I had made an agreement—not on paper and nothing was discussed with the record company—that we would continue to draw our Sun royalties but would leave all of our Columbia royalties alone. We agreed to never touch them, to just leave them in the bank as our retirement nest egg, rather than set up a formal retirement plan.

Over the years, we never took any money out of that royalty account, none of it. We'd get a statement from Columbia showing how much we'd made, but we just left that money in the bank. It was something to fall back on if we ever needed it.

Now, however, whenever the subject of retirement came up, John didn't want to talk about it. We thought something was strange, and when we started looking into things, we discovered that he'd gone to Columbia and gotten the label's execs to give him all that royalty money, every penny of it! Talk about letting the air out of a balloon. We knew the mental and physical shape he was in and the way he was blowing through money—and we just knew we weren't going see a dime of that retirement money.

⎯⎯ᴍᴍᴧᴩᴍᴍ⎯⎯

John was nominated in just about every category for the Country Music Association awards that year, and in October, at the group's annual convention, he won nearly all of them. John was named CMA's entertainer of the year and male vocalist of the year, won album of the year for *Johnny Cash At San Quentin* and single of the year for "Boy Named Sue," and he and June were named vocal group of the year. That was just icing on the cake, because afterward, everything got bigger and better for the Johnny Cash Show.

Not long after the CMA Awards, the *Nashville Banner*, Music City's afternoon newspaper, ran a huge article headlined "Johnny Cash: The Biggest Record Seller in the Universe." Not bad for two car mechanics and an appliance salesman who started out strumming on three battered guitars and traveled to dates in an old Plymouth with a bass tied on the roof!

Also in 1969, *Life* magazine did a big article on John and ran his picture on the cover. That was the talk of the country, especially among those in the country music world. It really was a delight to walk into a drugstore or pass a newsstand and see John on the cover of America's favorite magazine.

⎯⎯ᴍᴍᴧᴩᴍᴍ⎯⎯

Everything was running full speed ahead, and we were packing them in everywhere we played. In December, we sold out New York's legendary Madison Square Garden, the first time in history that a country music attraction had done that. Columbia recorded the concert, and while the resulting album was a good one, the label locked the master away and apparently didn't discover it until more than thirty years later. Columbia finally released *Johnny Cash Live At Madison Square Garden* in 2002.

The album is such a delight to listen to and includes Johnny Cash and the Tennessee Three, Carl Perkins, the Statler Brothers, Tommy Cash, and the Carter Family. The only person missing is June, who wasn't at the show that night. When John announced onstage that she was home "taking care of the family"—the latest addition to which was due in March—there was a huge round of applause from the crowd. It seemed that everybody, everywhere, including that sold-out crowd at Madison Square Garden, was thrilled that June was going to have a baby and that John was the daddy.

Everyone, it seemed, was hoping that baby would be a boy. John already had four girls—Rosanne, Kathy, Cindy, and Tara—with Vivian, and he loved them to death, but he wanted a boy real bad. He got his wish on March 3, 1970, when John Carter Cash was born.

PART THREE
THE SEVENTIES

The day John Carter Cash was born, March 3, 1970, was the day that Johnny Cash stopped doing drugs. No matter what you may have heard, no matter what has been printed, no matter who got credit for what, the moment John looked down and saw his infant son was the moment he quit drugs 100 percent.

Not only did he stop taking drugs, John also stopped smoking cigarettes. As a result, he started putting on quite a bit of weight, but that was very becoming to him. John always looked exceptionally good in his stage clothes, and no matter how much weight he put on, he always looked sharp. When he was dressed up a bit, like in his stage clothes, there was almost an aura around him, especially after he stopped doing drugs. He had charisma and a keen awareness of who and what he was: a superstar.

John's behavior always changed when he got straight, and this time was no exception. Those little naps he was once so fond of were now necessities, and he had to change his schedule a little to get them in. He couldn't just pop around town at all hours, like he'd done in the past.

Now straight, John had a powerful presence and a new air of confidence about him. Whenever he walked into a room, everyone's eyes would turn in his direction. At concerts, when he walked onstage, the crowds would go wild. And when he'd turn his back on the audience, like he did on the TV show, and then turn around and say, "Hello, I'm Johnny Cash," the applause would start all over again. Sometimes it would go on for several minutes, and you couldn't hear anything but hollering and screaming, and often we were almost blinded by all the flashbulbs going off. Many times, the only way we could get the crowd to sit down and listen was to start the show.

When John was onstage, especially during the first part of the show, whatever troubles people in the audience might have—at work, at home, in their personal or professional life—would all vanish. It was a good feeling to see how his presence and our music lit up their faces and helped them forget their problems for at least a couple of hours. It was very rewarding.

———◆———

We were rehearsing in Nashville that spring when John came up to me one day and said we'd received a call from Washington and that President Nixon wanted us to perform at the White House. "Man, oh man, that's good!" I told him. He sort of laughed and asked me if I'd "go up there and sort of case the place out a little bit." John's sister Reba had taken the call at the House of Cash, and there weren't many details, so I told him I'd get in touch with the appropriate contact person and, if necessary, fly to Washington to check things out.

Reba gave me the name of the contact, who turned out to be the private secretary for first lady Pat Nixon. She was delighted when I telephoned and told her who I was. "The president really wants Mr. Cash to come up and do a performance in the White House," she told me. She wasn't able to provide much information about the room where they wanted us to perform, so I suggested that I go up there and look around. "Now, this is not to say we will or we won't do the show," I told her. "It's just that we need to really know how to program ourselves, so to speak." She said, "We'll be glad to have you come up."

When I arrived at the airport in Washington, I discovered they had sent a long limousine (not the president's limo, I'm sure) to pick me up and take me to the back door of the White House. When I walked in, I was greeted by Mrs. Nixon's secretary, who showed me the room where we would play. It was a large room that could probably handle 300 to 350 for a concert. I told her what size stage we would need and other particulars, and she wrote them all down and said, "We can do all of that. All we need to know is when President Nixon will be available for the show."

I flew back to Nashville and told John about the meeting. He said, "What do you think?" I told him we should definitely play the White House. "OK," he said, "set it up and we'll give it our best shot."

At John's insistence, we brought some of our family along to the show in Washington. John and June brought John Carter; I brought along Etta and my son, Randy; and everyone else brought their wives. John and June toured the White House for an hour or so in the afternoon before we did the show and were introduced to President Nixon. He asked if they would like to have a place for John Carter and his nurse, Mrs. Kelly, to stay, which resulted in John Carter getting to sleep in one of the White House bedrooms.

We'd been on a lot of stages and had done a fair amount of television by that time in our career, but performing at the White House was awesome! President and Mrs. Nixon were the last to arrive, and they sat down right in front of us, no more than ten feet away. It was a very tight setup, with the stage just eighteen inches off the floor and the chairs elevated so that those in the back rows could see. When I looked over to the right and about halfway up the rows, I was delighted to see our old friend Tex Ritter sitting there. Tex had opened a number of shows for us and was a wonderful man. There were also a lot of other people from Nashville in the audience, in addition to our friends and families.

Performing in front of the president of the United States and the first lady was quite a treat, especially when we saw their expressions and realized they knew all of our songs! I figured that was quite an achievement. We played for about an hour, and Mr. Nixon called us back for two encores, after which we sat down and chatted with the president and some of the Congressmen. It was a night that those of us who were there will never forget.

The Billy Graham organization contacted John and invited him to appear as a special guest at a Billy Graham Crusade in Knoxville, Tennessee, on May 24. Naturally, we took them up on the invitation. It was the first time we'd ever performed at a Crusade, and all of us went to the date in East Tennessee.

Meeting Billy Graham was another big highlight of my life, and I'm sure everyone else felt the same way. I had admired the man for so many years but had never seen him except on television, so I was a little nervous when I found myself standing face to face with him. There were so many people at the Crusade, and they were so appreciative. It was wonderful that we were able to build a longtime association with Billy Graham.

The very next day after we played the Billy Graham Crusade in Knoxville, the Tennessee Three recorded an album for Columbia called *The Sound Behind Johnny Cash*. It got a lot of airplay, and several disc jockeys used cuts off the album as their theme song. For a long time after that, you could hear us almost anytime you turned on the radio.

The three of us never really pursued a recording career, because there was only so much we could do instrumentally and usually those things were our Johnny Cash songs. Still, a lot of people were interested in our music, and it's something I'm glad we did. I think we did three albums, and all of them featured instrumental versions of the Johnny Cash songs we'd recorded earlier.

At about that same time, John made a movie with Kirk Douglas called *A Gunfight*, which was released the following year. It was a good film, not one of those B movies you'd see at some rundown theater, and we were fortunate enough to do the soundtrack, too. This was yet another highlight in our career. Meeting Kirk Douglas was an honor in itself, and he later appeared as a guest on our television show. John also invited him to spend some time at his Hendersonville home, and the band went out one night and had dinner with him. We discovered that Kirk Douglas was not only a great actor, he was a great man.

Also about that time, Gregory Peck was filming a movie called *I Walk the Line*, the title of which was taken from our classic song. The studio execs asked us to do the soundtrack, which was a natural for the movie and which we recorded in April 1970. After that, with Carl Perkins's help, we recorded the soundtrack for *Little Fauss and Big Halsey,* starring Robert Redford. Both films were very successful and exposed our music to many new listeners. And, of course, it was really a pleasure to go into theaters and hear ourselves performing the soundtracks of popular Hollywood movies.

<hr />

When John Carter was about six or eight months old, John and June began taking him on the road with us. They brought along a nurse, Mrs. Kelly, to help with John Carter, and a bodyguard, Armando Bisciglia, a nice guy whose wife worked in John and June's home as a cook. It was Armando's job to look out for the family during that time of social unrest, when ransom kidnappings of celebrities and their family members were a real possibility.

John was the most protective father I've ever seen, and he went to great lengths to safeguard his young son. We often stayed in downtown high-rise hotels, and John worried a lot about that. Armando always carried a bag containing 200 feet of rope with him, so he could lower John Carter from a window to the ground in case there was a fire at our hotel. Whenever possible, I tried to book our rooms at hotels in the suburbs, where the buildings weren't as tall and there were usually secluded areas where John could take John Carter for walks without being disturbed by a lot of people.

We always had a security guard who would sit outside the door of whatever room John Carter was in. Sometimes John Carter would stay with his nurse, and sometimes he'd be in the room with John and June, depending on circumstances and how tired everyone was. Nonetheless, the guard was always close by. He would meet John's limo when it pulled up to the hotel, then go to the room and stay there until we left, although he occasionally would accompany father and son on walks outside the hotel.

I always made sure John told me when he was going to leave the hotel with John Carter, and many times I'd follow along behind them and keep watch, just to make sure nothing unusual happened. There had been so much publicity about John that by then just about everybody knew about John Carter, so I just didn't want to take a chance that somebody might try to harm either one of them. And I wasn't the only one looking out for them; everyone on the show helped keep an eye out for anything suspicious, and as a result, there were no problems.

John was also concerned about John Carter being exposed to cigarette smoke that had been absorbed by the carpets, bedding, and furniture in their hotel rooms. One day he told me, "When you book the hotels, I want you to make sure that there's no cigarette odors of any kind in the room. If there's any sort of cigarette odor, or any odor, I want the hotel to shampoo the carpets and clean the room. If we have to pay extra for it, we'll just pay extra for it."

He stopped, thought for a moment, then said, "On the other hand, let's don't check for odors, let's just have it done. Make it part of the arrangement to have all of the carpets cleaned and fumigated before we get to the hotel. That way, if John Carter Cash wants to get down on the floor and play, I won't have to worry about it, and we won't have no cigarette odors or contamination of any kind in the room. I want it spic and span from A to Z so John Carter can have free run of the place." That was an interesting request from someone who, just six months earlier, had been one of the heaviest smokers I'd ever known.

<hr />

All fathers love their sons, but there was an unusually strong bond between John and John Carter. Proud papa John would spend every minute he could with his baby boy while we were on the road, and they were always playing together. I think he would have been the same way with his girls.

John loved *all* his children. There was often the perception that he loved John Carter more than he did Rosanne, Kathy, Cindy, and Tara, because he spent so much time with his son and almost none with his daughters. But that's wrong—he loved his girls every bit as much as he loved John Carter. The difference was that John Carter came along in 1970 at the height of John's career, and when he saw that baby and decided to stop using drugs, a whole new world opened up for him. Now he was clean and sober and wanted his son with him at all times.

But when the girls were born, John was deep into drugs and didn't want anybody around him. If he'd had his head on straight, and if the girls had gone on the road with us, I'm sure he would have doted on them just as much as he did John Carter, because he loved all his kids from the bottom of his heart. But the girls were born in a different era, under different circumstances, and because they remained with Vivian after the divorce, it took longer for that special bond between father and daughters to develop. It was unfortunate, but that's the way things happened.

Things were going so well and happening so fast that our heads were practically swimming. Looking back, it was one of the greatest times in our lives. John and June were so much in love it was almost unbelievable, and the relationship they had with John Carter was so wonderfully close. They were together almost all of the time, at home as well as on the road.

Now that John was completely straight and back to being his old self, the closeness between us had returned, and everybody was terrifically happy. Even though we were very busy, we all stuck together, worked together, helped one another, and lived for one another.

The attitude of everyone working on the Johnny Cash Show changed—from the production man all the way up to John himself—and that happened because John had changed. When he stopped using drugs, John became a great person again. Our performances were much better, our record sales were soaring, we had a hit television show—everything was better. And everybody responded by giving their all. Every day, at every show, in every studio session, no matter what we were doing, everybody gave their very best to the Johnny Cash Show.

———◦———

With all that was going on, John didn't want to take any time off to prepare new material and go into the studio to record. And even though it was time to cut another record, we didn't have anything on tape that was worth releasing. Part of the problem was that we were involved in so many things that we really didn't have a lot of time to scout around for good songs, and John didn't have the time to write any. We were really hurting for a good song.

Sometime earlier, we had met Kris Kristofferson at the Columbia studio in Nashville where he cleaned up between sessions and worked as a handyman. The first day I met him, he was cleaning the studio and leaned down to pick up an ashtray sitting beside me. "You don't smoke, do you, Marshall?" he asked in his deep voice. I told him I didn't, and he said, "Good, I'll just take this ashtray and put it out back."

Kris, who'd flown helicopters in the military, had been trying to get songs to John, but Columbia had a policy that prevented employees from pitching songs to the artists. The label's brass told him that if he started pitching songs, they'd fire him, since they didn't want anyone to make the artists uncomfortable when they came to the studio.

Kris abided by the rules, but one day John heard a noise outside his house. When he looked outside, he saw a helicopter landing nearby in a small field where John would later build a tennis court. When he went out and walked up to the chopper to see what was going on, there sat Kris Kristofferson.

John didn't know his first name at the time, but Kris jumped out and said, "I didn't know any better way to get you out of the house and to hand you this tape, but I have a song I want you to hear." Naturally, John couldn't refuse a request from someone who'd gone to so much trouble to contact him, so he took the tape and soon listened to it. He called Kris later and told him that when he got the time he was going to record the song, which was called "Sunday Morning Coming Down."

A few months later, in July 1970, we worked up the song during an afternoon rehearsal for *The Johnny Cash Show* and
decided to perform it on TV that night. Kris was in the audience,
sitting almost in the top row of the balcony at the Ryman. There
were a couple of lines in the song that the producer didn't like.
One was, ". . . wishing, Lord, that I was stoned," which the network execs didn't want aired on prime-time television. John listened to his request and told him, "Well, I'll think about that."
Kris was worried, because he wanted the lines to stay; they were
part of his song.

Show time arrived, and when that particular segment rolled
around, John introduced the song and we performed "Sunday Morning Coming Down" just as Kris Kristofferson had written it. That
made Kris very happy . . . and the producer a little sad, although we
were able to convince him that everything would be all right. The
musical track of "Sunday Morning Coming Down" was taken off of
the TV show and released as a single, and it became a gigantic hit.
At that point, our last three hit records—"Folsom Prison Blues,"
"Boy Named Sue," and "Sunday Morning Coming Down"—had all
been recorded live onstage.

⚬⚬⚬

John's extreme generosity also returned about this time. Before he
got into drugs, he was always giving somebody something, as much
as he could afford, which at the time wasn't a lot. But if anyone
looked like he was down and out, or someone needed help or had a
family member who needed help, John was always there for them.
Unfortunately, he'd stopped doing those little acts of kindness during the drug years.

Now, however, it wasn't unusual for him to call a member of the
entourage to his dressing room and give him a check for a huge
amount of money. When that happened to me, I'd question him
about it and tell him, "Hey, John, you know this is totally unnecessary." But he wouldn't even discuss it.

I remember we were playing a large theater while on a tour of
Europe, when I heard John call my name from his dressing room. I
was upstairs getting ready to start the show when I heard him
holler again, "Marshall!" I yelled back and asked what he wanted.

"Come on down here," he answered. I shouted, "I'm getting ready to start the show in a couple of minutes." He hollered back, "Come on down here anyhow."

I went hustling down to his dressing room, which was at the bottom of the stairs, and when I walked in, June was standing there and John stepped into the bathroom. "Did he holler from here?" I asked. "Yeah, he's in the bathroom. He just wanted to give you this," June said, handing me an envelope. "Well, I got to start the show!" I told her, but I opened the envelope and discovered a check for a huge amount of money. I said, "This is totally unnecessary." She said, "Marshall, it's just something that he wants to do. Just take it. It's something he wants to do, and he wanted me to give it to you. He'll be up onstage in just a few minutes."

That's the way John was. When he was straight, he was the greatest human being I'd ever known in my entire life—and I've known a lot of people! For a pretty good while there, he'd been one of the cruelest people I'd ever known, but now, finally, the old John was back and we were all pleased to see him!

<hr />

In the fall of 1970, a few days before Thanksgiving, John came up to me and said, "Marshall, I want to buy June a ring, and I need to have it here by the day after tomorrow." When I asked him what kind of ring he was interested in, he said, "I want a big diamond." That's all he said. "Well, do you want a perfect stone, or what do you want?" I asked. He said, "I want a perfect stone, the biggest you can buy."

My brother Hershel was a jeweler, and he was the first person I called. I told him what John had said, and he asked me, "What does he call a big ring?" I said, "The biggest that you can find." Hershel said, "Does he realize how much money this is going to cost?" I said, "I don't think he cares."

Hershel spent the better part of that day making phone calls, and when I rang him back, he told me, "I can't find anything in this part of the country. Something like that will have to come out of New York." I related that conversation to John, who told me, "Well, tell him to go to New York and get it and try to have it here the day after tomorrow. When can he leave?"

I called Hershel back and said, "If I bought you a prepaid ticket, could you fly up to New York and go in all the places and see what's the best you can come up with?" He said he could do that, and then I told him, "Well, he wants it here the day after tomorrow."

I arranged for Hershel's airline ticket, and the next morning he began scouting all of the city's wholesale diamond houses. He called me back and said he'd found two stones. One was 5.2 carats, and the other was 8.2, and each of them cost a *lot* of money. When I told John the price and asked which one he wanted, he answered, "I want the big one." I asked if he was sure, and he said, "I want the big one. Can he have it here by tomorrow night?"

I called Hershel and told him what John had said. "These people gotta be paid for this thing," Hershel said. I told him I'd send the money to him by wire transfer within a couple of hours, to which he replied, "Well, that's only the diamond. I'll have to set it in a ring. But while you're getting the money, I can get that done."

By the time he was able to get the stone placed in the setting, it was too late to get a flight out of New York for Nashville, so the next morning I called my travel agent and had him book a series of flights that would get Hershel into Nashville about an hour before the TV show was to start. I sent Armando Bisciglia, John's chauffeur at the time, to pick Hershel up at the airport and take him downtown to the Ryman. The plane landed about thirty minutes late, so when the car finally pulled up outside the Ryman, I grabbed the ring, took it out of the box, and rushed into John's dressing room.

"Here it is, John," I told him. "Oh, man, thank you, Marshall!" was all he said. He didn't ask any questions about anything; he just went out onstage. While he and June were doing some little bit, he reached into his pocket and pulled out the ring. "Lookie here, baby, I bought you a Thanksgiving present," he said as he gave her the ring, which was the most beautiful thing you'd ever want to see in your life.

That was just something John wanted to do for June, I think maybe as a way of making up for lost time, for the bad days when everybody was suffering—mentally, physically, financially, and every other way—while he was throwing away everything on drugs. Now that he was straight, he just couldn't do enough for people. It didn't make any difference who it was, friends, acquaintances, or total strangers, he just couldn't do enough for people. If we stopped at a truck stop to fuel up, he was liable to give somebody at the next pump his last guitar or one of his black suits or whatever. It seemed like he just couldn't give enough away.

John did benefits all over the United States, and one day I told him, "John there's a children's home near Senatobia, Mississippi, that depends on contributions to exist. It's a good place for children who've lost their fathers and mothers or have been abandoned, and some of them are a little sick. It's just a wonderful place, and I'd like to impose on you to take the show down there and do a benefit for them." He said, "You set it, and we'll be there." And that's exactly what we did.

I set up a fundraiser concert at the Farrow Manor Baptist Children's Home, and John took the whole show down there, which cost him a lot of money. We supplied the sound, the lights, and everything else, and we raised about $30,000 for the home. John paid all of the expenses and never asked for anything in exchange; he was just so happy to do a good deed for people in need. Some of the kids at the show came backstage that night, and John met them, talked with them, shook their hands, rubbed their heads, and he almost looked sheepish at times because everyone was making a fuss over him for doing a good turn.

During that period, I don't think that John turned down a single request to do a benefit. Whether it was something I personally wanted to do or something that someone called to tell me about, John always agreed to perform, paid all of the expenses, and never even asked how much money we raised. He always pretty much knew, though, just by looking at the size of the crowd. I, of course, would always give our accountant a breakdown of how much we'd raised and how much the benefit had cost us.

34

Most people had read about John's drug problems in newspapers and magazines, but now when he walked out onstage, everybody in the place knew they were seeing a different man—the real Johnny Cash—and they were so appreciative. They loved him and wanted him to be straight and to do the things he did best: make music and entertain.

It didn't matter if there were 20,000 people in the audience or just 1,000, every person in the place—fans, cast and crew, building management, ushers—was just thrilled to death to see John looking, acting, and performing so well. The magic and charisma were back, and everything was going great.

The extent of John's popularity with the fans became apparent to me when we flew into Pittsburgh to do a show. As we were approaching the city, the pilot came back into the passenger cabin and said, "Mr. Grant, I just got word from the airport that we have a small problem, and I'd like to know what you want me to do about it." I asked, a little nervously, "Well, what's the problem?" The pilot said, "They tell me there are about ten thousand people inside and outside the airport just waiting to get a glimpse of John and the other people on the show as they come through the terminal. It's causing quite a problem, and we don't know how to deal with it."

I suggested that, to avoid the crowds, we have our ground transportation pick us up at the gate as we got off the plane and leave someone from the crew there to secure our baggage. And that's what we did.

John felt a little bad about avoiding all those fans, but I told him I'd made the choice for security reasons, and thought it was the best thing to do. That night at the concert, there was an enormous sold-out crowd of about 20,000, and when we got onstage, he apologized for what we had to do at the airport.

Now that John was truly straight—he'd gained a lot of weight, looked great, and was enjoying tremendous success with the TV show and hit records—the media were continuing to give June the credit for breaking his drug habit. Many of the stories sounded as if Vivian had gotten John started on amphetamines and couldn't get him to quit, and then June had come along and finally got him to stop. But that wasn't the case at all.

Many people had worked very hard to get John to stop taking drugs—June, Nat Winston, and myself included—but we all failed. In fact, at the height of his drug abuse, we just did the best we could to keep him alive and showing up for concerts. But now that John was doing so well, the media were focused on June's role in his recovery, and the question some of the articles seemed to raise was: Why couldn't Vivian have done that?

Well, the truth is that Vivian tried everything she possibly could to get John to quit. But she was living in California raising their children, and John seldom went home between tours, so she found herself facing an almost impossible task. I don't think she really understood what she was dealing with, because while John was always a bit unpredictable when straight, he was totally unpredictable when he was strung out on drugs. And Vivian just couldn't figure out how to reach him, no matter how hard she tried.

With due respect to everyone involved, the facts are that Vivian Liberto did not get John to start taking drugs and June Carter did not get him to stop. John did that all by himself, and the day he stopped doing drugs entirely was the day John Carter Cash was born. I think that, with all the exciting and positive things that were happening at that point in our career, John was pretty close to kicking his bad habit—although it could have gone either way—but the birth of his son was the extra push he needed to straighten up completely.

Over the years John told many stories about "quitting" drugs and his subsequent "recovery." He told reporters very believable tales about having hallucinations and feeling like splinters were running under his skin when Dr. Winston had locked him away at home for that thirty-day cleanup, and he told them about all of June's efforts. But the truth of the matter is that, except for a few clean-and-sober periods, Johnny Cash was never truly free of drugs from the late 1950s until the day his son was born.

⚬⚬⚬

Everyone who knew John was surprised when he showed no signs of withdrawal whatsoever when he stopped taking amphetamines. And that confirms my belief that, despite all that has been said and written, John was not physically addicted to drugs. Yes, he used them as a crutch to overcome fatigue, and yes, he would often get out of control when he was taking them. But I believe he took those pills not because his body craved them, but because he liked how they seemed to mask whatever was making him feel bad—fatigue, troubles at home, guilt over the hurt he'd caused others, or anything else that was bothering him. He didn't *have* to take drugs; he *chose* to take them.

It was the same way with cigarettes. John smoked on and off for years. He smoked really strong cigarettes loaded with tar and nicotine, but when he'd decide to quit, he could just put them down and never show the first sign that he wanted or needed one. I'd ask him, "You having a problem? You gonna have a nicotine fit?" And he'd say, "Naw, I'm fine." He might not use tobacco for a year, and then one day, just because he wanted to, he'd light up a cigarette and start smoking regularly again. He never showed any signs of withdrawal from cigarettes or drugs. When John got ready to quit—he just quit. And that was vintage Johnny Cash.

The television show had become such a tremendous success that Harold Cohen, the producer, ordered a brand-new Rolls-Royce as a gift for John. It came off the boat in New York, and John asked if I'd be interested in going there to get the car and drive it back to Nashville. "Of course I would!" I told him. W. S. Holland wanted to go, too, so the two of us flew up and went over to get the Rolls, which was solid black and beautiful.

Before we'd even cleared the New York city limits, the car's left-rear window rolled down all by itself, and no matter what we did, it just wouldn't roll back up! We drove all the way back to Nashville with that window down, and when we got there, I told John I'd take it to the Rolls dealership, which was on Broadway.

I pulled into the service department and told the service writer about the problem. "Well, let me see what could have happened," he said as he got in the car and pushed the window button. That damned window rolled up without a hitch! "What's going on here? What did you do?" I asked him. "I haven't done anything. I just rolled the window up," he said. I'd been around a lot of cars, so that really baffled me. I sat in the driver's seat and rolled the window down . . . and rolled it up . . . and down . . . and up. . . . There was never a problem with that window the entire time John had the Rolls, but I'm still wondering what happened on that trip down from New York.

Another very popular television show of the era was *This Is Your Life*, hosted by Ralph Edwards, who contacted us about doing a show on John's life. Through the efforts of many people, we were able to set that up in Nashville in early 1971, while we were taping *The Johnny Cash Show*. The people who were featured on *This Is Your Life* never knew they were going to be on the show, so everything was kept very hush-hush. Only a few people, including June and myself, knew what was going on, and June in particular made sure that John was kept totally in the dark.

One night, just after we'd finished taping our show, June went over to John and said, "John, there are some people that have come in here to see you," and out walked Ralph Edwards. John had the most puzzled look on his face when Ralph came over and started talking to him. He was totally surprised, and so were a lot of other folks. Many people John had known during his life—guys he was in the service with, one of his schoolteachers from Dyess, Arkansas, old friends and new—came out one by one and reminisced with John, sharing their memories as the cameras rolled. I was very honored to get to say a few things about the early days of our career. It was all very powerful and moving.

If you knew how to read his face, you could tell how John really felt about something, and that night, I think he was overwhelmed and very impressed that Ralph Edwards had come to town to do a show on him. *This Is Your Life* had been on the air for quite some time, and just about everybody in America watched it, so it was very exciting and a really great night for John. He deserved it, and I was glad to see it done for him.

One of the best-written songs I've ever heard is "The Man In Black," which John wrote in 1971. We recorded it later that year, and it just fit John to a T. It's about a man who wears black to remind us of all of the unfortunate people out there that life has ground under—the poor, the hungry, the elderly, the sick, prisoners—the underdogs that John always wanted to help.

It was such a personal song, and audiences could see that, and when we performed it onstage, people would just be mesmerized by his deep, expressive baritone voice. I loved to play "The Man In Black," and John always did it well. We played it every night for years and years, and it definitely became his signature song.

People always associate Johnny Cash with the color black. Part of that, of course, is because he wore only black onstage for years, and part of that is the result of the song. There have been many imitators over the years, but the original Man In Black was and always will be Johnny Cash.

In March 1971, after nearly two years and fifty-eight shows, ABC canceled *The Johnny Cash Show*. We had enjoyed a very good run, and I was extremely proud of the work we'd done, but like all television series, sooner or later it had to end. Now that we weren't facing the pressure of doing a weekly TV series, I thought John might become a little more interested in recording and come up with some great songs, but that wasn't the case.

He was more interested in spending time with June, taking trips with his family, and enjoying more time alone. He and June had gotten an apartment in New York City, and whenever they could get off from touring, they'd spend a couple of weeks there resting, attending the occasional Broadway show, or just getting away from everybody. The apartment was good for them and gave them a place to go where they could just be themselves.

June was an avid shopper and spent countless hours wandering through stores all over the Big Apple. John really wasn't a New York type of guy, so he didn't go out on the streets too often. Sometimes they would invite a family member to spend time with them, but usually they stayed there by themselves—just the two of them, and they enjoyed that tremendously.

Johnny Cash was a spiritual man and a great Christian. In November 1971 he, June, and a small film crew went to Tel Aviv, Israel, to film *The Gospel Road*, a musical documentary about the life of Jesus Christ. We had already laid down the soundtrack, and John had done some of the narration before going over to do the filming. He put his heart and soul into that project, financing it himself and pulling together all of the people he needed to make this phenomenal movie.

John never intended to make money off *The Gospel Road*, although all of us would have liked to see him get his investment back, which he probably didn't. The movie was sort of a testimony, and John wanted to use it to help other people find Jesus. It was really an extension of Johnny Cash.

He and I sat down and talked about it one day, and we decided to try to contact some influential people and see if we could find a way to use the movie as a way to raise money for charity. I talked to Kemmons Wilson, founder of the Holiday Inn hotel chain, who was involved with several charitable organizations, and asked him what he thought, adding that we would love to work with him in some way. As it turned out, Kemmons adored Johnny Cash and was very pleased that someone from John's organization had approached him to help.

We got together and decided to show the film in theaters and charge admission, with all the money to be donated to a charitable organization that Kemmons Wilson sponsored. The plan was for John and June to make an appearance at every showing, which we hoped would attract a lot of people and raise a lot of money.

The movie premiered in Memphis at the Park Theater on Park Avenue, a nice movie house that has since been torn down. Tickets sold out almost immediately. Five minutes before the start of the film, John got up onstage and talked about the movie and his life, and introduced some special guests, and then the movie began. It went over great! We did this for a while at every showing, and one day we were contacted by the Youth For Christ organization in San Diego to see if they could utilize the movie in some way.

I talked to John, and he was thrilled at the possibility of being associated with Youth For Christ and felt that we could really do some good. We agreed that John, June, and I would appear at every showing. I carried a copy of that 32-millimeter movie (which I still have in my possession today) to theaters and other places from coast to coast and border to border, and we raised a lot of money for Youth For Christ and several charitable organizations.

We worked with Youth For Christ for about a year, and John paid all of our expenses, which were considerable, to appear at the showings. However, he cut no corners. He wanted everything to be first class, and he wanted to book the movie into the best places possible. All of the money—and I mean ALL of the money—from screenings of *The Gospel Road* during this period was turned over to Youth For Christ for their use.

Since we did the movie fundraisers between concerts, other appearances, and recording sessions, we were away from home a lot more than we wanted to be. Sometimes John, June, and I would finish a six-day tour and then stay on the road for another five or six days to appear at the movie screenings. John and June were together, but since Etta didn't travel to those dates, that meant she and I wouldn't see each other for two weeks or more at a time. I didn't mind that too much, nor did Etta, because we felt that we were doing a lot of good for a lot of people. It was very rewarding.

━━◦◦◦━━

To get away from everything and recharge their batteries, John and June started going to Jamaica. In June 1972, John came to me and he said that he wanted to do a couple of benefits on the island to help the children there. "I want to take the entire cast and their husbands and wives," he said. "We don't have to do that," I told him, but John said, "No, I want to do that. I want everybody to come over there. Let's set these benefits so that there are a few days between them, and I want Etta and everybody else to come and enjoy themselves." I said, "If that's what you want to do, that's what we'll do."

When I told everyone about his plans, they were all gung-ho to go. I set up the travel and bought almost a briefcase full of airline tickets. We stayed at a resort on the coast, and everybody had a real blast. When John was straight, he wanted to do things for people, especially the folks who worked with him and had done so much and suffered so much with him. It was such a thrill that everything was going so well. Things couldn't have been more perfect.

We were flying to almost all of our dates now, a rarity at the time for a country music act, but the shows were so far apart that traveling by plane was really the only way we could make them on time. There were eighteen people in our entourage, and enough luggage to nearly fill a train boxcar. This created quite a headache for me, since I handled all our travel arrangements.

I had inherited the job of road manager (a much-misused term—I think "general flunky" is much more accurate) from day one, because somebody had to look out for the business side of our career and I was the one who stepped up to the plate to do that. I took on a lot of responsibilities, the biggest of which was to make the shows work—all of them—from A to Z. I coordinated all of the air and ground transportation, lodging, and just about everything else associated with the organization.

Things never slowed down when I got home. I may have been off the road, but I still had to handle everything, and believe me, there was always something that needed handling. Countless people from Nashville and the House of Cash and even John's family called constantly because they felt that whatever they wanted or whatever information they needed should come through me, since I was on top of everything. That helped keep everybody on the same page, but it was very time consuming and difficult to do.

When we were on the road, I'd always get a limo for John and June and a bus to ferry the rest of the cast to the hotel. I'd go into the hotel with John and June to make sure they got checked in OK, and when the rest of our group arrived, I'd have all of their keys and would hand them out. The next morning, we'd go through the same procedure in reverse.

Coordinating all the travel and booking all of the hotels, airlines ground transportation was becoming a full-time job. As our itinerary expanded, Artist Consultants, especially Molly Fleming, and my travel agent in Memphis, Ruth Noble of World Travel, were able to take some of the load off me and really helped make things easier.

We played a lot of international dates during the seventies, in Japan, Australia, New Zealand, Europe, and just about everywhere that we had time to go. We were playing so many shows in so many different countries that whenever we returned home, we were so tired that it took a long time to rest up. And by the time we did, it was usually time to go again. It was a matter of supply and demand: we were trying to supply the world's demand for the Johnny Cash Show. And there was a *lot* of demand for the Johnny Cash Show.

At one point, we did a three-week tour of Europe, came back to work a short tour in the States, and then headed to Australia. London is six hours ahead of Memphis, and when we got adjusted to the time difference so we could sleep, it was time to return home. Back Stateside, we barely had time to readjust our body clocks before we were off again to Australia, where it was a different day and an eighteen-hour time difference from Memphis. When we arrived Down Under, we were so blooming tired that we walked around in a daze, but the shows had to go on. That was hard on all of us, but on John in particular because, after all, it was the Johnny Cash Show, and in one sense he carried most of the load.

As the decade progressed, shepherding a large group of musicians to and from dates all around the world became one hell of a job and started to get the best of me. It wasn't because I was too old and worn out to handle things, it was because there was only so much one person could do. And it seemed as if there was always more that needed doing.

There were only a couple of people on the show that I could always count on to help make sure everything ran smoothly. One was our promoter, Lou Robin, who always took care of business 100 percent. Lou and Artist Consultants would book the dates, and I'd make sure everyone played them and got back home. Whenever I got into a situation that was completely over my head, he was the only one in the entourage who would come to my rescue, and he did, many times.

Lou was absolutely fantastic at tying up loose ends, and he was a professional in every sense of the word. For the most part, no one else seemed to care. Their attitude was, "I'm part of the Johnny Cash Show, and I'm hot stuff, so don't bother me." I could ask some of them for a small favor and they'd just look down their noses at me. I finally figured out that if something needed to be done, I'd have to do it myself, which is why I had to wear so many hats, big and small.

Another person who was a great help was Jay Dauro, our very efficient production manager and lighting director. Jay made sure that all of our equipment was set up on time and worked with the tech people in the buildings to ensure there were no glitches. It took about five hours to set up all of our stage gear and sound and lighting equipment, and Jay saw to it that, whenever we went into a building to do a sound check and returned later to perform, everything was ready to go.

Jay was a big dude who had the agility of a much smaller person, and he ran wide open all the time. It took a big load off my mind to know that the technical part of our show was in such capable hands. Jay was something else, and he'll always stand out in my mind as one of the best employees we ever had.

❦

Our touring schedule was a real hardship for our wives and children, who often wouldn't see us for a month or more at a time. June traveled with us, but she had a nurse to help her with John Carter and a bodyguard to help take some of the load off so she could work. John realized how tough these extended absences were on the families of our cast and crew, and that really bothered him because he had his family with him and we didn't. But since we were in the business of entertaining, we just had to weather the storm and keep the wheels turning.

The old saying "the show must go on" often means missing birthdays, anniversaries, and other special occasions. I wasn't there for my son Randy's high school graduation. I wasn't there when he graduated from college, and I've missed more birthdays than I can count, but that's the nature of the business. I'm just thankful that I had an extraordinary family who stood by me through thick and thin.

My wife, Etta, was always a tremendous help and made countless sacrifices over the years to keep the home fires burning and everything on an even keel, but she never once complained or asked for anything in return. I was so fortunate to have somebody who could understand what was going on and could go along with it. There's no question (and John knew this, too) that if it hadn't been for Etta, we never would have made it in the music business. Her little head was working for us all the time, and she managed to do some things that I just simply couldn't have pulled off.

Etta was the lady behind the scenes and loved everybody in the organization. She's a remarkable person, one in ten million. She's always been the love of my life and always will be.

John loved Etta as much as he did any of his sisters, and he and June both would send her little gifts of appreciation. John would often say, "Take this and give it to Etta for her help." Sometimes he'd just say, "Take this and give it to ol' Etta." June would do the same thing. Our home today is filled with countless tokens of love and appreciation from John and June.

⚊⚊⚊⚊

John's home in Hendersonville was just twenty miles north of the studios on Nashville's Music Row, but he didn't much like going into the city to record. As a result, in 1972 he decided to build his own state-of-the-art recording facility at the House of Cash, which over the years also became a popular museum.

That made it a little easier to get him into the studio, but when he did, his mind often wasn't on recording. We'd had so much success with our records that it wasn't a priority with him anymore; he seemed content just to kick back and enjoy life. John (and to some extent, the rest of us) looked on recording as something that musical artists need to do occasionally, and when those occasions rolled around, we'd pack our bags, leave the wives and kids at home, and head for the studio for what sometimes could be a very long time.

One benefit of the House of Cash was that it had living quarters upstairs, including five bedrooms, so if John wasn't feeling inspired to lay down any tracks for three or four days, which sometimes happened, we had a convenient place to stay. We never knew when one of those moments of musical magic might occur, so it was always worth going there to see what John might do. Sometimes he'd show up without anything to record and would sit down and start writing a song that we'd later cut.

Those upstairs bedrooms also meant that when John needed to rest, it was easy for him to do so. When he was straight—and believe me, now he was totally straight—John would have to take a break every afternoon about two o'clock and go lie down for a two-hour nap. It was just something he had to do, and as long as he needed that nap, we knew he wasn't taking drugs. Long experience with John had taught us that anytime he didn't take that break, trouble was not far around the bend.

The Statler Brothers were having tremendous success, putting out hit record after hit record while still opening the show for Johnny Cash. In 1973, John decided it was time for them to go out on their own because he knew they could make a lot more money as a headline attraction. They could also be self-contained and set their own itinerary—basically work when they wanted and stay home when they didn't.

John and I talked at great length about the best way to accomplish the split—we certainly weren't going to just toss them out of the nest and hope they could fly on their own. The plan that we ultimately took to them was that John would take them on a few more tours, and then they would leave the Johnny Cash Show and go out on their own. He did that to help them because the Statlers were young, vibrant, very ambitious, and it was time for them to make their own mark on the concert trail.

After another couple of tours with us, the Statler Brothers got their own bus, hired a driver by the name of Dale Harmon, and began charting their own very successful course through musical history.

From the time the Statlers first began touring with us in 1964, you could see their popularity growing with each passing day. The music world had been a little slow to accept the Statlers because they were a quartet and all the other quartets at the time were gospel groups. But with all the exposure they got with us on the road and on the weekly *Johnny Cash Show*, that started to change and people began to recognize them for what they were: great guys and great entertainers.

They were determined from the very beginning to be successful in show business, and it was evident that was going to happen. They didn't have a No. 1 hit record to follow up "Flowers on the Wall," but they never gave up and they started feeling their way in the business to see exactly what they wanted to do. They had initially signed with Columbia in the late sixties, but they didn't get a lot of satisfaction from the label and in 1970 switched over to Mercury, where the great Jerry Kennedy would produce them.

I had met Jerry, who was a great guitarist, early in our career when he was a staff musician on the *Louisiana Hayride*. He later moved to Nashville and became a manager and a producer at Mercury. When the Statlers called Jerry and asked if he would be interested in signing and producing them, Jerry took them right on, and that was another turning point in their career. He believed in them, as we all did, and they quickly started to assemble the right musicians to back them, which was extremely important.

The Statlers were some of the greatest songwriters to ever come down the pike, and while they were on Mercury, they would write some of their greatest hits, among them, "I'll Go to My Grave Loving You," "Do You Know You Are My Sunshine," and countless others.

They were such a pleasure to be with on the road, and we all had so much fun with them, especially Carl Perkins. Carl and Harold Reid had a little thing going, with Harold playing the part of a little Mexican that Carl called Snappy, who would do some strange and funny things. Their easygoing rapport was an extension of the closeness that existed among everyone in the organization at the time. There were no problems of any kind; everybody loved one another, and it showed everywhere—in the studio, at concerts, and everywhere we presented ourselves to the public.

We all knew the Statlers were destined to go to the top. They had the talent and the business sense, and they worked hard all the time to be successful. One thing John always neglected was the business part of the music business. He never put much emphasis on money, and he didn't treat music like a business, which in later years would come back to haunt him.

But with the Statlers, it was totally the opposite. They set themselves up as a business and treated music as a business. When they went out on the road, they didn't go out to party, they went out to entertain people. And that they did—they were some of the greatest entertainers to ever walk out onstage and were incredibly professional. There were no bad notes, no missed cues, just perfection from the word go. For the entire time they were part of the Johnny Cash Show, I was fortunate enough to play bass with them, and I enjoyed every minute of it. If I had it to do all over again, I'd do it in a heartbeat.

The fact that the Statler Brothers started from scratch with nothing, and today, years after their retirement, remain the most award-winning act in the history of country music, says a lot—about their talent and about them as individuals. They became successful because they took care of business and put first things first. If they had a problem, they would sit down and talk it out. If they went into the studio to do an album and had a list of twenty songs, they would sit down and vote on which songs they wanted to do until they had pared the list down to the number they needed.

Just like John, Luther, and myself in the early days of our career, the Statlers were always prepared when they got to the studio. They had their parts worked up, and all they had to do was teach a song to the musicians and they were ready to cut it. The Statlers could cut an album faster and better than anybody else in the business. And they never made a bad record during their entire career.

By this time, the Statlers had the talent and the experience to change anything they wanted when they got to the studio, but they chose not to. Instead, they would work up everything in their office in Staunton, Virginia, before coming to Nashville to record. They knew it was very wasteful of time and money to go into the studio unprepared because those twenty-five or thirty people sitting around waiting for the session to start were on the clock and had to be paid. Many artists go into the studio with too much ego in their back pocket, intending to spend a lot of the label's money. But that wasn't the case with the Statlers. They would go in and cut an album before most people could get their guitar case open, and it would always be high quality.

Their ability to focus on the business side of entertaining—always being prepared, "reading" an audience and giving them what they wanted—gave the Statler Brothers unparalleled longevity among country music vocal groups. Even today, if they chose to, they could go out and fill major concert halls, produce top-selling records, or do pretty much anything else they wanted.

The Statlers' departure left a big hole in the Johnny Cash Show, especially during the finale when everybody came out, which was by far the strongest part of the show. Without those four very talented voices, some of the songs just didn't sound right anymore. For instance, the powerful "Were You There When They Crucified My Lord?" was so barren without the Statlers' soulful harmonies that we had to cut it from the finale, along with a couple of other songs. We worked for months and finally got the finale to where it worked again, but it was never as strong as it had been. Still, we kept working and moving forward.

⊸⊸⊸⊸

Coordinating all the aspects of the Johnny Cash Show's tours was a continual problem, and John and I talked quite a bit about how we could improve the situation. One option was to buy a bus, or maybe two, but John really didn't like the idea of traveling on a bus with everyone else. We eventually decided to buy a plush motor home for John and June, and to either charter a bus for the remainder of the cast and crew or have them continue to fly to the dates. I bought a 1973 Blue Bird motor home, which at the time was the top of the line. June was very skeptical about riding with just anyone, so she asked if I would drive John and her everywhere they went.

If the opening tour date was quite a distance away, say, on the West Coast, we would all fly to the first city, and I would have Fred

Mathews, a driver I'd hired, bring the motor home to the first date. Then I'd drive John and June around for the rest of the tour, and Fred would meet us at the final date and drive the motor home back to Nashville while everyone else flew back home. That worked out pretty well and greatly simplified things.

John never got in a big hurry when we were driving from town to town. Sometimes we'd be going down the road and he'd talk June into cooking a meal. Even if we were cutting things a little close, we'd pull off under a shade tree or stop at a rest area and June would cook. That was something John wanted to do, and he was in such great shape, we'd never say, "Hey, man, we can't do that, we gotta go."

He enjoyed it so much, and it was good for all of us to lay back a little bit and do some of the things we wanted to do. Even though our itineraries were very strenuous, some of the best and freest times we ever had were when we were going down the road in that motor home.

Johnny Cash (left) and the Tennessee Two, Marshall Grant (below at left) and Luther Perkins (below at right) charted a distinctive course through musical history.

All photos from the author's collection.

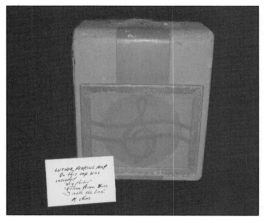

This Silvertone amplifier (above) and Martin guitar (right) were the band's earliest instruments and were used by Luther and John on all of the group's recordings for Sun. • Luther, John, and Marshall in Tampa in 1956 (below). John signed the photo in his later days and gave it to Marshall as a memento.

Jackie Gleason (above left) introduces Johnny Cash and the Tennessee Two, who made their first national television appearance January 19, 1957, on The Jackie Gleason Show *(above right, left). • Later that year, they became regular members of* The Grand Ole Opry *(below).*

John and Luther onstage at a date early in the band's career (above). • *The Tennessee Two were named Instrumental Group of the Year for 1957 by* Country Song Roundup *magazine (below).*

John onstage and in a promotional photo from the 1950s
(above). • Music legend Roy
Orbison (below at left) with
Luther and Marshall.

Early on, Johnny Cash and the Tennessee Two played many small venues where audiences crowded close to the musicians (left page). As their popularity soared, bigger halls with stages were the norm (right page).

The band often went out on package tours with Opry *stars during the 1950s and '60s (above). • Luther, John, and Marshall show off some of their early stage attire (right).*

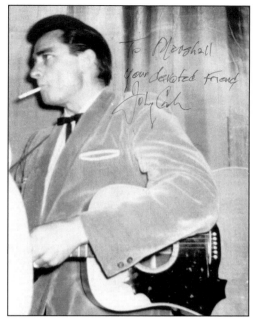

More pictures from the early years, signed by John and given to Marshall and his wife, Etta, some four decades later.

Drummer W. S. Holland was added to the lineup in 1960, and the group later became Johnny Cash and the Tennessee Three *(above)*.
• Promotional photo from John's 1961 movie Five Minutes to Live *(below)*.
• John does his impression of Elvis Presley *(right)* as Marshall looks on.

*Lovely and talented June
Carter (left, above) joined the
Johnny Cash Show in 1962.
Mother Maybelle Carter and
June's sisters, Helen and
Anita (below), would some-
times come along, and in
1967 they would begin tour-
ing full time with the Johnny
Cash Show as the Carter
Family.*

Scenes from the early 1960s: John and June (above), John and Luther onstage (right), and the Tennessee Three relaxing backstage between sets.

The group made its first trip overseas in 1959 and later played numerous international tours. John, June, the Tennessee Three and Carl Perkins (left) head for Ireland. • John and first wife Vivian (above) leave for Europe. • Members of the Johnny Cash Show in Korea in 1962 (below).

The Statler Brothers joined the show in 1964, and when the Carters were also on hand, it made for a big lineup onstage (below). • The portrait above includes (standing, from left), Luther Perkins, W. S. Holland, Marshall Grant, Johnny Cash, and Statler Brothers Don Reid, Phil Balsley, Harold Reid, and Lew DeWitt, and (seated, from left) Helen, Mother Maybelle, June, and Anita Carter.

*In the studio with
John and Luther.*

John and June in the 1960s (above).
• John weaves a spell onstage
(right). • Music great Carl Perkins
with Marshall (below).

Johnny Cash and the Tennessee Three onstage in the sixties (above). • John relaxes backstage (left). • Marshall, W. S., and Luther strike a pose on a hotel balcony in Los Angeles.

"Ring of Fire," with its Mexican trumpets, was a huge hit for
Johnny Cash and the Tennessee Three and sparked numerous
music industry awards (above). • Marshall named one of his racing
boats (below) after the landmark song.

Marshall Grant's house at 4199 Nakomis Street in Memphis (above). • John strums his guitar backstage between sets (left).

The January 1968 show at California's Folsom Prison was both a frightening and thrilling experience for the group. The concert also spawned a top-selling album, Johnny Cash At Folsom Prison.

John proposed to June onstage during a show in London, Ontario, in late February 1968, and on March 1 of that year, the two were married in a small church in Franklin, Kentucky. At left is the first photo ever taken of the newlyweds. • The Tennessee Three and their wives (below) were among the handful of attendees at the ceremony. From left are W. S. and Joyce Holland, Marshall and Etta Grant, John and June, and Luther and Margie Perkins.

In August 1968, Luther Perkins died in a tragic fire at his house in Hendersonville, Tennessee. His death came some fourteen years after he, Marshall, and John (below) began a musical journey that would forever change the face of modern entertainment.

A few weeks after Luther Perkins's death, Bob Wootton (above center), became the new guitarist for the Tennessee Three. • In the studio in the late 1960s are (below, from left), Marshall Grant, W. S. Holland, Bob Wootton, Carl Perkins, and Johnny Cash.

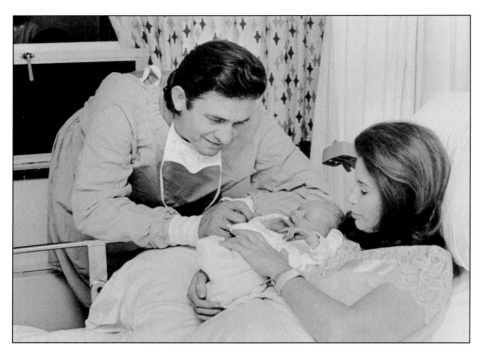

March 3, 1970, the day John Carter Cash was born (above) was the day Johnny Cash stopped doing drugs. Within a matter of months, John and June were taking their son on the road with them. • Proud papa John and John Carter (right) at a tour date in the early 1970s.

THE WHITE HOUSE

WASHINGTON

April 23, 1970

Dear Mr. Grant:

The White House evening with Johnny Cash was
a great success, as you know, and I understand
that your assistance with the many arrangements
necessary did a great deal to make it so. Mrs.
Nixon and I were especially pleased that you and
your colleagues could be a part of this occasion
which has given such bright memories to all of
us, and I want to thank you for your generous
cooperation and your many courtesies.

With my best wishes,

Sincerely,

Richard Nixon

Mr. Marshall Grant
4199 Nakomis
Memphis, Tennessee

*A thank-you letter to
Marshall from
President Nixon (left)
after Johnny Cash
and the Tennessee
Three played a com-
mand performance
at the White House.
• John shakes hands
with Ralph Edwards
(below), host of the
popular television
series* This Is Your
Life, *after John was
a surprise guest on
the show in 1971.*

John and June were very
much in love and it showed—
onstage, at industry events,
and in private.

The Carter sisters during the 1970s (above, from left) Helen, June, and Anita. • John performs on the CMA Awards Show (left). • John and June sing soulfully during a taping of ABC's Johnny Cash Show (below).

The 1975 Blue Bird motor home (above) made life on the road a little easier for John and June. • Marshall always screened John's phone calls when the group was on the road (right). • While working a show for the Youth For Christ organization in California in 1976, John and June received honorary university degrees (below).

To Marshall, thanks for being part of it all

John

Marshall and Etta stand atop a mound in the ancient city of Jericho in this photo taken by Johnny Cash during a trip to the Holy Land in 1977.

Marshall and the Statler Brothers meet with President and Mrs. Reagan at the White House following a 1984 performance there.

In 1994, TNN hosted a tribute marking the Statler Brothers' thirtieth year in show business, airing it as a special episode of Nashville Now. From left are Marshall Grant, Nashville Now co-host Lorianne Crook, June Carter, Don Reid, Harold Reid, Johnny Cash, Jimmy Fortune, Nashville Now co-host Charlie Chase, and Phil Balsley.

John and Marshall perform on an all-star tribute to Johnny Cash on March 6, 1999, in New York. The show was John's final public performance, and his appearance brought the house down—a fitting tribute to a legendary entertainer and a great man.

We were doing many other things in addition to touring. John had gotten a lot of exposure through our television show and was beginning to make guest appearances on several other shows. Among his many appearances were a couple of guest shots on the popular *Columbo* television series starting Peter Falk, and I was lucky enough to get on camera, too.

John was great in those guest shots, whether they were musicals, dramas, murder mysteries, Westerns, or whatever, and they really showed the diversity of his talent and proved to new audiences just what a great entertainer he was. He was so natural in the parts he played, they seemed to be a part of him. He was a monster entertainer—on every stage. John also hosted or was a presenter at the CMA Awards show just about every year during the decade.

We left home on Christmas Day 1973 for Los Angeles, where we were to begin filming an episode of *Columbo* the next morning. Carl Perkins had a part in that particular episode and was on the plane with us. When we arrived in L.A., Lou Robin met us at the gate and pulled me off to the side and said, "Marshall, I don't know what to do about this, but I'll let you handle it. We got word about an hour ago that Carl's brother, Clayton, has committed suicide."

Boy, that was tough to hear, because everybody knew and liked Clayton, and I was sure the news would be devastating to Carl. I talked things over with John, June, and Lou, and told them to walk toward the baggage claim area while I spoke to Carl. John chose to stay with me, and as Carl stepped out of the jetway, I pulled him over to the side and told him what had happened to Clayton.

When I asked what he wanted to do, he said, "Of course I've got to go back." I said, "You don't worry about it. I'm gonna go over to that service agent and get you a ticket back home on the very next plane." Fortunately, there was a plane leaving within the next hour, and I was able to book Carl on board. W. S. Holland offered to fly back with him, so we put the two of them on that flight back to Memphis. We went to the hotel and the next morning, with heavy hearts, went to the *Columbo* set to begin filming. The writers changed the script to make up for Carl's absence.

Carl Perkins was one of our dearest friends. He was a superb entertainer, a wonderful guy, a talented songwriter, and a loving father and husband. But Carl had a problem with alcohol. He never got sloppy drunk while on the road, but he did drink a good bit. One night after a show in Los Angeles in the mid-seventies, a friend of Carl's came up to the room in a Sunset Boulevard hotel that Carl was sharing with W. S. and myself. Carl and his buddy got absolutely plastered and stayed up all night, and the next morning he was crying and carrying on, as Carl would often do when he felt remorseful after a drinking binge.

Later that day, we were going to go by John's house in Casitas Springs to see Vivian and the kids before heading up the coast to our next show. Carl was still pretty drunk, and as we approached Casitas Springs, he started crying. "I can't go up there," he said. "I can't go up there and let Vivian and those girls see me like this. I just can't do it. Marshall, if you don't mind, pull off on the beach here somewhere and let's talk about this."

I pulled over at the first little spot I got to, and we got out and walked down to the beach. Carl had a fifth of whiskey with him, and as we walked, he was crying and carrying on because he was so embarrassed that he couldn't sober up enough to go see Vivian and the children. I told him, "Carl, we don't have time to sit under a shade tree while you get sober; we gotta go. I don't really know what to do."

We walked a little farther down the beach, and as we got closer to the water, he looked at me and said, "Gramps, I'll tell you what I'm gonna do. I'm gonna take this bottle, and if I can throw it in the water, I'm never gonna take another gulp of alcohol as long as I live. But if it don't make it to the water, I'm gonna go over there and pick that bottle up and drink every last drop of it."

"Hang on just a minute, son," I told him. "Let's get a little closer to the water!" When we were about fifty feet from the water, I said, "I believe you can make it from right there—let her rip!" He wound up real good and threw that bottle as hard as he could, and sure enough, it made it into the ocean, although just barely. "I'm never going to taste another drop of alcohol as long as I live," he promised. "Carl, I hope you can live up to that," I said. "If you don't, we're all still behind you—but that would be great."

When we got back into the car, I said, "Carl, what do you think? Do you want to go see Vivian and the kids?" He said, "I'll go up there and sit in the car while y'all go in and see them." John was already there when we pulled into the driveway, and everyone but Carl got out of the car. The girls came running out, and we started playing with them and then went into the house. Vivian asked where Carl was, and I told her that he was out in the car and hadn't come in because he'd had a little too much to drink. "Oh," she said. We visited for thirty minutes or so and then got back into the car and drove off. The kids never saw Carl, and he never saw them except when they came running out of the house.

The next day, Carl came to me and said, "Gramps, let me tell you, I meant what I said about the bottle. But you're gonna have to stick with me. From now on, if it's at all possible, if you and W. S. are sharing a room, I want to stay in there with y'all. If I don't, I won't ever be able to live up to my promise. I gotta be with you all the time. I want to go to the restaurant and eat with you. I don't

211

want to go in no bars. I just want you to stay with me all the time!"
I said, "Carl, if that's what you want, that's what we'll do!"

From then on, I always tried to book the three of us into a single large room with three beds, or into two rooms with a connecting door. Sometimes the best I could do was a room with two beds and a rollaway. Carl always took the rollaway, and I felt a little bad about that because some of them were just awful. I often told him that we should take turns sleeping on the rollaways—just like John, Luther, and I did early in our career—but Carl said, "No, I'm the one here that's causing all the problems, and I'll be the one that sleeps on the rollaways."

Carl was true to his word. I never saw him drink another drop of alcohol—he may have, but I never saw him do it, and I always respected him for that.

Carl was a great guy with an enormous amount of talent. Not only was he a great singer—rockabilly, gospel, ballads—he was one of the greatest guitar players I've ever known, but above all else, he was a great person. His songwriting ability was unparalleled. John recorded his songs ("Daddy Sang Bass" is one of my favorites), the Beatles, Elvis—in fact, just about everybody in the music business at some point in their career has recorded a song that Carl Perkins wrote. The amazing thing was that Carl could write such great songs in a matter of minutes. I don't think it took him more than fifteen minutes to write "Blue Suede Shoes."

Carl Perkins and his family will always be in my heart as long as I live. He was one of the dearest people I've ever known, and I'm thankful that show business brought us together.

Late in the summer of 1974, John and I spent a week in the Stone Mountain, Georgia, area filming an in-depth documentary about locomotives called *Riding the Rails*. It was quite an experience. We'd go out on location at different times each day, and sometimes we'd work an hour, sometimes two, and sometimes we'd be out there till after dark.

We were staying in a hotel south of Atlanta, and one day while taking my daily walk I noticed a bus parked up on the upper side of the parking lot. I kept walking past it, but on one of those laps around the parking lot, a young man stepped out of the bus, came up to me, and said, "Aren't you Marshall Grant?" I told him that I was, and as I looked at him, he seemed awfully familiar, but I just couldn't place him. "I'm Duane Allen with the Oak Ridge Boys," he said. Well, that rang a bell all the way home.

I asked Duane what he and the other Oaks were doing in Atlanta, and he said, "Well, we knew that you were staying down here, and we hoped to get to see you or John. We'd like to do some work with you. You don't have the Statlers with you anymore, do you?" I said, "No, they're out on their own and doing pretty good business, too, just rolling right along."

Duane expressed interest in playing some shows with us, and I told him, "The only thing we have open right now is Las Vegas next April. We have Carl Perkins, the Carter Family, and June Carter with us, but we could add you on in Vegas." His eyes lit up and he said, "Oh boy, that would be great!" I told him I'd talk to John about it and would let him know. We exchanged phone numbers, and later that day I told John about our conversation and said it might be wise to take the Oaks to Vegas since we wouldn't have the Statlers with us.

John thought for a second and then said, "Well, I think you're right. Get with their people and see what we can get worked out." We reworked our arrangements to accommodate the Oak Ridge Boys, and they played the Las Vegas Hilton with us April 2-12, 1975. They did a fantastic job, although they didn't join us onstage for the finale the way the Statlers had. Basically, they just did their show, and we kept the rest of our show intact.

We took the Oaks back to Las Vegas on several occasions, and they always did a superb job. I don't think playing Vegas with the Johnny Cash Show did all that much for their career, although it wasn't very long after their first appearance with us that their popularity exploded. They're still doing great business today, and while I'd like to say that I had a hand in their success, I really can't because, just like the Statler Brothers, the Oak Ridge Boys were destined to make it big in the entertainment business. They're as solid as the Rock of Gibraltar and have become country music legends. Not bad for another quartet that everyone said couldn't survive outside of gospel music.

I learned early on that you had to be careful what you said around John, because if he heard you say you wanted something, he would often do his darnedest to get it for you.

In early 1975, we wrapped up a tour of Florida in Gainesville, and the next morning, just after I'd pulled the Blue Bird onto the interstate for the trip home, I saw a silver blur growing larger in the rear-view mirror. June was sitting up front with me, and in just a matter of seconds that silver blur shot by us with only a whisper of sound.

"My lands, Marshall, he's flying, ain't he?" June said. "Yeah, he really is," I said. "But, June, that's my favorite car right there, and one of these days, I'm going to get me one." She asked what kind of car it was, and I told her, "That's a silver 1975 Mercedes 450 SEL, the top of the line. It'll go fast, and that's exactly what he's doing with it! It's a great car, and I want to own one someday."

A few weeks later, we were in Las Vegas playing our first shows with the Oaks. On April 4, June came to me and said, "Marshall, we're going to have a little get-together in our suite in the morning, and we'd like to invite you up." I asked what time, and she replied, "Oh, I don't know, about eleven o'clock in the morning or something like that, if you want to come up." I told her I'd be there.

The next morning when I arrived at their suite, there was a huge crowd there, probably thirty-five or forty people, including the Oak Ridge Boys, several people from the hotel staff, the entire cast of the show, and some friends we'd made in Vegas. I walked in and acted very nonchalant as I said, "Man, what's going on here?" June had invited me up to their suite, but I thought it was just going to be a brunch with John, June, the babysitter, and John Carter. There was a lot of food, and everybody was loading up plates and standing around visiting, eating, telling jokes, and just having fun.

This went on for about forty-five minutes, and nobody said anything in particular to me. I was just part of the crowd and was enjoying talking to everybody, but it seemed a little strange that June had invited me up for what I thought was going to be a small brunch and all of those people were there. Finally, John got up on the dining-room table and began talking, and he was holding what appeared to be a scroll in his hand.

John was always great at putting words together, and some of the things he said that day were absolutely beautiful. He spoke from his heart for about fifteen minutes, never looked at any notes, and at some point it suddenly dawned on me that it was our twentieth year in the music business!

I still treasure what he said, but I was absolutely stunned when John said, "We found out one thing that this man wants more than anything else. We can't do enough for him, but we can at least give him what seems like would be his most valued present at this time." Then he unrolled the "scroll," which turned out to be a picture of a red 1975 Mercedes 450 SEL. "Now, this isn't like the one he wants. We found out that he wants a silver one, but this is the only picture of the identical car we could get at the dealer here. The exact car he wants is a silver 1975 Mercedes 450 SEL—and if anybody would like to see it, it's sitting out back on the loading dock— so let's go see it!"

I think my jaw was still on the floor as most of the people in the room headed for the elevators or stairs to go down to the loading dock to look at the gorgeous gift from John and June. I found out later that everybody in the room knew what was going to happen, except for me!

I still have that car today. It's under a special cover in a very tight, specially built garage where I keep special mementos I've collected over the years. Etta and I have driven it quite a bit, but if you open the door, it still smells brand new. It's in immaculate shape, not a scratch on it, and has 30,000 miles on the odometer—not bad for a car that's more than thirty years old! I'll treasure that Mercedes forever and will pass it along to my son, who I hope will pass it on to his son, and so on down the line. As far as I'm concerned, it's my most prized possession and will always be in my family.

As I said, you had to be very careful about what you said around John. When I talked to him later about the car, he said it was June's idea but he jumped at it. Apparently, my remark to her that morning on I-75 in Florida planted a seed in her brilliant mind that "a silver Mercedes is what we need to get Marshall for his twentieth year of being together with John."

⸺⸺⸺

Maybe it was the new car that got us to thinking we needed to upgrade our two-year-old motor home, which was beginning to show some wear. We'd been pretty happy with the Blue Bird, so I ordered a brand-new 1975 model from the factory. It was a little bigger and definitely more modern.

I was still driving the motor home between dates, but it was starting to become too much for me to handle. In addition to being John and June's "bus driver," I was playing bass for all the acts on the show, serving as master of ceremonies, and handling the merchandise sales, although Lou Robin often helped with that.

I also screened all of John's telephone calls, because it seemed everybody in the world wanted to talk to John. By the time I got to my room, the phone was always ringing. Answering the phone during the day wasn't so bad, but if we stayed in town overnight, which we usually did, the phone would ring almost constantly because people had seen the bus outside and knew where we were staying.

I had to get a certain amount of sleep to be able to drive safely, but it got to the point where I wasn't getting enough sack time, and

I started having problems, such as severe muscle spasms, especially in my neck. At times, when I hadn't slept very much, I'd get up in the morning and my neck would absolutely be killing me.

In addition, as road manager, I was the guy everyone on the show came to whenever there was a problem. It was my responsibility to help everyone along, and I tried my utmost to do that, no matter who or what time it was. But with so much to do, and only so many hours in the day, it was getting to the point that I was so tired I was afraid that I might fall asleep at the wheel of the motor home or wouldn't be able to react quickly in an emergency. I didn't want to take any chances, so I finally told John that I couldn't handle everything and needed some help.

As a result, he hired a man named George Shaw, a really nice guy from Bristol, Tennessee, who tipped the scales at somewhere between 300 and 350 pounds. George moved to Nashville and started driving the Blue Bird, which was a tremendous help, and I began to feel much better about things.

There was still a lot of turmoil, however, as our brutal touring schedule and changes in personnel on the show were making it harder for everyone to get along. By 1975, we were working about 200 dates a year, which meant that, with travel time and off days, we were away from home at least 250 days. It started to bother me an awful lot that I was away from my family so much, especially Etta.

In addition to keeping the home fires burning while I was away, she was constantly busy handling all the business-related activities—bookings, lodgings, travel itineraries—anything and everything that I normally handled when I was there between tours. The phone rang all the time, and she was so busy she had very little time for her personal life. It was a job that would have kept at least five or six people constantly hopping, yet she and I were handling things pretty much by ourselves. We never gave up, but as time passed, it got to be more and more of a problem.

It never fails that when things are going great, someone has to throw a monkey wrench into things. John told me one day that a certain married band member seemed to be making a play for one of his sisters whenever she came around. I told him, "John, this

217

thing works two ways. You should think long and hard about it. Do you want me to talk to him, or do you want to handle it?" He said, "No, I wouldn't want you to talk to him. Since it's my family, I think I should handle it. But I'm gonna say something to him, and if it continues, we're gonna have to replace him."

"That's entirely up to you," I said. "I can understand your feelings. We'll have to handle it the way you see fit. But let's give it a chance. Say something to him and say something to your sister, whichever sister it is, because it works two ways." He said, "I'll let you know what happens."

Maybe six months or so later, John asked me if I'd seen any "fooling around" between the couple in question when they were in the same vicinity. "No, I haven't," I told him. "In fact, I never saw anything in the beginning. You told me about it—and it was kind of a shock—but as far as I'm concerned, there's nothing going on, and from what I've seen, there never has been. I think things are just fine. Whatever you said, or whatever you did, it fixed the thing. So let's just move forward with our lives and our careers." And that's what we did.

Throughout the 1970s, we were suffering for hit records. We were recording mediocre songs and mediocre albums, and Columbia Records was complaining because we weren't delivering any credible material. We really didn't need a hit record because our concert crowds were good, everything was going smoothly, and it seemed that John's career would soar on forever even if we never put out another top-seller. To supply the public's demand for Johnny Cash material, Columbia had been re-releasing some of our past hits.

It was just so difficult to get John into the studio because his heart just wasn't into recording, and a big part of that was that our busy schedule was taking a lot out of him mentally and physically. Sometimes the band would gather at the House of Cash for a two-, three-, four-, or maybe a five-day session to record an album. John would come in, pick up his guitar, sit down on a stool, and literally start trying to write songs.

Sometimes we'd stay for several days but accomplish nothing. Oh, we'd record something, but it was usually thrown together with no thought and no arrangement. That became evident when the disc jockeys began passing on our new songs and instead played our old standards, all the way back to "Hey Porter," "Cry, Cry, Cry," "Folsom Prison Blues," and songs from our live concerts and the TV show, like "Boy Named Sue" or "Sunday Morning Coming Down."

You could never count John out, though. If he made up his mind that he was going to make some good records and cut a hit song, he would do it. I think history speaks for itself. We'd go for a long dry spell, and then all of a sudden he would decide what it was he wanted to do and come up with some great songs, like "Ring of Fire" or "Boy Named Sue." But there were long stretches in between when we recorded some pretty mediocre stuff.

⁂

The worst thing in the world you could do was try to encourage John to go into the studio and record something, because he insisted on doing everything at his own pace and in his own way. That's what made him so different—nobody ever produced John. You can talk here about Sam Phillips, Jack Clement, Don Law, Frank Jones, and all those other great producers, but they were producers in name only when it came to our recording sessions. We always did things our own way, and when we could get decent material, it always worked.

I've always believed that if a record company lets an artist do things his way, hire the musicians he wants, and do the arrangements he wants, he'll come up with something good. But so many producers, especially those working with new artists, go into the studio and say "OK, here's the song you're going to sing; here's the key you are going to do it in; here's the musicians that are going to do it with you; and you're going to do it right now." When that happens—and it happens all the time—it becomes the producer's music, not the artist's music, and the songs all tend to sound the same.

That never happened with us. We always did things our way. Whatever we recorded, whether it was live or in a studio, was Johnny Cash's music. It had a distinctive sound, and that was one of the many reasons he enjoyed such longevity as a performer.

As I said before, John *performed* on record. While many artists would just sing on a record, John never did that. When he decided to do a song, he got into it head over heels. We did a wide array of songs, from one end of the scope to the other, that a lot of other artists wouldn't even have thought about doing. But we did them, and while not all of them turned out to be hit records, they were all part of John.

※

Because I was involved in all aspects of the Johnny Cash Show while we were on the road, I had the opportunity to become acquainted with a wide variety of people in the entertainment business—talent buyers, agents, managers, local radio disc jockeys, building managers, stage managers—and all of those contacts helped me tremendously. I kept a ledger with their phone numbers because most of them were good people and I wanted to stay in touch with them.

If someone did me a favor or helped me out a bit, I'd always make sure I called that person to say, "Hey, man, I really appreciate all you did." If there had been a problem at one of our shows, I'd call the building manager and say, "Man, I'm sorry about that. That shouldn't have happened, and I wanted to call you and apologize." Taking time to do those things paid dividends the next time we were in town, and way on down the line.

I always tried to start our shows exactly on time, but sometimes that was a problem because if John got hungry, he'd often have me pull the motor home over so June could cook something. When I knew we were running behind schedule, I'd say, "Hey Man, we can stop and cook, but you know we're running pretty tight here." And John would usually say, "Ahhh, it'll wait. Don't worry about it, we'll make it."

There were plenty of times we made it just by the skin of our teeth. When we'd roll into town late, I'd park the motor home by the back door of our hotel and get us checked in, then we'd run to our rooms and get cleaned up, jump back into the motor home and rush over to the building, where I'd park, run inside, pick up my bass, and go out onstage to start the show.

※

With such a large entourage and so many dates to play, we should have been traveling in two buses all along and scheduling the tours so the distance between cities was shorter. That would have been the simplest and most efficient way to do things by far, but for some reason, neither John nor June wanted to do that.

June had traveled on tours with bands earlier in her career, and she was never really comfortable with it. She didn't like the idea of being cooped up on a bus with a bunch of other people, especially if it was a long haul between dates. June always used to say, "A bus ain't the place to pull off your boots and let your stinky feet fill the air." The motor home was more homey and comfortable, and June much preferred that whenever we had to travel over the road to tour dates.

As a result, John and June pretty much set up our tours they way they wanted. We'd fly to the first date, travel in the motor home to the others, and fly back home after the final date. And if the dates in the middle were too far apart to drive between them, we'd fly to all of them. That was fine for John and June, but they weren't thinking of the people trying to coordinate everything.

Sometimes I'd set up a tour just exactly the way John wanted it, and then the day before we were set to hit the road, he'd call me up and say, "Marshall, I don't think I want to do it that way. Let's do this and let's do this . . ." It wouldn't be too long before we'd be rearranging the travel itinerary for the entire entourage—the day before we were scheduled to leave. John never thought twice about things like that.

One time, about a week before we were to leave for an Australian tour, I had made all of our travel and lodging arrangements, and a member of the cast asked me—in John's presence—when we were going to leave, when we were going to arrive, what the tour itinerary was, and when we were going to come back home. I told the person the particulars and didn't think any more about it, particularly since we were out on another tour at the time and there were other matters that I needed to tend to.

As that tour went on, John asked me a couple of questions about Australia and what we would be doing there, and I answered those. Not long after we got back home, he called me and said, "I know you've put a lot of work into that Australian tour, and you've got it all set and it's probably the way it ought to be, but I don't want to leave on that day—I want to leave a day later. And I'd like the whole cast to go over a day later, too."

When you're taking eighteen people halfway around the world, you can't just flip a switch and change things. So I called my travel agent, and we worked feverishly for a couple of days to change our transportation and lodging arrangements. We had planned to stay a night in a hotel in Honolulu, but we had to change that, and we also had to change our arrival time in Sydney and several other things that had already been set. John was very spontaneous when it came to things like that, and because he was straight as an arrow at that point in his life and wanted things to be just so, I don't think he really gave much thought to what was involved in making them happen.

You had to be careful when John was around, because if he overheard you, he'd start thinking and often would come up with a "better plan" that suited him. If I had just called that cast member over to the side and said, "Here's what you need to know . . ." things would have been a lot simpler. But I didn't; I made the mistake of answering his questions in front of John. And that cost me a couple of days of work, plus we had to take less desirable flights.

I began to notice a change in John somewhere around 1975. He wasn't doing drugs, but he certainly wasn't acting like the same person. I attributed the change to our grueling schedule, and we sometimes had to postpone dates to catch up on our rest. John wasn't the only one feeling strain; everybody in the organization felt overworked.

Most of the touring we were doing was unnecessary because John had overcome the financial problems caused by his drug abuse and by now was a very wealthy man. The money was still going out pretty quickly, however, in part because John wanted to help everybody, but also because, as he and everyone else knew, we were taking way too many people out on tour with us, especially when we went overseas.

He wanted to take John Carter with him everywhere, and I don't blame him for that, but that also meant having to bring along the nurse and bodyguard. Plus, we were still carrying a big cast, including the Carter Family, although sometimes Mother Maybelle's health didn't allow her go, but we'd always take Robbie Harden or someone to fill in for her. All of that was very expensive, considering the cost of airline travel, hotels, and food.

John just couldn't say no to anybody at that point. If he saw someone who was down and out, regardless of who it was, he'd give him money and usually try to take care of the person's family as well. But there was only so much he could give away before it started taking a financial toll. I think that sometime during 1975 John began to realize he had to stop giving away so much cash because he wasn't progressing financially anymore.

Our cast and crew were paid very well, but that really wasn't the problem. There were always other people around with their hands out, and John would fill those hands up. He'd been doing that for so long it was very difficult to stop—he couldn't help it; that's just the way he was. But when he realized that all of us on the show were working ourselves half to death, it began to bother him.

John never put a lot of emphasis on money. He made a lot, spent a lot, and gave a whole lot away. As a business practice, that's generally a bad thing. John was never good at business or at handling money—as all of his children know today.

—————

I always tried to arrange our travel so that we'd arrive at the next hotel early in the day, giving John plenty of opportunity to rest. I knew that if he didn't get enough sleep and started to feel fatigued, there was a chance he might start popping pills again to stay awake. That just scared me to death, so I made it a priority when coordinating our travel plans to make sure he could get plenty of sack time.

It got to the point that if John was napping and June needed something, she'd come to me. That was fine with me, because neither of us wanted to interrupt his rest, so we'd just let him sleep.

In October 1975, we were on a tour of Japan and were staying in a Tokyo hotel that was only partly Americanized—there were no bathrooms in our rooms! Those were located downstairs, so if you had to use the facilities, you had to take the elevator to a lower floor. To make things even more interesting, both men and women had to use the same bathroom. That didn't bother the guys too much, but June and the rest of the Carter Family didn't like it at all.

When June got the urge, regardless of what hour of the day or night it might be, she would call me and say, "Marshall, I hate to tell you this, but I gotta go to the bathroom." I'd meet her downstairs and check out the bathroom to make sure it was unoccupied and then stand guard outside the door, keeping men out and allowing only women to go inside. We worked around Tokyo for the better part of a week and stayed in that hotel the entire time. June was my war buddy and companion, and she was such a delightful person that I would do anything for her—even if it meant pulling guard duty outside a strange bathroom in the middle of the night.

<hr>

John and I often reminisced about things that we'd done early in our career, when Luther Perkins was alive, because remembering those days always seemed to brighten his spirits at a time when he needed a lift. One escapade that would always crack us up took place while we were driving home from New York after our appearance on *The Jackie Gleason* Show in January 1957.

We were coming into North Carolina when John said, "Boy, I wish we would run up on some snow somewhere. I sure would like to have some snow cream." John really loved snow cream (it's just like ice cream, except it's made with snow). Since I'd been born and raised in the Tar Heel State, and knew the area well, I told him, "We're not going to get into any snow until we get to the top of Soco Mountain, and there'll be plenty of it there. John asked if I was sure, and I told him, "Absolutely. I know there will be, no question about it, this time of year."

We stopped in the little town of Black Mountain and bought a dishpan (which I still have), some plastic bowls and spoons, and all the ingredients we needed to make snow cream. When we got to Soco Mountain, sure enough, we started seeing a little snow along the side of the road, and there was more of it the farther we drove. When we got to the top of the mountain, boy, there was all sorts of snow! It wasn't exactly clean, however, as it had been there a long time, but we stopped the car and walked a little way off the road until we found a patch that looked good.

We filled the dishpan, went back to the car, and whipped up a fine batch of snow cream. There was a park bench nearby, and the three of us were sitting there enjoying our treat when all of the sudden, we heard a strange noise coming up the bluff toward us. "What *is* that?" John asked, and Luther and I replied at the same time, "I don't know!"

We found out real quick when a big Smoky Mountain black bear poked his head over the rise. I guess he'd smelled our snow cream and wanted some for himself—and here he came! We moved pretty darn fast for a couple of car mechanics and an appliance salesman. We grabbed the dishpan and the bowls and spoons, jumped in my little '54 Plymouth, and just tore down the road off Soco Mountain! The last thing I saw in the rearview mirror before we rounded the bend was that bear sniffing around the bench where we'd been eating and looking after us as we zoomed away.

One of the highlights of John's life occurred on March 10, 1976, when he was honored with a star on Hollywood's Walk of Fame. June and I attended the ceremony with him when the sidewalk plaque was unveiled, and it was a very exciting moment for all of us.

John really treasured that star and liked to talk about it. He often would jokingly compare himself to the big movie stars of the time, but unfortunately, he never did become a big star of the silver screen. However, he certainly deserved having his name enshrined on that Walk of Fame star, and you can see it at 6320 Hollywood Boulevard.

⊸⊸⊸

In March of that year, everyone gathered at the House of Cash for a recording session. John arrived about thirty minutes late, which wasn't unusual, and didn't have anything prepared. He did, however, have some songs someone had sent him, and he started singing a verse and chorus from one of them, just him and his guitar. I sat beside him, as I did a lot of times, and familiarized myself with the song and started playing bass along with him.

We worked on the songs for about half an hour, but they didn't strike us as being very good, except for one called "One Piece at a Time." It told a clever little story about a General Motors employee who was stealing a car piece by piece. After a while, John put down his guitar and said, "Guys, do whatever you want to do. I'm going to go pick up John Carter at school and go take a nap. I'll be back up here at five o'clock or so."

I said, "John, before you leave, why don't you put down that song about the car? Let Charlie turn on the machine, and put it down with just you and your guitar. Let us work on it and lay down a track, and when you come back you can put your voice on it. I think it's a hit record."

"You think so?" he asked. "I really do," I told him. "It's real catchy, and it's original." He said, "Ah, you just relate to it because you used to be a mechanic." I told him that was probably part of the reason I liked it, but I said I really thought it had the potential to be a hit for us. John picked up his guitar, started a tempo that felt good to him, and then laid down the whole song, from start to finish, before he left to pick up John Carter.

The rest of us put our heads together, made up our charts, and after three or four takes, we laid down a track. About five o'clock, John came back looking rested after his nap. "John," I said, "I want you to listen to this track and put your voice on it—because I still think it's a hit record." He wrinkled his nose and said, "Ahhh." I told him, "Just listen to it and lay your voice on it one time and let's see how it sounds." He rolled his eyes a little bit but said, "Wee-l-l-l, OK."

Charlie Brad, the engineer in the control room, rolled the tape and John laid down a vocal track. After the first take, I said, "What do you think?" and John replied, "Well, it is a little different, isn't it?" I told him, "I like it. I think we need to work with it and get it in the bottom of the groove, but I think it's a hit record." After about three more takes, it felt real good, and John said, "You still think that's a hit?" I said, "John, I know it is. You just mark my words, I know it's a hit record—in my heart, it's a hit." He said, "Well, OK, I hope you're right." We fiddled around in the studio after that and didn't come up with anything else during the entire three days we were there.

Probably a month went by, and on the day we left for a European tour, that quirky little record was released. We were in Europe for the better part of three weeks, and when we got back to the States, "One Piece at a Time" was the No. 1 record in the nation. It had been some time since we'd had a hit record—everything we put out would make the record charts but only rise into the twenties or thirties, never the Top 10—but "One Piece at a Time" changed all that.

About a year after the release of "One Piece at a Time," a man walked into the House of Cash and told the manager there, John's sister Reba Hancock, that he wanted to talk to Johnny Cash. "You can't do that," Reba said, "because he has a concert in Dallas tonight, and he's packing and getting ready to go and he's running a little bit late." The man replied, "Well, I sure would like to talk to Johnny." Reba again explained the situation to him, adding, "I'm sorry sir, but he's probably already left for the airport." And at that very moment, in walked John.

He was in fact on his way to the airport, but he'd stopped by the House of Cash to pick up something before he left town. The man introduced himself to John, saying, "My name is Bill Patch, and I've got something I want to give you." John, antsy to leave, told him, "Man, I don't have time; I'm late getting to the airport. I've got a concert tonight in Dallas, and I gotta go. I just don't have any time to talk to you right now."

The fellow wouldn't be put off and told John, "Wait a minute. If you're going to Dallas, I came to town on my Lear jet, and if you don't mind, I'll just drop you off in Dallas and I'll go on home to Oklahoma." It turned out that Bill Patch was a coal strip-miner who lived in Miami, Oklahoma, and was very wealthy—although you wouldn't know it to look at or talk to him. "OK," John said after a moment, "if you're that determined to do it, let's go. I gotta get to Dallas."

As they drove to the airport, Bill told John that he had a car built exactly like the one described in "One Piece at a Time," and he basically wanted to give it to John. "I want to sell it to you for a dollar," he said, "and then if you ever want to get rid of it, I'll buy it back for a hundred thousand. That was an offer John couldn't refuse, and when we finished that tour, they worked out all the arrangements and Bill Patch had that car delivered to the House of Cash in an enclosed van. That car was one of the most amazing things I've ever seen! And if you listen to "One Piece at a Time," you can visualize it.

We became very good friends with Bill Patch after that. Bill was building a civic center in Miami, Oklahoma, about ninety miles northeast of Tulsa, and when he and John were talking about it, John said, "I'll come help you build that. We'll do a benefit show and help build that little civic center."

When time came for the concert, Bill flew down to Nashville and picked us up in his Lear jet, making several trips to ferry the entire cast and crew to Miami. When we got there, we literally landed in his back yard! After we touched down on a 5,000-foot runway, Bill turned the jet around and taxied to his home, which was right next to the airstrip, and pulled the plane into a bay right under the house. All he had to do was get out of the jet and walk up a few steps into his den. It was the most phenomenal thing I've ever seen.

Bill also had a hanger there, and after the show he threw a party inside it for the cast and some of his friends. As the night progressed, I went to Bill and said, "You know, it's getting a little late. I got a lot of stuff I need to do tomorrow, and I need to get back to Memphis." Bill smiled and said, "Not a problem!" I climbed aboard the jet with W. S. Holland and Bob Wootton, and Bill flew us right back home and then returned to Miami for another load. John and June spent the night with him at his home and flew back to Nashville the next day.

Bill Patch was a marvelous man, and we became very close friends. He'd fly down to visit with John and June, and I often talked with him and his wife, Janine. Bill came down with cancer and battled it hard for a while, and I talked to Janine almost every day to get an update on his condition. Then, early one morning, she called to tell me that Bill had passed away during the night. It was a terrible loss.

I stayed in touch with Janine, who later married a fellow by the name of Ronnie Dunn. They moved to Nashville but didn't have a place to live, so John invited them to stay in a cabin in the woods on his property for as long as they wanted. He and June had also become close to Janine, and they came to know and like Ronnie.

After the couple had been in the cabin about a year or so, Ronnie teamed up with Kix Brooks to form the vocal duo Brooks & Dunn, and they've made some musical history of their own. I still talk to Janine occasionally and consider her a great friend. I'll always admire the way she stood by Bill during his illness, and I'm happy she's the wife of a superstar; she deserves that.

<hr />

As 1976 progressed, I could definitely see signs that John was beginning to falter in some ways. There again, I think it was the effects of our schedule, but I watched him very closely because I was concerned that he might turn to amphetamines again to cope with his fatigue. He didn't, though; he just gritted his teeth and "played through the pain." But as time wore on, I definitely noticed signs that the road was starting to take a toll on his health.

I talked to him as much as I could to try to keep him in a positive frame of mind. We talked about the silly things we'd done early in our career, the pranks we played on one another in the hotels and backstage. That cheered him up a little, but it would only last so long. I tried to keep him focused, but I could see he was going through some changes.

By this time, John and June had several places where they could go to get away from it all. They still had their apartment in New York City, as well as a retreat in Virginia, where June had been born and raised, and one in Bon Aqua, Tennessee, about fifty miles west of Nashville. They also had purchased a lovely home overlooking Montego Bay in Jamaica and had renovated a house in New Port Richey, Florida, that was owned by Mother Maybelle.

When we'd finish a tour, they would often head for one of these retreats to rest up. Now, that wasn't always necessarily a good thing because it kept John away from his other family members and friends a little too much. If he and John Carter and June went to New York or Jamaica or wherever, that left his other children at home. And after all, Rosanne, Cindy, Kathy, and Tara were John's children, too, and he didn't spend nearly enough time with them. They were precious, wonderful kids, and they still are today. I think that if you're in show business, you have to keep your priorities in order and make sure you share yourself equally with all your family and loved ones.

On January 29, 1977, we kicked off a tour in New Haven, Connecticut. The band and I checked into a hotel, and John had come in a little earlier by Lear jet. The building where we were scheduled to play was literally just around the corner, so a little before 5 p.m., the band and I headed over to do a sound check.

As we walked up to the stage door, the guard on duty took a look at us and our instruments and said, "Ahhh, Mr. Cash's band. Good to see you. Mr. Cash is already here." *Uh-oh*, I thought, *we got a problem!* John never showed up for a sound check when he was straight, so I naturally feared the worst. I hurried inside and maneuvered up about three steps, then turned left into a hallway that led to the stage. Right at that moment, John came walking off the stage, and when he saw me and the rest of the guys, he made a left turn into his dressing room and closed the door. *Oh my lands, we got a problem!*

I carried my bass out on the stage, pulled it out of its case, and plugged it into the amplifier—and then I slowly walked over to

John's dressing room and went inside. He looked me straight in the eye, and I stared right back at him and said, "Why, John? Just please tell me why? You've had all these good years. You've got the world by the tail. You're *THE* Man in country music. You have a great family, a great wife. You've got everything a man could possibly dream of. Why have you turned your back on them?"

He got this sort of sarcastic look on his face and said, "Marshall, let me ask you something. You've never gone through the change of life, have you?" I said, "Well, no, John, I haven't. Besides that, I don't think that's what's wrong with you." He said, "You'll see. I'm going on that stage tonight and I'm going to knock those people out, and tomorrow it's going to be a new world. I'll be over this thing by tomorrow, and I'll be all right. So you just don't worry about me, because when I get over this little problem, I'll be all right."

I told him, "John, I really hope so. I really hope so. Let's wait and see what tomorrow brings, and we'll wait and talk about it some more. If that's the case, I want to be the first to apologize to you. But, John, let's don't go down this route no more. Let's not do that, 'cause we'll never survive it. There's just no way to survive it."

"There's nothing wrong with me!" he said. "You think I'm on drugs? I'm not, I'm just simply going through the change of life."

"OK, John, let's let that lay a little while, and we'll talk about it as time goes on. I'm going out there and rehearse with the band and get the ol' show ready to go. We'll see you when you walk out onstage."

"I'm going to walk onstage, and I'll be a better man than you've ever seen me!"

"I'm really looking forward to that, son. Have a good day, and I'll see you onstage."

That night, we started the show as usual, with the Carter Family segment and the band playing a couple of instrumentals. We then took a ten- or fifteen-minute break to reset the stage for John. Usually, during the break, I'd go to the dressing room to check on him to make sure everything was all right, but on that particular night I didn't, because I knew he was already in the building.

John walked onstage into the lights, but when he turned toward me, I could see that he was in worse shape than when I'd seen him that afternoon. I just wanted to stop the whole show, go backstage, and sit down and cry. However, John did a decent show, and I don't think anyone in the audience knew he was less than 100 percent. The man was an entertainer from the word go, and no matter how strung out he might be, he'd always have the crowd in the palm of his hand. And that night in New Haven was no different.

No one in the audience—or in the cast and crew, for that matter—noticed anything unusual about John that night. No one but June. She looked so sad onstage, and her eyes said it all. She and I looked across the set at each other, each of us silently asking the other, "Are we going to go through this again? Is this what's going to happen?"

It had been seven years since John Carter's birth, and Johnny Cash had been totally drug free during that entire time. We all had hoped for the best, but June and I had known all along, deep down, that there would be some bad times. We just didn't know how bad they were going to be. We wondered what was in store for us all now that our worst fears apparently had been realized. What did John have in store for us?

John pretty much kept his drug use under control throughout 1977, but he never did straighten up completely; he always had something in his system. However, he was reasonably easy to get along with, and we worked together with no animosity. Sometimes he and I would sit and talk, never about drugs, but I would sort of beat around the bush to let him know that I was very, very concerned about his using them.

It really didn't seem to make much difference what I or anyone else thought about it, that's just the way John was. He was very self-centered in some ways. If he was straight, he would listen to anything you had to say and you could always come to an agreement. But if there was anything at all in his system, that didn't happen; everything had to be done his way, although that wasn't necessarily the best way to go.

Johnny Cash was one of the greatest teachers I've ever known. I learned so much just by watching what he did, what he said, and how he conducted himself. He may not have set a good example all of the time, but he still was a great teacher. I don't think he actually intended to teach anyone anything, although you could often learn what *not* to do by observing how his actions hurt himself and those around him. If you looked at John with an open mind and open eyes, by the time the day was done, you would always learn something from him, be it good or bad.

44

Noted evangelist Billy Graham wanted John to appear March 23 on one of his Crusades in Asheville, North Carolina, which was very close to where Billy lived. John, June, and I flew into Asheville and were met at the airport by Ruth Graham, Billy's wife, who took us to the downtown Hilton Hotel in her car. Ruth was driving and kept looking around to talk with John and June, who were in the backseat.

After the second or third close call on the highway, I finally told Ruth, "I tell you what, if you'll just pull over to the side and let me drive, you can turn around in the seat and talk to them all you want." She laughed and said that sounded like a pretty good idea, then stopped the car and switched seats with me so they could continue their conversation as I drove to the hotel.

We did several Billy Graham Crusades and enjoyed them very much, as John would always get himself straight enough to do a good job. On May 15, Billy invited us to perform on a Crusade at the

University of Notre Dame, just outside of South Bend, Indiana, where a crowd of 43,000 people was on hand.

The Crusade the next day was in Omaha, Nebraska, and I was having trouble getting flights there from South Bend. Normally, I would have had all the travel and lodging arrangements worked out way in advance, but the Crusade appearances had come up sort of quick, so I'd only made reservations as far as South Bend. Cliff Barrows knew I had been struggling with the travel arrangements all afternoon, and he came to me and said, "Marshall, let me talk to Billy. If he doesn't have to go home right after the services today, maybe I can get his Lear jet and get the pilots to run you over to Omaha."

I told Cliff that would be a lot of trouble and expense, and that I'd manage some way. "Oh, no," he said, "you guys have done us a great favor; let me see what I can work out." He called me in about an hour and told me, "Marshall, it's all worked out. There will be a car at the Crusade; just take all of your belongings with you, and they'll take you directly to the airport and fly all of you nonstop right into Omaha." That's exactly what happened, and everything was really slick from there on. All of the people with the Billy Graham organization were and still are wonderful people. It was a great experience for John, June, and I to do those Crusades with Billy Graham, one I'll never forget.

⸻

On August 16, 1977, Elvis Presley died. John and Elvis hadn't seen much of each other lately and at that point weren't what I would call bosom buddies. They were now two of the biggest entertainers in the world, not the up-and-coming singers who had spent so much time on the road together pulling little pranks to keep each other amused. Still, Elvis's death hit John real hard, because despite all the years and miles, he loved Elvis and Elvis loved him, and they had so much respect for one another.

I thought the way that Elvis died might shake up John enough to throw away all the amphetamines, start over, and do a little better, but that didn't happen. I also expected that when John started using drugs again, his intake would soar, but thankfully, that didn't happen either. He seemed to have pretty good control of things.

Some days were worse than others, and the problem was always there, but everything kept rolling along pretty smoothly. There were no problems within the organization, and we were all very grateful for that.

⸺⸱⸱⸱⸺

That summer, we were called to the House of Cash to record an album. John came into the studio before we started the session and asked me to go upstairs and talk with him about something he wanted to do. "Marshall," he said after we'd sat down in his office, "I want to take everybody on the show—everybody and their wives—to the Holy Land." He'd already been to the region when he filmed *The Gospel Road*, and he and June had been there on other occasions, but none of the rest of us had ever seen that part of the world. John loved the place and had talked so much about it.

"I want you to check and see what we can get worked out," he said. "Now, I know a tour guide over there; his name is Joe Jahshan, and I want to use him. If you'll get all the airlines figured up and see what we can do, I'll get in touch with Joe Jahshan or put you in touch with him to work out all the details. I really want him, because we've been over there before and he was a tremendous help and has become a great friend. He's even come to my house and visited, and I want to use him as a tour guide." He added that he wanted to go over in October, when it wouldn't be so hot.

There were about thirty people that he wanted to take. He said, "I want everybody to go first class. I want them to stay in the first-class hotels, which we'll get Joe Jahshan to set up, and all of the food and all of the expenses will be paid for one hundred percent." I said, "John, that's great, but isn't that carrying it to the extreme a little bit? After all, these people have got to eat even if they stay home. I don't see why you should be obligated in any way to furnish everybody's food and all the amenities." But he said, "No, that's what I want to do. All these people that I'm thinking about are very special to me and have done a lot for me. It's just a little payback time."

He told me Joe Jahshan's brother-in-law was a travel agent in Toronto. "Before you buy the tickets," he said, "I wish you'd check with John Jaber and see if you can get them through him because I think the tour will work better if these two could work together, because they do that often with groups. I'd feel pretty good if we could work everything through them." I told him I'd check it out.

He gave me John Jaber's number, and I called him and told him what we wanted to do. "I'd like you to give me an estimate on the airline tickets," I told him, "and we'll let your brother-in-law take care of everything over there. But just get me an estimate on the airline tickets." He said he'd work up the numbers, then added, "You know, with this many people, I can go with you and it won't cost you or anyone else. The airlines will give me a free round trip just to be your guide." I said, "That would be good. We're probably going to need that." Since I had never been to the Middle East before, it was a little strange and I welcomed his help.

John wanted Etta and me and W. S. and his wife, Joyce, to fly with June and him from Washington's Dulles airport to Paris on the Concorde. Everyone else would travel first class on a regular commercial flight.

After about a week or so, John Jaber called and gave me a price on all of the tickets. I had also gotten a price from Ruth Noble at World Travel, and John Jaber's was $12,000 higher than Ruth's. I went to John and told him, "John, I know you want to use John Jaber, and I can understand that, working with Joe Jahshan over there. But the tickets through him are a little over twelve thousand dollars more than if we get them here in the States from Ruth Noble and World Travel."

He said, "Well Marshall, I understand what you're saying, but I feel that it would work smoother and slicker if we bought them through John Jaber. I appreciate all the work, and I realize that twelve thousand dollars is twelve thousand dollars, but I don't want anything to go wrong. This is new territory for all of us, and for something to go wrong would be terrible."

"I have no problem with that," I told him, and that's what we did. After a few days, I worked out all of the fine details with John Jaber. He was a good travel agent, no question about it. He had booked a lot of overseas tours, around-the-world tours for a lot of people, and you could just tell by talking to him that he was a professional.

October 22, we gathered in Nashville and caught an American Airlines flight to Dulles, and from there it was on to Paris, London, and Tel Aviv.

Our tour guide, Joe Jahshan, met us at the airport in Israel, and it was first class all the way. We had a great bus to travel all over the Holy Land, and he was a great guide. I still marvel at everything he told us and everything he knew. You couldn't ask a question he didn't answer correctly, with lots of pleasure. He loved all of our people, and we loved him. We were just one big, happy family.

We didn't get much rest over there. We didn't get into bed until late at night, and we got up early the next morning to head out again. John wanted to utilize all of the time we had over there, and he wanted us all to see everything possible. He and June had seen much of the region before, but he wanted to make sure all the people from the show saw it, too. These were the people closest to John in his life, and he wanted them to experience the trip that he and June had enjoyed more than anything else they'd ever done. It was certainly a highlight of my life and I think everyone else's too. I don't see how anyone could have topped that trip.

John and I talked about doing a couple of shows somewhere, maybe to help with some of the expenses, even though he wasn't concerned about those. He also wanted everyone to see a bit more of Europe, so we added a couple of days on the Continent on the way back home. We played shows in Vienna, Austria, and Frankfurt, Germany, and everyone in our group enjoyed those cities, especially those who hadn't been there before. We arranged to play those dates to give everyone a chance to do some shopping and sightseeing. It was a remarkable trip, to say the least.

—————

We had been back home only a short time before we hit the road again for yet another concert tour. We loved playing concerts and all of the people who turned out for them—and we were drawing huge crowds everywhere. Our touring schedule was frantic, and I could see John changing. The more hectic our itinerary got, the more amphetamines he'd take.

Every once in a while, something would come along that would slow down John's drug use. One of those events occurred in

February 1978, when Billy Graham invited us to go to Las Vegas for five days to appear on a Crusade. We looked at that as a chance to do a lot of good, and to rest up a bit, too. John, June, and I and backup singer Jan Howard flew out, and we all stayed at the MGM Grand Hotel.

It seemed, during that time, as if John had gotten himself about 95 percent straight. You wouldn't know he had any drugs in his system unless you knew him really well. June and I both knew he was still taking amphetamines, but I'm certain nobody connected with the Crusade knew it, because he was straight enough to be the old affable J. R.

Billy Graham and Johnny Cash were a great combination. They were so compatible in so many ways. Both had tremendous charisma, and when they were onstage together, it was an event. I will always treasure the time I spent with John and June on those Crusades.

We flew behind the Iron Curtain in April 1978 to play a series of shows in Prague, Czechoslovakia. There was a nice coliseum in the city, and we sold out two shows a night there on April 10 and 11, drawing more than 44,000 people. The promoter said he could have sold out at least four more shows, but unfortunately, we had other engagements and couldn't remain in town.

About three weeks later, on May 4, we recorded with the great Arthur "Guitar Boogie" Smith in a studio in Charlotte, North Carolina, and the following day were scheduled to perform at Carowinds, the big theme park south of the city. John had asked Etta to come along on that tour and she'd accepted.

On our first night in Charlotte, John said he wanted to go to a nice restaurant and spend a little quality time with "just the two of y'all." When Etta and I got there, we were taken to a private room in the back. As we walked in, a whole slew of people stood up and started singing "Happy Birthday," and among that group was my entire family—and I mean all of my brothers and sisters and cousins. It was then that I realized it was my fiftieth birthday and John and June had pulled a big surprise on me.

I stood almost motionless for a while as everyone hollered and sang and had a ton of fun. There was a beautiful cake that was probably six feet tall by four feet wide, and everybody starting urging me to get a knife and cut myself a piece. As soon as I cut through the frosting, the top of the cake popped off and my youngest sister, Aubrey, poked her head out through the hole. That was such a special surprise! I found out later that Randy, my only child, was supposed to be in that cake, but his plane had been delayed in Memphis and he couldn't get there on time. He finally arrived just as everything was winding down.

About halfway through the party, John told me I had a phone call. When I picked up the receiver and said hello, a voice on the other end said, "Marshall, Roy Orbison." I was stunned but managed to say, "Roy! My lands, it's been forever since I've seen or talked to you!" He said, "I just wanted to call you on your birthday and wish you a happy fiftieth. I remember the good times we had out at your house on Nakomis, when we used to come in to record. You'd invite us out and we'd barbecue and just have a lot of fun. I think about it often and I appreciate it so much." It was so good to talk to my old friend. Unfortunately, that would be the last time I would ever speak to him.

Everyone—my family, John, June, the band, myself—had an awesome time that night. It was a birthday party I'll never forget. And it was all arranged by John, who was in great shape and took part in it like the friend he truly was, and my loving wife, Etta. I must say it came as a total surprise to me!

Through the decade, John had done many wonderful things to help countless needy people. On June 10, 1978, his efforts were recognized when he was presented a United Nations Humanitarian Award during the international organization's annual Citation Dinner in New York City. He certainly deserved it. It was a great night, and he was praised to the hilt. John felt very honored to receive the award, and I thought it might even help him take control of his drug problem, which was definitely making a comeback.

⚊⚊⚊⚊⚊

Some good songs were being sent our way, but John really and truly wasn't interested, so our recording career continued to suffer. We were in the studio in July working on the *Gone Girl* album, which was being produced by Larry Butler, our piano player on the road. Larry had a song called "The Gambler," which we all liked. It was one of the first things we recorded at that particular session. It came off well, which made me happy because it was the first thing that we had cut in a long time that had any commercial value whatsoever. And we really needed a hit record.

John didn't keep his composure very well. He kept going into the bathroom, and every time he'd come out he would be a little higher. Finally, during that daylong session, he got out of control and started arguing about a lot of things with Butler, who just wanted John to do the best he could do and record some good songs.

Jerry Hensley, our guitar player, a great guy who was a first cousin to June Carter Cash and a fantastic musician, was sitting by my side in the studio. Larry Butler came into the studio to move Jerry's amplifier because it was bleeding into my bass amp, and Jerry jokingly said, "Say, Butler, when did you lose control of this session?" He said, "Oh, I don't know, about an hour ago, but you just wait and we'll get all evened up."

We continued to work but accomplished nothing else that day, since John was determined not to do anything that Butler wanted. The band members were determined to do the best we could, but nothing came together so the session just sort of fizzled out. John was blaming everybody in the studio for all the things he thought had gone wrong, but the person he should have heaped all the blame on was himself.

The only decent song we recorded that day was "The Gambler." In fact, we cut a fantastic version of the song—everybody, John included, had really done a fantastic job—but things had gotten so out of control at the session that nothing came of it.

For Larry Butler, it was payback time. Butler also produced Kenny Rogers, and the day after our session, he brought Kenny into the studio and recorded "The Gambler." Just ten days later, the single was released, and it would become one of Kenny Rogers's greatest hits. Our version was still in the can, however, and the album wasn't finished yet.

That session marked the turning point in John's recording career because nobody could deal with him in the studio. His drug problems were getting worse.

Luckily, that same month we did a session with Waylon Jennings that turned out pretty well. We recorded "There Ain't No Good Chain Gangs," which reached No. 2 on the national charts. The song wasn't a career builder for either John or Waylon, but at least it was a hit record and sold lots of copies. And it kept John on the radio for a while.

By the time "Chain Gangs" was released, Kenny Rogers's version of "The Gambler" was climbing the charts. John wasn't in a very good mood there for a while, but as I said earlier, the only person he could really blame for missing out on a great opportunity was himself.

When John was taking amphetamines, he had a tendency to blame other people for things that went wrong or weren't to his liking. That's exactly the opposite of what his normal behavior would be if he was totally sober. When he was straight, he'd take responsibility for anything he did, or didn't, do. But when he was strung out, somebody else got the blame, and many times it was June or I. When he was sober, we could do no wrong, but when he was blown out of his mind, we couldn't do anything right.

46

John called me one day in September 1978 and said, "You know, Marshall, September sixteenth we're playing Puyallup, Washington, and Muhammad Ali and Michael Spinks are fighting on the fifteenth at the Superdome in New Orleans, and I've got some tickets." I said, "You have? You got tickets to that fight?" He said, "Yeah, I've got six—that's all I could get my hands on that were together—but we need to check and see who all wants to go. We could swing by New Orleans to see the fight and catch a flight on out to Puyallup, and it should work out pretty good. Why don't you check and see what kind of flights we can get, and we'll go see the fight. And find out who wants to go see the fight, but just remember, I've only got six tickets and can't get anymore unless they're up in the balcony or something."

I checked everything out, and it was almost impossible to get a flight from either Nashville or Memphis to New Orleans and from there to Seattle. There were no direct flights, and the only connections were through Los Angeles, which was going to be a problem. I didn't want us to cut things too close, because once we got to Seattle we would still have to travel quite a way to the concert site.

I called John back and I said, "This is real tough. It's going to be iffy whether we can do this thing and get into Seattle in time to make it on down to Puyallup." He said, "Well, what if we were to fly into Dallas, check into a hotel there on the fifteenth, and then go on down to New Orleans and see the fight and come back up to Dallas?" I told him I'd try to set that up.

There wasn't anything that would work, and I called him back and told him so. He said, "Maybe we can get a Lear jet out of Dallas, go down to New Orleans and back up to Dallas, and then catch a flight to Seattle." I said, "Well, let me check that out."

As it turned out, there was a Lear available from Executive Jet in Columbus, Ohio, which I did business with frequently. "Well, let's do that," John said when I told him. John, Jan Howard, two members of the band, and I decided that we wanted to see the fight, and we flew into Dallas, checked into an airport hotel, went over to the private jet facility, and flew down to New Orleans. When we landed, we had an awful time getting transportation because the city was so bogged down with the huge fight crowd that you couldn't find a taxi or a limo. After several phone calls, however, I finally was able to secure a limo to pick us up and take us to the Superdome and back to the airport after the fight.

When we arrived at the huge arena, about an hour before fight time, we went in the front door just like everybody else and found our seats. Someone from Muhammad Ali's entourage saw John sitting there and came over and asked if he'd like to go back and meet Ali. "Of course I would!" John exclaimed. When he stood up, so did I, and I told Ali's man, "I have to go wherever he goes because there are a lot of people here and he has to have somebody with him. I don't have to go in to see Ali, but I gotta go to the dressing room door." He said, "That's not a problem; come right on."

When got to the dressing room door, the fellow told me, "Come right on in." John and I went in, and there was Muhammad Ali sitting there in a chair, still fully clothed, looking sort of relaxed. He said, "My man, my man, my man! Johnny Cash—that's my man right there." Ali stood, and he and John embraced a little bit, and we talked and had an unbelievable time. We talked about the upcoming fight, but Ali wouldn't predict the round in which he would knock out Michael Spinks. "I'll whup him," he said, "but I won't predict a round. He's pretty tough."

"Ahhh, you'll knock him out," John said. "I don't know, Johnny, I don't know," Ali said. "We're going to give it our best." We talked for about fifteen minutes or so and then went back to our seats. By the time we got there, it was about thirty minutes to fight time. John signed a multitude of autographs and met a lot of people, but enjoyed being out in the audience. It was a great fight, but it did go the distance, with Muhammad regaining the heavyweight championship—by a unanimous decision—for a record third time.

Afterward, when our group went outside to get our limo, it wasn't there. We tried to flag down a cab, but they were all full, and every limo that pulled up wasn't ours, wasn't ours, wasn't ours. That went on for about two hours, and I finally walked about half a block away from the Superdome and flagged down a taxi. I offered the driver nearly quadruple the regular fare if he would take us to the private air terminal. I think I paid $200 to get us all to the airport, but we really needed to get there.

Our pilot was waiting and flew us back to Dallas. When we arrived, it was about five o'clock in the morning and we had to catch our flight at nine. We all laid down for a bit and rested our eyes, then got up and caught our nonstop flight into Seattle. The promoter picked us up at the airport and drove us down to Puyallup for the show, and everything worked out just fine. Seeing Michael Spinks and Muhammad Ali vie for a heavyweight championship was another highlight of my life, and it happened because John wanted to see that fight and, out of the goodness of his heart, wanted us to see it, too. We all had a ball!

———

When he had to, John could always come down and be straight enough to do whatever he wanted to do—no matter what it was. In October 1978, he hosted the twelfth annual Country Music Association Awards Show. This was about the fifth or sixth time he'd hosted the show, and he always did a fantastic job. It seemed like the CMA show was made for him.

One of the things that made John so great was that if there was anything he wanted to do, and he set his mind to it and stayed straight, he could handle it better than anyone I ever knew.

———

Mother Maybelle Carter's health had started to fail earlier in the year, making it difficult for her to go on the road. Jan Howard or sometimes Robbie Harden would fill in for her on those dates, and everything worked very smoothly. Still, all of us missed Mother Maybelle. If there were anyone on earth who could have taken my mother's place when she passed away, it would have been Mother Maybelle Carter. She had grown up in Virginia, and I had grown up in North Carolina, so we had a lot in common, and many times we'd sit backstage and talk about the old times.

Sadly, on October 23, 1978, Mother Maybelle passed away. For nearly everyone in the cast, it was like losing one of our own parents. I'll always miss her, and I'll always love her. I was very honored to be a pallbearer at her funeral.

B y 1979, drugs had become John's top priority. Things were going in the wrong direction for us all, and the only person responsible for that was John. Sometimes when things were really bad, I'd say, "Well, it can't get any worse," but somehow it always did.

John was missing lots of dates, and when he did show up for a concert, he couldn't sing. He could get himself in condition to perform, but his voice would be gone. The same was true for recording sessions: he would get straight and come into the studio, but because he'd been wiped out for so long, his voice would be rough and unresponsive. The magic was totally gone.

When he tried to record, it put everybody in the studio in a very awkward position. Everyone tried to do his best and everyone was very supportive of John, but he couldn't sing, he couldn't keep tempo, and he'd forget the words—they'd be right there in front of him, but he couldn't read them. It was obvious that something terrible was going to happen.

June was having a terrible time dealing with all the pressure and problems caused by John, and it looked as if there would be no end to it. When we'd finish a tour, I was able to go home and sort of get away from the situation, but when June went home, she was still right in the middle of everything. I often thought about her and wondered how she was coping with it. John's behavior was really taking a toll on her, and there was no letup in sight. She would occasionally go to their apartment in New York and spend a week or two shopping to get away from all the problems.

On a couple of occasions, she sought advice from doctors and at one point even checked herself into the Mayo Clinic in Rochester, Minnesota, for help. Over the years, she and John had been treated at the clinic for various illnesses, and one of the doctors there who understood both of them pretty well told June when she checked in: "Your biggest problem is being the wife of Johnny Cash. You'll have to do something about that before we can do anything for you."

John called one day while we were on the road and made an unusual request regarding his hotel accommodations. "From now on," he said, "I want a two-bedroom suite with a living room between the bedrooms. I don't want to ever have two bedrooms and the living room off to the side. I want them in a row, with a door coming into the bedrooms from the hallway, and I always want a living room between the bedrooms. From now on, don't put John Carter in the suite with June and me. When John Carter comes along with Mrs. Kelly, give them a separate room. Put them across the hall or next door, but don't put them in the suite with us."

"OK, that won't be any problem," I told him, although I couldn't really understand why he apparently wanted separate rooms for June and himself. But if that is the way he wanted it, and considering his frame of mind, I certainly wasn't going to argue with him. I just did it.

The reason for the new setup, I soon discovered, was that John was making telephone calls to people he shouldn't have been calling and he wanted privacy and a bedroom all his own. Even though they were staying in the same suite, he and June were totally out of communication when they were at the hotel. He didn't visit her room, and he wouldn't allow her into his. On rare occasions, they would order room service and eat together in the living room, but they very seldom went out together to the hotel coffee shop or a restaurant.

John was adamant about those living arrangements. On a couple of occasions, I had problems finding a hotel with the layout he wanted. When I called to tell him, he said, "Keep looking until you find it. I want the living room in between the two bedrooms."

<hr>

In addition to touring, we did a lot of recording during the first half of 1979, but nothing we did was really significant. We cut two or three albums, but there wasn't a song on any of them that would be a huge hit or help our career, although a few of them did make it into the Top 10. John's drug use had made him so hoarse that his voice sounded terrible, and at times it would get so bad he couldn't talk. He'd come to the studio anyway and try to sing. We recorded some of the worst stuff in our entire career during the first six months of 1979.

In mid-July, however, John got himself into pretty good shape, and we did a television special for CBS called *The Unbroken Circle: A Tribute to Mother Maybelle Carter*. He did a fantastic job, and the show was nominated for an Emmy. Kris Kristofferson was the host, and the performers, in addition to John and Kris, included Lynn Anderson, the Carter Family, Ray Charles, Larry Gatlin, Emmylou Harris, Waylon Jennings, Willie Nelson, Linda Ronstadt, and many more.

The beginning of the end of Johnny Cash and the Tennessee Three started in late July 1979 at the Front Row Theatre east of Cleveland, Ohio. June had begun to suspect something was going on and was really interested in just who John was making phone calls to so late at night. She'd step out of her bedroom, go into the suite's living room, put her ear up against his door, and listen. I don't know who all he'd been calling, but in the early morning hours after our show there on July 29, the final night of a three-day stand, John had been talking to Jan Howard trying to figure out what was wrong with June.

John had been calling Jan an awful lot, because he wasn't in any frame of mind to figure things out for himself, which he could have, if he'd just stopped, looked, and listened to what was going on around him. I guess he needed someone to talk to, and he figured that Jan, who was best friends with June, almost like a sister, would be a good source of information.

"Too much pressure," Jan would tell him. "She's going through a lot."

Jan was sort of caught in the middle between June and John, and she was trying to help both sides. Being in the middle is not a pleasant place to be. I've been there, so I know. In fact, I was always in the middle, protecting June and trying to pacify John, and when worse came to worst, I was always on June's side—because she was always right.

Jan was never part of the discussions June and I had about how to deal with John, but she was always there for both of them. June would call and talk to her, and John would call and talk to her, so Jan got to hear both sides, and I think she was a big help to both of them.

⸻⫯⸻

When John called Jan's room somewhere around two or three o'clock that morning, June was listening through the door. Maybe she heard something she didn't want to hear, I don't know, but John was alone in his room when he made the call. However, a certain band member, the same one who John had earlier thought was making a play for his sister, was in Jan's room. John's call sort of scared the living daylights out of that band member, who perhaps thought he'd been caught in the middle between John and his "girlfriend" and would have a tough time getting himself out of that situation.

I had no idea what had gone on because I'd been in bed sleeping. July 30 was a travel day, and we were headed to Omaha for a week's stand. Our flight was about 10 a.m., but it was a good hour's drive from where we were staying all the way across town to the airport on the west side of Cleveland. I got up pretty early to get everything ready, get everyone checked out of the hotel, and take care of all the other details I always handled, then went down to the coffee shop and had breakfast.

There were a couple of other members of our entourage there, but no one said anything. After I finished breakfast, I walked back upstairs where I met the band member in question in the hallway, and he told me what happened. I think it had dawned on him that there might be some sort of relationship between John and Jan

Howard, so in order to protect himself, he had called John and told him that he was in her room when John had called early that morning. The band member told me that he'd informed John that he had been seeing Jan for quite sometime and had told him, "If you're thinking about getting serious with Jan Howard, you need to know that, because it's been going on for quite some time and we are making plans."

June was in her bedroom getting her things together to go to one of two places: to Omaha or back home. She came out of her bedroom, walked into the living room, and knocked on John's door. When he opened it, she told him, "This is the turning point. If Jan goes to Omaha, then I go home, and that's just all there is to it. I'll take John Carter and go home, and it's all over."

Needless to say, John sort of panicked. He'd managed to get some sleep, so he was in good enough shape to understand exactly what June had said, and he was pretty sure that she meant it.

I was in my room packing when John called. "Marshall," he said, "where's Jan and the rest of the band?" I told him I had just put everyone in the rental cars and they were headed to the airport, and that I was going to wait and go with June and him in the limo. "I need to talk with Jan," he said. No one had cell phones in those days, and I told him that it would be tough to reach her, since she was on her way to the airport. "I've got to talk to Jan," he said, "and I've got to talk to her right away."

"John," I told him, "the only thing I can do is take the limo or a rental car and drive all the way across town to the airport, and hopefully I can catch them before they get on the plane. That's the only thing I can do." He said, "Well, I gotta talk to her."

I drove as fast as I could across town. It was pretty early in the morning, and traffic was terrible, but I managed to make it to the airport. When I got there, I jumped out of the car, ran inside the terminal, and, as luck would have it, found myself at the head of the concourse leading to the gate where our plane was waiting.

I ran to the gate and saw Jan handing her ticket to the gate agent. "Jan, hold up just a minute," I hollered, then walked over and pulled her off to the side. "We've got to get to a phone and call John,"

I said. "What's the problem?" she asked. I told her I had no earthly idea what was going on but that John had sent me to the airport to find her so that he could talk to her before she got on the plane.

I got permission from the gate agent to go onto the plane and talk to the band. I told them, "You guys just go on; everything's arranged. We have rental cars reserved in Omaha, so get two of them and go to the Ramada Inn. I'll call and make sure everything is taken care of; you're pre-registered."

I went back into the terminal and walked Jan up to the lobby to find a phone. I dialed the hotel and asked for John's room. When he picked up, I said, "John, I've got Jan here. We're at the airport, and I caught her as she was getting on the plane. Here she is."

I handed Jan the phone, and when she said hello, there was a god-awful quietness and the look on her face was just terrible. I went over and sat down in a chair about twenty feet away. Jan listened without saying a word for what seemed like five minutes or maybe longer, and then she suddenly dropped the phone and let out a blood-curdling scream that could be heard all over the airport.

I went over to her and said, "Jan, come on over here and let's sit down now. Come on, let's go." She kept screaming, and I said, "Jan, let's just walk up here a little bit, because people are looking at us pretty hard." I led her to a place where there weren't many people and was able to get her calmed down enough to talk. She told me that she couldn't go to Omaha, and added, "I guess I won't be going with you guys again."

I asked her what the problem was, and she said, "I don't know. I really don't know. But a band member has told John something, and I don't know what's going to happen." At that point she broke down. I never felt so sorry for anyone in my life. I said, "Jan, I don't know what to say, but I know one thing for sure—we can't stay here; we gotta go back to the hotel or whatever. I'll buy you a plane ticket and send you anywhere in the world you want to go."

"I don't want to go anywhere," she said, but I told her again, "We can't stay here." I talked to her about thirty minutes, and she calmed down a little bit, then said abruptly, "I want to go back to the hotel." I asked if she was sure, and she said, "Yes, I want to go back to the hotel." So we went outside and got into the rental car and drove all the way back across town to the hotel.

When we got back to the hotel, I walked up to the girl at the front desk, told her who I was, and said, "We want to keep my room, Ms. Howard's room, W. S. Holland's room, and John and June's suite. Would it be possible to keep them for another night? I'll just check everybody out in the morning, and we'll catch the same flight out to Omaha." She said that would be fine.

I took Jan to her room, unlocked the door, and carried her luggage inside. Then I sat down and said, "Jan, what can I do for you? No matter what it is, what can I do for you? I don't understand all of this." She looked at me and said, "I'll be all right. Don't you worry, Marshall." I said, "You call me anytime. I won't be out of this hotel; I'll be in my room or in the coffee shop." She said, "I'll keep that in mind, but rest assured, I'll be all right. I'll probably stay here tonight; I'm not sure, but I'll let you know."

I went back to my room, which was just up the hallway four or five doors, and called John. "I just want you to know that Jan is back in the hotel, back in her own room," I said. I told him that I had offered to fly her anywhere she wanted to go, and even offered to send her to Memphis to stay with Etta. "I said that whatever she wanted to do, I'd take care of it," I told him, "and it was her choice to come back to the hotel, and there wasn't a lot I could do about that." John said, "That's all right. Don't you worry about it. If she wants to come back to the hotel, that's just fine. We'll get this whole thing sorted out."

49

I know in my own mind that what happened that day in Cleveland was the beginning of the end of a lot of things. And while some of them took quite some time to run their course, it was definitely the beginning of the end of Johnny Cash and the Tennessee Three.

I'll always believe that if that certain band member had kept his mouth shut, June would have left John and the tour and gone home, which is what she should have done at that point. She should have taken their son and gone back to Nashville, because if she had, John would have been so shaken that she could have dealt with him and gotten him straightened out, and they might have been able to have a normal life together. That would have been the best thing that could have happened—for all of us.

June was a brilliant person and knew how to deal with John. She knew that if she'd confronted him about his behavior before the incident in Cleveland arose, it probably wouldn't have fazed him. But now, because of the way things had unfolded, June had the upper hand, and there was no way John was going to give up his wife and son, no matter what was going on.

I'm confident, beyond any shadow of a doubt, that if June had left him that day, John would have bent over backwards to put everything back together. He would have done an about-face, they would have patched up their relationship, and there's a very good chance that they'd both still be alive today. There's no doubt in my mind that, with all of the stress June was under from all of the things that were happening, she was headed for the grave.

I talked to John several times throughout that day and night, and on one or two occasions went down to their suite to see how he and June were doing. It seemed that everything was all right, but it wasn't the most enjoyable place to be. I didn't get involved in their personal business; I just checked on them because I was concerned about their well-being. Before I finally went to bed, I told them what time we were leaving the following day.

I talked to the band member involved, and he pretty much told me everything that had happened, although I didn't understand why he did that. If he in fact had been in Jan's room at 2 a.m., and if he'd been doing what he told me he'd been doing, he should have kept his mouth shut. But instead he called his wife and told her he'd "saved the organization." I believe that if he'd kept his mouth closed, things would have been different today.

The next morning, I went down to tell them we were ready to leave and make sure their luggage was out in the hallway for the bellmen to take to the limo, a routine that I had set up years before for all of our cast and crew to make sure our baggage made it to the next stop on the tour. W. S. Holland and I were going to take the rental car and go to the airport ahead of John and June to reserve a spot for them in whatever VIP waiting lounge was available, another routine I had set up years earlier.

We all made it to Omaha and even had a little time to rest before heading over for our first show at the city's big Aksarben (Nebraska spelled backwards) celebration. John had managed to get himself into pretty good shape, and we played to a packed house of about 8,000 people that night.

All of our shows at Aksarben were sold out for the six-day run, which was very encouraging to me and certainly must have been for John, who seemed to be getting better each night as our August 5 finale approached. I thought, *Hey, maybe June got her point across, and John's going to straighten up and toe the mark and act like a good husband, and everything's going to be good again.* I remember especially well that John looked to be coming back to himself a bit and was moving around onstage like he used to. I really thought things were looking up.

But early on the morning of our last show, not much after sunrise, John called me and said, "Marshall, I want to bring Jack Clement in here today. He's got a song that I gotta hear." I said, "My lands, John, you're going home tomorrow morning. Are you sure it can't wait?" He said, "No, this is a song I have to hear tonight."

Something told me there was something bad wrong, but John had been in such good shape the night before, perhaps about 90 percent sober, that I put that thought aside. "I want to bring Jack here," he said. "I want him to have a first-class ticket, I want a seven-passenger black limo to meet him at the airport, and I want the biggest suite in this hotel for him. And I want to get him in here today."

I called Ruth Noble, my travel agent in Memphis, then called John back and told him, "We can get Jack here, but he has to change planes and it'll be about six o'clock this afternoon before he gets in. You know the first show is at seven, and you'll be leaving about six." He said, "That's OK. Just make sure his hotel suite is in order and all, and I'll listen to the song tonight."

I called Ruth again and arranged for Jack's prepaid airline ticket, the limo, and hotel accommodations, then called him and gave him his itinerary. He arrived about six that evening and was driven to the hotel to check in.

That final show went really well, as everyone was upbeat and John was in a fabulous frame of mind. He'd been getting better each night and was closer to being his old self than he'd been in quite some time—and that was really nice.

Afterward, I made sure everyone had transportation back to

the hotel, then went inside the arena to take care of some final details. I talked to all the production people and to Don Romeo, the promoter, and thanked them all for doing a great job. Then I headed for the hotel, arriving about forty-five minutes after everyone else.

———

We were staying on the fifth floor, and when I stepped off the elevator to go to my room, I was surrounded by more chaos than I'd ever seen in my life. Helen Carter was running up and down the hallway looking for me.

"Marshall, June's a-dyin'! She's a-dyin'" Helen wailed in her Virginia accent. "Well, where is she?" I asked. "She's in my room, and she's a-dyin'!" she sobbed. Helen took me to her room, which was right by the elevator, and when she opened the door, there was June lying on Helen's bed. I asked Helen, "What in the world is going on here?"

"Marshall, John fired all of us," she said. "He what?" I asked, wondering if I'd heard her right. "He fired all of us—all of the Carters!" I asked her if he'd also fired June and everybody else, but Helen said, "No, just the Carters." I shook my head and asked, "Why in the world did he do that?" She said, "I have no earthly idea. He came down to our rooms and called us all together and fired us all!"

I asked if June had been there when it happened, and Helen said no. "Well, how did she find it out?" I asked. Helen said, "Well, I told her. It was just more than she could stand." Then I asked how come June was in her room, and she said, "I don't know, I don't really know."

We put some cold washcloths on June's head, but she wasn't responding a whole lot and I was getting very concerned. Helen wanted to call an ambulance to take her to the hospital, but I said, "Helen, let's think about this a little bit. I don't know how bad a shape June is in—I'm not a doctor, but obviously she's in pretty bad shape—but if we call an ambulance to pick up June Carter Cash and take her to the hospital, there are going to be a lot of reporters asking a lot of questions that right now none of us can answer. I need to talk to John about this and see what he wants to do. It's his wife."

Helen looked at me and said, "Marshall, he's pretty bad." I asked where he was, and she said, "He's down in Jack Clement's room."

I went down the hall and knocked on Jack's door. John answered the door, and the only thing he had on was his pants; no shoes, no shirt. He flung the door open so hard that the doorknob punched through the wall and stuck right there. He didn't say a word, just turned around and went back into the room.

"John we've got a real serious problem down here," I said as I followed him inside. "What's the problem?" he mumbled. I was stunned, because John was obviously in terrible shape now but had been happy and upbeat less than an hour and half before. "June is in Helen's room and she's passed out," I told him, "and Helen wants to call an ambulance and take her to the hospital. I don't know what to do; it's your call. I'm not going to call an ambulance unless you say so. But I can tell you right now, if she goes to the hospital, the headlines in the paper tomorrow are going to read, 'June Carter Cash Hospitalized' and they'll probably go into some details here, so we got to think about this."

"Well, where is she?" he asked again. I said, "She's up in Helen's room," at which point he went tearing up the hallway, barefooted, wearing nothing but his pants. The door to Helen's room was open, so John walked in and went over to the bed where June was lying and said, "What's wrong with you?" When there was no response, he reached down and slapped her pretty hard on both cheeks a couple of times and said, louder this time, "What's wrong with you?" June didn't even grunt, and Helen said, "John, she's a-dyin'! Don't hit on her; she's a-dyin'." John said, "She's not dying. She ain't gonna die." But Helen insisted, "Yes she is! That's all there is to it—she's a-dyin'!"

John turned around and stalked out of the room. I followed him back down to Jack's room and asked him again what he wanted to do. "Marshall," he said, "I don't know what *you're* gonna do, but let me tell you what *I'm* going to do. I'm gonna get my little boy, and I'm gonna leave, and y'all can do anything you want to." I asked, "Do you want to send June to the hospital or not?" He replied, "I don't care. Do whatever you want to do with her. It don't bother me one way or the other."

When I got back to Helen's room, Anita was there with her. I said, "Girls, we saw what happened here as far as John is concerned, but we still got a problem if we take June to the hospital. If you all want to take her, I'm not going to call the ambulance, but I'll look up the number for you and one of you can call. But I can't do it, because I'm getting involved in a family situation here that I just shouldn't be involved in. I just want to help, that's all I want to do. I suggest we work on her ourselves and see if we can get her revived a little bit. I think she just fainted, and that's about it."

Anita agreed to that, and we started bathing June all over with cold washcloths. She began to come around a bit, and finally, little by little, she was able to talk to us. I still considered it to be a family affair, so after I'd spoken to June a few minutes, I said, "Girls, I'm going to leave now. If you need me anytime during the night, don't hesitate to give me a call. I'll be here immediately; I'm just down the hall."

Things calmed down, but every so often I'd stick my head out the door to see if anything unusual was going on. There wasn't, so I went to bed. I lay there for a couple of hours wondering what in the world was going to happen and what to do, if anything. I finally dropped off but woke up pretty early the next morning after getting maybe four hours of sleep.

I went down to the coffee shop about 6 a.m. and had breakfast, and by the time I finished, everybody else was getting ready to go to the airport. I went down to John and June's suite and found June there with John; apparently the girls had taken her there while I was sleeping. I felt a little bad that I hadn't been able to help them, because I'm sure it was a struggle to get her to the suite.

"Look, guys," I said, "I checked and there's a later flight that doesn't leave until about eleven o'clock, and I can get on the plane with you. It's going to Nashville, but it lands in Kansas City and I can get off and catch a flight to Memphis and you can go on to Nashville. Why don't we catch that later flight, so you won't have to be in such a turmoil here?"

They agreed, but when it came time to leave, June was so weak she couldn't walk. We got a wheelchair from the hotel and managed to get her in it, then rolled her down and put her in the car.

At the airport, I got the airline's passenger service rep to bring another wheelchair out to the car and I wheeled June from the curb to the VIP room. We waited there for fifteen or twenty minutes, until they called us for our flight, and I wheeled her onto the airplane. John sat down beside her, and I sat in the seat right behind them. It was a short flight to Kansas City, and when I got off the plane, I told them, "I just wish you the best of luck in the world. We've got some real serious problems that we need to put a lot of thought to, and I'll pray for you. Go on home and enjoy your time off, and I'll be talking to you."

<hr />

Now we had a situation where John definitely had the upper hand, not only on June but on me and everybody else. If that certain band member had just let everything blow up while we were in Cleveland, if he hadn't called John, all of the pieces would have fallen into place and June would have had the upper hand. She would have taken John Carter and left John, and John would have been so shaken that he would have gotten himself together, kicked the drugs, gone back to June, and started rebuilding a happy life.

But the way things turned out, she had nothing. Her family had been fired from the show, she was a physical wreck, and now there was no way to reconcile the problems we had. It was a terrible situation, and from that point on, things just got worse.

Three or four days after we got home from Omaha, John called me and, surprisingly enough, was in pretty good shape. He talked sensibly and he wanted to talk about several different things. But then he started in on the situations in Cleveland and Omaha and asked me what I knew. I said, "I don't know anything about it other than my involvement at Aksarben with June, and as far as what happened at the Front Row Theatre, I didn't know anything had happened until I got up the next morning. Things just weren't working right, and I started inquiring around and I found out there were some problems that night."

He asked me what I knew about the band member, and I said, "I only know what he told me. He said that he was in Jan's room about two o'clock in the morning and that you had called and he got scared because he got to thinking he might be messing with your girlfriend. I told him, 'Man, Jan is not John's girlfriend; she's a friend of the family, but not a girlfriend, I can guarantee you that. John and June have some problems they're trying to get sorted out, and he's talking to Jan, he's talking to a lot of people. He's going through some bad times. He can't control his drug addiction, and he's just got a lot of problems with his career and his family and his marriage, and he needs help. I think he was talking to Jan to get help.'"

"What else did he tell you about himself and Jan?" he asked. I said, "It wasn't too good, John, it wasn't too good. I think we better leave this thing alone because it could backfire in all our faces, and whatever happened has happened. The pages can't be turned back, so let's leave it alone and go on with life and try to put the pieces back together again."

But he wanted to talk about it, and he indicated that he wanted to keep that band member at home during our next tour, and maybe forever. "John, you can't do that," I said. "That won't work because it'll plant a seed somewhere and it'll explode in our faces. We need to put that whole situation behind us and move forward; we got to do that. There's no sense in dwelling on it. Turn it loose and let it be."

"What do you think happened between Jan and him that night?" he asked. "I don't know," I said. "I only know what he told me. He told me that he was involved with Jan and after hearing the conversation between you and Jan and two a.m., he knew he had to do something. So he called his wife and told her that he'd 'saved the organization.'" This was his way of covering his own butt.

"I told him, 'Man, it just don't work that way. Things like this just don't work that way at all. It's going to be a problem from here on out. No matter what happens in the organization or in their personal lives, it's going to be a terrible, terrible problem. And I think that I was probably right because it's already been a problem for everybody, and Jan Howard at this point is totally destroyed."

John had no response to that, but a moment later he said, "June and John Carter and I want to go to Jamaica for a few days, and we'll get things all worked out, don't you worry about it." He asked me to arrange their airline schedule and added, "When we get over there, these rental cars that you've been getting, those little-bitty things, I don't like them. See if you can find us a full-sized car."

The past couple of weeks had been a nightmare, but judging from my conversation with him that day, John appeared to be coming around. I figured that all of the problems had made him take a hard look at what he'd been doing, and that maybe he'd finally taken a turn for the best. It was very encouraging.

———⌇———

A couple of hours after John and June were scheduled to arrive at Cinnamon Hill, their home about fifteen minutes from the airport in Montego Bay, I called to make sure they'd gotten there safely and that everything was all right. June answered the phone, and when I asked how things were going, she said, "Marshall, everything is just fine. We got the bigger car, and we appreciate that very much. John's in pretty good shape. He's taking a nap right now, but that's great. Everything is just fine, and hopefully we'll stay here a few days and rest up a little bit, and everything will be all right."

That was very short-lived because the very next day John was messing around in town and found a bunch of pretty powerful amphetamines. That night he got blown completely out of his mind and went out driving on the island. He was tearing around pretty fast, ran through a construction zone, and wrecked the car. He told me later that a two-by-four had punched through the windshield and broken his nose. I don't know about that, because his nose never did sit on his face very straight; it sort of leaned a bit to the left.

He pretty much totaled the car, and I talked to the rental company several times and had everything taken care of. The police investigated and found that John didn't have a driver's license, but then again, he never did. Luckily, because he was practically an icon in Jamaica, having done so many benefits for the island's children and helping so many others, they didn't arrest him. It was obvious that John had a supplier in Jamaica, because that wasn't the first time he'd gotten wired there.

June was so distraught over his behavior that she left and flew to New York City, where she stayed in their apartment.

———⌇———

A day or so later, John called me from their house in New Port Richey, Florida, and he was still in bad shape. He said he wanted a boat so he and John Carter could go fishing. I told him I didn't know anybody who had a boat down there, but if he'd give me a little time,

I'd see what I could come up with. I went right to work on it and called him back later to tell him I'd found a couple of places that could take them fishing. "Don't worry about it," he said. "I bought a boat."

I was very surprised and said, "You've already gone out and bought a boat?" He said, "Yeah, John Carter and me want to go fishing, and I bought us a large boat. I paid a hundred thousand dollars for it." I said, "My lands, John, I'm sure I could have come up with a boat for you to use down there for a couple of days, maybe with a guide and everything." He said, "We didn't want no guide; we wanted a boat all of our own. Tomorrow we're going out fishing, and we're gonna go wherever we want to go."

"John," I said, "you've got to be very careful out there. You don't know those waters, and you've got John Carter along with you. You gotta be very, very careful. You get lost and go in the wrong direction, and it could be real dangerous."

He didn't get lost, but he did manage to run out of fuel. The Coast Guard towed him back to the dock on the little canal right in front of their house. He put some gas in the tanks but couldn't get the engine started, which was a godsend because, considering the shape he was in, he certainly had no business piloting a boat anywhere, especially out in the Gulf of Mexico. He called me and asked if I knew what might be wrong. I owned some racing boats and could make them go pretty good, so I guess he figured I'd have the answer.

I said, "John, I don't even know what kind of boat you've got. Is it an inboard or an outboard, and just what size is it?" He said, "Well, it's a big boat, and it's got the motor down under a big ol' thing here in the middle. I said, "Man, I just don't know what's wrong with it. Is it out of fuel? Does it have a diesel engine, or does it run on gasoline?" He said, "I don't know. But I guess it was out of fuel. We put some in, but it still won't run."

"What kind of fuel did you put in it?" I asked. "We put some gas in it," he said. "Well, that could be the problem right there," I told him. "You've bought a big boat, and it could have a diesel motor in it, and you just put gas in it. You better leave it alone and find somebody that knows what they're doing to come check it out. Call the dealer wherever you got it and have them come check it out."

He didn't like what I was telling him about the boat. I guess he thought I could just pull a rabbit out of the hat and tell him exactly what to do. But truth be told, if I had known what was wrong with it for sure, I wouldn't have told him because I didn't want him to get that motor started again. He had no business operating a boat in the condition he was in, especially with his son on board.

In the meantime, I called June in New York and talked to her a little bit about the problems she was having with John, and she was pretty much at her wits' end. She didn't know what was going to happen, or when, and she said she was actually fearful for her life. John was more out of control than he'd ever been, and we couldn't see how things could get any worse. We were wrong.

The saddest part of the whole affair was the way John's drug problems affected not only him but his family, friends, and everyone associated with the Johnny Cash organization. Most of the family stayed away from him, because he was impossible to deal with. When John was straight, he loved his family, parents, and friends to death, and they loved him. But at that point in time, few people ever saw him when he was straight, and nobody meant anything to him except his drugs and his drug-abusing friends.

Most of the people with the show thought that John would live forever, that he could do anything he wanted to do, that he could punish his body with drugs as much as he wanted, and everything would be all right. After all, he was *Johnny Cash!* He was a legend; he was indestructible; you couldn't harm him. But now it seemed that John was approaching the point of no return, and if he didn't pull himself together soon, there would be no turning back and very bad things would happen. But somehow he kept hanging on.

He couldn't lie down, couldn't sleep; he prowled around all night long, fumbling with things, doing nothing. And he was about the same during the day. He'd be so wired, he'd stay up sometimes for a week at a time, and it wouldn't be until he ran out of his stash of amphetamines that he would finally crash and go to bed. And he'd come down hard, usually passing out and sleeping for fourteen or sixteen hours at a stretch. When he'd wake up, he'd be in fair shape—at least he'd be coherent enough that you could talk to him and sometimes reason with him. That didn't happen very often, however, and it was really tough for those of us who cared about him.

The problem was that too many people in our entourage just looked at him as a source of income. They kind of thought of him as a big corporation, one that was tough as nails and could survive any sort of downturn and bounce back to the top. A lot of times he did, but it was now getting to the point that, unless something was done, John was heading for the big crash from which there would be no recovery.

Everybody connected with the show did their part, did their job, and were very dependable. They were all troupers, always ready to go. No matter where, what, or when we were scheduled to perform, they were ready to get on a plane, get on the bus, and get on the stage to play a great show. The problem was, nobody lent much of a hand when it came to dealing with John. With June and I pretty much the only ones fighting him when he was really strung out, it was tough. It's a thousand wonders that one or both of us didn't lose our lives somewhere along the line.

I was very concerned about June, who was still in New York. John had dropped out of sight, and nobody knew where he was. I called everywhere I could think of—the House of Cash, friends and business associates in Nashville, the house in New Port Richey—but no John. I was hoping he hadn't gotten his boat running and gone out on the Gulf and gotten lost. I wasn't terribly worried, because he'd disappeared a lot of times before, and I had sort of gotten used to it.

On August 20-25, 1979, we were scheduled to work the South Shore Music Circus in Cohasset, Massachusetts. Somehow, by the grace of God, I suppose, John and June had gotten back together. I think John had gone to their New York apartment and gotten himself back under control a bit. They showed up at the Music Circus, which was one of those in-the-round theaters we liked so well, and things went reasonably well. John wasn't clean by any means, but at least he was there and ready to do the shows. The first night was sold out, and he performed well.

We always stayed at the same hotel there, Kimberly's by the Sea, and all of the rooms had a balcony overlooking the bay. We were on the second floor, and John and June's room was right next door to mine; the only thing separating us was a banister on the balcony. On the third day of the engagement, I was sunning myself on the balcony when John came outside wearing a bathing suit. He wasn't completely straight, but I could talk to him a little bit.

I noticed that one of his knees had a nasty-looking cut. The flesh was rolled almost inside out, so to speak, and you could see the bone in his knee. "John, what in the world is wrong with your knee?" I asked. "Ahhh, I cut it a little bit," he replied. I said, "That's not cut a little bit, John, that's bad news and it's liable to set up an infection. We need to go to the emergency room and get that thing sewed up." He said, "Naw, there ain't no need to do that."

"That thing looks horrible to me," I told him, "and you're going to have an ugly scar there even if it don't get infected and become a real serious problem." He said, "Naw, it don't even hurt." I could believe that; considering the shape he was in, I don't think he could feel anything.

He went back inside after a while, and June came out and said, "Marshall, I've been antique shopping around town, and I bought John an antique wooden typewriter. I want him to come back out and look at it here in the sunshine. Would you come over on our side and just sit and talk to him a little bit? He just needs somebody to talk to in the worse way, and this typewriter will be a good conversation piece."

I told her I'd be glad to do that, and pretty soon John came back out and sat down with me on the balcony. A couple of minutes of later, June brought out this magnificent old typewriter, the likes of which I'd never seen before or since. "John, what in the world is that thing?" He said, "Man, I don't know. It looks like a typewriter." I asked if it was made of wood, and he said, "Yeah, it's made out of wood."

That got a good, long conversation going about that typewriter, and we pecked on the keys a little and just played with it like a couple of kids. At least it was something to talk to him about, because it was almost impossible to start a conversation with him otherwise. We must have talked and played with that antique typewriter for about half an hour. It was getting to be late afternoon, so I told John I was going to go back to my room and get ready for that night's show, and that I'd see him at the theater. "All right, we'll be there," he said.

❧

The hotel was about five blocks from the Music Circus, so everybody in the cast changed clothes in their rooms and then went over to the show. Just before 8 p.m., I gave the usual countdown to show time, since I knew John was in his dressing room, which was a trailer out back, and could hear the announcement. Lou Robin, our promoter, came over to me and said, "Marshall, John wants to see you in his dressing room." I told him we were just three minutes away from starting the show, but Lou said, "Well, you better go back there because he is pretty adamant about it and he wants to talk to you a minute."

I hurried out to the trailer, and when I saw John, I couldn't believe my eyes. He'd obviously gotten really high after I'd left his hotel room, and he'd found a lot of gauze and bandaged his entire head, from the chin on up. All you could see were his eyes, his mouth, and a small hole at the end of his nose so he could breathe—the rest of his head was completely covered. He looked exactly like a mummy!

When I walked in the trailer, I stopped dead in my tracks and couldn't say a word. He looked at me and said, "Marshall, I've been listening for years and years and years to you giving that silly countdown. As of right now, it stops. When you give that countdown, you lock me into something that I've got to do, and I don't want to deal with anything that I've got to do. I know I've got to go out there and perform, but not in four minutes, or three minutes or two minutes or one minute, so we'll never give that countdown again. As a matter of fact, we're never going to start another show on time again as long as we're in the business. They'll all be at least twenty minutes late from now on!

"If you insist on giving that countdown for all these people that you talk about, I'll send somebody to tell you when you can start the show. On second thought, I don't want that countdown no more. No more! I'll send somebody everyday to tell you that I'm ready, and then you start the show."

I said, "OK, John, if that's what you want to do. That's just exactly what we'll do. How long before you'll be ready now?" He said, "Twenty minutes. You go back and tell everybody that the star of the show will be ready in twenty minutes. You can see that I'm not ready. I had to re-break my nose. I went to the doctor over in Jamaica after that two-by-four came through the windshield and broke my nose, but they don't know how to set a nose. So I re-broke it and set it, so I need to stay here a little bit while my nose heals, and then I'll be ready to come out onstage."

I said, "OK John, just let me know what you want to do, and that's what we will do." I certainly wasn't going to argue with him about it at that point.

I went backstage and told the band and tech people, "Guys, it's going to be a little while longer—I don't know how long—but John's not ready." That's all I said; I didn't mention the bandages on his head or anything else. In about fifteen or twenty minutes, someone came out of the trailer and told me, "John says it's OK to start the show now." I turned to our group and said, "OK guys, let's go to the stage, no countdown, no nothing. We'll walk onstage and do the normal thing."

We always opened with a medley of well-known Johnny Cash songs, after which Bob Wootton would kick off "Folsom Prison Blues" and John would walk onstage. When he stepped into the spotlight, the audience jumped to their feet and began to cheer and clap, but when they saw all of that gauze on his head, the applause stopped and everyone just stood and stared. In a matter of seconds, the building got as quiet as midnight in the middle of a desert.

I thought that Jerry Hensley, who was standing right beside me, was going to die. He quit playing his guitar, because he didn't know what was going on, and looked at me and sort of grinned, wondering what to do next. "I don't know, Jerry," I told him. "Let's just do what we're supposed to do. We'll talk about it later."

John looked so ridiculous, and at the end of a song, the people in the audience weren't sure what they were supposed to do. We struggled through the rest of the show, keeping to the usual routine, but at the end, when the audience would normally give us standing ovation after standing ovation, John just walked off the stage, and no one out front knew what to think. I was sure that someone with the media or in the audience had taken a picture of the bizarre scene onstage, and that it would appear in the paper the next day. Thankfully, that didn't happen.

Before heading back to the hotel, I had a talk with the entire cast and crew about the situation, since everyone wanted to know what had just happened. I told them everything that had occurred when I went to John's dressing room before the show, and then said,

"Guys, I have no earthly idea what's going to happen. Let's just go back to the hotel, and we'll see what tomorrow brings."

———

I got up early the next morning, as I always did, to take care of a lot of details and make a lot of phone calls. When I walked out onto my patio, I saw our big, black Blue Bird motor home, our "bus," sitting in the parking lot and wondered what in the world it was doing there. I called the hotel switchboard and asked if George Shaw, our bus driver, was registered, and then had them ring his room. When he answered, I said, "George, did I wake you?" He said, "Well, yeah, I drove all night and I'm just getting in here, but I'm OK."

"George, what are you doing up here?" I asked. "John's got limos to take him back and forth to the show, a limo to take him to the airport. I told him before we left that you wouldn't be needed on this tour, that you could have the time off." George said, "Well, he called me yesterday and wanted me to go by the drugstore in Hendersonville and pick up a prescription." I said, "Are you telling me that you drove all the way from Nashville to Cohasset [about forty miles south of Boston] to bring him a prescription?" He said, "Yep, that's what he wanted, and that's what I did."

I asked George if he'd given the prescription to John yet, and he said he hadn't. I started to tell him to give the vial of pills to me, but I thought that might get George into trouble, so I just let things run their course.

Sometime during the day, George gave John his prescription, which wasn't a real prescription at all; he had an arrangement with the drugstore to supply him with whatever he wanted, whenever he wanted it. He knew that if he had the drugs shipped to him by FedEx or another delivery service, either June or I would probably intercept the package and dispose of it before he could get his hands on it. But if he had George drive up from Nashville and hand deliver the package to him, he wouldn't have to worry about us destroying his stash.

———

It was very obvious at that point that drugs had totally taken over John's life. As bad as things had been, they were now worse and sliding farther downhill fast. There was no doubt in my mind that June and I were both in trouble with him, because we were constantly trying to keep him away from drugs. I knew he saw us as his two biggest enemies and would go to great lengths to try to get around our precautions.

But, come hell or high water, we weren't going to change, although John was now so wired that he wouldn't sleep for an entire tour, which meant we couldn't search his room for drugs whenever he crashed. For the entire four or five days we were in Cohasset, he never went to bed and would sometimes get down on the floor and start searching his briefcase and do other silly things.

John was doing a lot of silly things now that the drugs were really taking control of his life. Take that big cut on his knee, for instance, which he got while he was trying to figure out why the new boat he bought wouldn't run. The boat was tied up alongside a pier, and rather than walk down a flight of stairs and simply step on board, John decided he'd jump down onto the deck.

The hatch over the motor was open, and instead of landing on the deck, John plunged through the opening and landed on the motor. It's a wonder the fall didn't kill him, but the only apparent damage to his body was that nasty cut on his knee, which he said he didn't feel.

I know he didn't feel that cut while he was in Cohasset, and the next time that I saw it, it still hadn't been sewed up and John still wasn't feeling any pain. He was in terrible condition, as bad as I've ever seen any man at any time in my life. And it was getting to the point that he couldn't perform, couldn't do anything. He was just staying totally blown away all of the time.

Earlier that year, in the spring, we'd done a tour of Michigan that included Traverse City, Muskegon, Ann Arbor, Saginaw, Kalamazoo, and some other places where no air service was available. I'd told John that because we couldn't carry everybody on the motor home, we should charter a bus so the entire cast and crew could travel to the dates together. "And," I said, "I think we strongly need to consider buying a bus. It'll be cheaper, more dependable; we can all travel together and keep the show together. I think it would work out real well."

He consented to that, so I called the rental company in Indianapolis and was told they had a bus that probably would fit the bill. It was a custom MCI executive coach, really nice and almost new, that had been outfitted with several booths and chairs and had a lot of sitting room throughout the interior. The only thing missing was bunks to sleep in.

The bus met us at the airport when we flew to Michigan to start the tour, and we all got on board. John couldn't get over just how much he liked that bus, and everybody else did, too. I started talking to him about buying a bus, and one day when we arrived at the next town on our itinerary a little early, I asked if he'd be interested in seeing the engine and other mechanical offerings. "Yeah, I'd love to do that," he said.

I raised the back hatch and showed him the motor, saying. "Now, you know that with our Blue Bird and Dodge motor homes, all the engines were up front and they were very noisy. But with this, the engine is here in the back, and everything is quiet. And it's not made to go camping in; it's made for travel. We could get one made something like this and we could travel in it, or we could have some bunks, especially for you and June. If the rest of us just had comfortable seating and all, we could make it that way."

He asked me how much it would cost, and I told him I really didn't know but would find out if he was interested. "I'm very interested," he said. "Let's check it out and see what we can do." I told him we could contact the factory and buy a shell, then customize the interior just the way he wanted it. You can draw it up, and we'll do it exactly the way you want it," I said. He told me to check it out.

I called MCI's representative and he quoted me a price. I also discovered that the only company customizing interiors at the time was Executive Coach in Columbus, Ohio, a class act from the word go. The price tag for the bus and the customized interior was pretty high, about $400,000. "John," I said, "I know this sounds a little high. But if you think about all the money we're spending for airline tickets, for chartered buses, and for rental cars in a year's time, it's really pretty cheap. And it just really makes a lot of sense if we get into a bus." He said, "Let's do it."

I ordered the bus shell, paying the retainer out of my checking account. It was built in Canada and took about three months to complete. When it was ready, I sent George Shaw to Canada to ferry the bus down to Columbus, where the custom work would be done. Things had really gone smoothly, and I was very excited because I was on the verge of realizing one of my fondest wishes: to be able to get on a bus, head down the highway, and leave the driving to someone else.

Shortly after the custom work had begun on the bus, I got a phone call from John. "Marshall, I been thinking about this bus," he said. "Here's what I want. First of all, I just want eight seats up front for the band, and then I want a stateroom right behind those seats for me, then I want the next stateroom for June, and then I want John Carter in the very, very back of the bus. I want John Carter to have a door of his own at the back, and I want June to have a door of her own, and I want a door of my own, and y'all can use the door that comes with the bus."

"John, we may have a little problem with that," I said. "First of all, as I told you before, the engine in these buses is in the back, and there's no way we can put a door in the back because the engine takes up the whole space. I can check it out, though. Now, because of the big bays for all the luggage, adding doors on the sides may pose a problem, too. I can get with Executive Coach and see if it's possible to do, but I don't think we can put a door in the side."

"Well, I want a door in the back for John Carter," he said. I told him I'd check out everything I could. I certainly wasn't going to argue with him, because he was borderline coherent. I could talk with him, but I couldn't make much sense out of what he said.

As I suspected, the people at Executive Coach told me it would be impossible to add the doors on the sides and in the back, and John didn't take it too well when I told him. About three days later, he called me—in even worse shape—and said, "You know Marshall, I've always heard that you were a good mechanic and I thought you knew something about buses. But now I find out that you don't know anything about buses. I've talked to a man that knows all about buses, and here's what we're gonna do.

"You're right about one thing: the engine is in the back of that bus, there's no doubt about it, and that can't be changed. But I got a man who can put a door in the back of that bus for John Carter. Here's how it works: All John Carter has to do is push a button right beside his door, the engine swings out, swings all the way out and stops—all of this is electric—and then the steps come down and a red carpet rolls out about three feet from the steps. That's how John Carter's room can be situated. We can do that; you just don't worry about it. That can be done.

"Then I know you're going to ask the question, 'What are you going to do about the radiator?' That's all worked out. You're right, the radiator does create a problem. But what happens here, all the water that's in the engine goes down in a reservoir under the bus when the engine swings out. Then when the engine swings back in, it's automatically hooked up—all the radiator hoses, all the electrical plugs, all the fuel lines and everything are all automatic. They fasten back in, they hook back up, the water pumps back in from that reservoir, and you're ready to go in ninety seconds. And you said it couldn't be done. Well it *can* be done—easy!

"And as far as the doors on the side, that's not a problem. It's being designed now to put those doors in. I don't want nobody coming through my stateroom. I want June to have hers, and I want John Carter to have his, like I explained to you. And I don't want nobody in the show to come past the door that leads into my stateroom; I don't want anybody back there. It's all worked out. You don't worry about the bus anymore; I'm taking care of it. It'll all be the way I explained it to you, and I'm taking care of it. All I need to know is the contact for those people up in Ohio and the person that you're dealing with."

I told him the man I was dealing with was Luther Monroe, and I gave him Luther's phone number. I said, "OK, John, if this is what you want to do, you go right ahead and take care of it. That's fine. I wish you luck, I really do." He said, "You don't worry about it. You don't have to worry about it anymore because I have a guy that can do it."

The first thing he did was charter a Lear jet, all by himself, for the first time in his life; I had always handled those arrangements for him before. The jet flew into Nashville and picked him up, then took him to the Executive Coach plant, which is located on the airport property in Columbus.

After he'd told the people there how he wanted the bus customized, I got a phone call from Luther Monroe. "This man is crazy!" he said. I replied, "Well, I've been trying to talk to him, and he's taking it over, so you're going to have to deal with him. I'm out of the picture now." Luther said, "Well, he's talking about things that are totally ridiculous and absolutely impossible to do. Now, if he wants somebody to do this, we'll just have to pass on it, because we can't do it. He says he's taking it over and has a man to do everything he wants. Well, he just needs to take it to that man."

"That man" didn't really exist, so Executive Coach finished the custom work inside the bus, which I have not seen to this day.

———————

John's condition continued to worsen throughout the spring and summer. I think that when June forced him to send Jan Howard home from the tour after our stand at the Front Row Theatre was the turning point in everyone's life, especially mine and John's and June's. It's impossible to explain just how ridiculous John's behavior was. Up to that time, he would periodically get off drugs for a little while and you could talk business with him—he was never completely straight, but at least you could communicate with him occasionally. In general, you just kept moving forward and did what you had to do and hoped that would please him.

John made several trips by Lear jet to the Executive Coach plant in Columbus, and somewhere along the line, as fall approached, he fired George Shaw and hired another driver, Roger Morton, a real nice guy from Alabama who had been our equipment-truck driver. John had Roger come to Nashville, and then the two of them flew to Columbus to check on the custom work. Roger later told me that was the most unbelievable trip he'd ever taken in his life.

When they arrived, John was all wiped out and was trying to explain how he wanted them to customize the interior of the bus. He was so far gone, no one could understand what he was talking about. They finally drew up a floor plan, gave it to him, and told him that layout would be an ideal situation for him, based on what he had told them. I later saw the floor plan, and it showed eight seats up front, with John's room behind those seats, then June's room and then a room in the back. There were no extra doors on the sides, nor a door in the back. And everyone wanting to go to the back of the bus would have to walk through John's room. I'm told that's the way the bus was built.

———————

As the 1970s drew to a close, John's drug problems were getting worse, seemingly by the day. Crowds at our concerts were beginning to fall off, and there were rumblings of dissatisfaction from Columbia because our records weren't topping the charts like they used to.

The only person who was to blame was Johnny Cash, and that bothered him a lot. One of the reasons John never got completely clean anymore was that, whenever he started looking back at his career and thought about all the people he'd hurt and how his relationship with June had deteriorated, he just couldn't cope with it. He always wanted to blame his troubles on someone else—and generally that was me, although I don't know why he felt that way. Nothing made sense anymore, and when things looked like they'd gotten about as bad as they could get, they just got worse.

PART FOUR
The Eighties

My last tour with the Johnny Cash Show started in Chico, California, on February 19, 1980. About a week before that, Reba Hancock had called and told me John was having a financial crisis and she had no idea what to do about it. She couldn't talk to him, so I was next in line. I didn't mind, since I'd been there from the beginning and owned part of the business, and even though John and his drugs had totally taken over the business, it was only natural that she would call me.

She was very concerned about John's upcoming bills. I told her, "Reba, I don't know what to say. But whatever it takes to keep him from going bankrupt, or keep this from getting into the media in any way, just let me know what it'll take to pay everything up and I'll take care of it personally. And we'll just have to work with it from there on. I owe everything that I have to John, and I may as well put it all back into him. We have some real problems, problems that we'll be lucky if he even lives through, let alone get his career back in order to where he can square up all of these debts and get everything straight in his life.

"I don't really think it's going to happen," I told her. She said, "I know it's not." I said, "We've got some dark, hard roads ahead of us, no question about it." I told her to pull together all the bills that needed to be paid, let me know what the total was, and I'd do the best I could to take care of the situation.

As usual, I figured out all of the routing for the tour and decided that everyone could leave home on the day of the show, fly to Chicago, get together with everyone else on the tour, and then everyone would fly together to Sacramento. There, I'd arranged for a charter bus to pick us up and take us to Chico for the opening date, and then take us from there to the remaining tour dates.

───◦⦿◦───

We got to Chicago in the middle of the morning on the nineteenth. I looked around and everyone was there except June. John looked to be in terrible shape.

The following day, February 21, looked to be a very hard day, because we'd been asked to do a show at Soledad State Prison, about 130 miles southeast of San Francisco, at one o'clock that afternoon, after which we'd still have quite a ways to go over the mountain to get down to Bakersfield for a performance there that evening. John was still coming down, and that made me very happy.

───◦⦿◦───

Everything went all right at Soledad, and we loaded everything back onto the bus and headed for Bakersfield. With all of the traveling and worry, I was exhausted, so I went to the back of the bus and took an hour's nap. When I awoke, I really didn't know where we were, so I walked up front, through the lounge where John and somebody else were sitting, and sat down by the driver.

"Hey, man, how we doing?" I asked. He said, "We're motoring right along." I asked what route we were taking and what time he thought we'd get to Bakersfield. When he told me, I said I was going to go back and take another nap and would probably sleep until we got into town.

I slept until we were about ten miles from our destination, then got up and got ready to handle our check-in. When we pulled up in front of the hotel, I went inside, just as I always did, and got the rooming list and all of the room keys, which I handed out to our entourage. John had calmed down a little more, which made me even happier.

He did a good job at the show that night, and when we got back to the hotel, John called me. He was in even better shape and said, "Marshall, June is coming in tomorrow, and we need to make arrangements to go by the airport and pick her up and then go on down to Anaheim. Could you arrange that?" I said, "Sure, but John, if you want me to, we can go on down to the hotel, and I'll come back to LAX and pick her up." He said, "Well, OK, if that'll work, you can do that."

We rolled into Anaheim and checked into the convention center hotel, and I drove up to the Los Angeles airport and picked up June. She didn't look good at all, but I didn't ask her any questions; we just chatted about nothing in particular in the car on the way back to the hotel. I had told everybody earlier that I would have all the instruments brought over to the hotel and we'd have a rehearsal with June.

When we got to the hotel, I gathered everybody together and we rehearsed for a while in a meeting room. The June Carter I knew wasn't in that room—she looked like a whupped puppy and was not at all herself. I don't know what all had happened, but she told me she'd had to have some dental work done. I didn't ask her any questions, but from what Bob Wootton had told me and what I had seen, I believe John and June had had a serious row. And I think that when John started coming down and realized what he'd done, he started trying to make things up to her, as he had done so many, many times before.

At that night's show at the Anaheim Convention Center, John was about 75 percent straight and June was just barely mobile. Afterwards, we went back to the room, and you could tell that John was still coming down, that he wasn't taking any more drugs, and that everything was fine.

The next day, February 22, we were scheduled to play a show at Claremont College east of Los Angeles. John had called me the night before and told me that Rosanne and her husband, Rodney Crowell, wanted to attend the show and bring their baby, who was just a few days old. "That's just fine," I said. "What would you like me to do?" He said, "Well, I just want you to make sure that they can get in all right, through the back door and right backstage." I told him not to worry, that I would take care of it.

It appeared that he was still getting straighter and that the old John was coming back. And when good ol' John started to return, everybody connected with the show began to get happy. You can't imagine what a difference that made throughout the organization. Everybody was thrilled to see him, including June, although she still wasn't doing too well herself.

About thirty or forty minutes before show time, I took Rodney, Rosanne, and their beautiful child backstage to see John, who was just so happy to see his new grandbaby. He was about 90 percent sober and did a good show that night, and really seemed to enjoy being with his daughter and her family.

John called me later that night and told me that when the tour ended on February 26 in Yuma, Arizona, he and June were going to attend the Grammy Awards show in Los Angeles the next night. "Then there's four days off before we have to play that private party thing in Houston. Are y'all going home?" I told him I thought everyone was tired and would like to go home and rest.

"Well, whatever y'all do is all right," he said, "but when we get through with the Grammy Awards, I'd like for you to make arrangements for myself and June and Rosanne and Rodney and the baby to go to Las Vegas to spend this time off. You think you could put us up where we could get the room arrangements we require?" I said, "Man, don't worry about it. I know the people at the MGM Grand very, very well. I'll call the manager and get it all set up and let you know."

I called the MGM Grand the next morning and told the manager what I needed. He said, "You just let me know exactly what you want, Mr. Grant, and it will be taken care of. And it will be all on the house; you don't have to worry about anything. Give me the flight numbers, and we'll pick them up at the airport, bring them in the back door with heavy security, and put them in the rooms you've requested. It will all be taken care of. You don't have to worry about a thing."

After we finished the show in Yuma, I had the bus driver take us to the Phoenix airport and arranged for John and June to fly back to Los Angeles. I had a limo pick them up and take them to the airport, and everything was set up with the hotels. I felt a little uncomfortable about not going with them, because I usually went everywhere they went. But in this particular case, that was just the best I could do, so I caught a flight for Memphis and home.

The next morning, Reba Hancock called me from the House of Cash. "Marshall, do you realize that John is here in town?" she asked. I said, "No, he was supposed to be at the Grammy Awards last night, and I got everything all set up for them to go to Las Vegas with Rosanne, Rodney, and the baby." She said, "Marshall, I'm telling you, he's in town. He's here in Nashville, and he's upstairs with E. J. Butler [our bookkeeper], and he is blown out of his mind."

"You've got to be kidding me!" I said. "This can't be true; there's no way. I don't see how he could have even gotten there." She said, "Marshall, believe me when I tell you, he's here, and we don't know what to do. We know what you told us—they were going to Vegas and all—but he is here!"

I didn't really know what to do. I tried to call June at the hotel in Los Angeles where they should have been, but they had checked out. I supposed that June was in transit, since she normally would have called me, but I don't think she felt too good about giving me the bad news.

I called Rosanne and asked her what had gone wrong." She said, "Marshall, my daddy called me this morning at four o'clock, and he was in such bad shape that I really didn't know who I was talking to. After a while, I realized that I was talking to my daddy, and he wanted to call me and tell me that the trip to Las Vegas was off. We wouldn't be going to Las Vegas. That's all I know. I don't know where he is. I don't know anything. I just know that we were supposed to leave in the morning to go to Las Vegas. We're packed and ready to go, and now it's off."

When I told her that Reba had just called and told me John was in Nashville, Rosanne couldn't believe it.

—◁◁◁◁◁| |◁◁◁◁◁—

I knew we were in trouble, and looking back, I knew that it had started at the Front Row Theatre in Cleveland when John was forced to do something he didn't want to do. Then that certain band member got right in the middle of it and made things worse. He told his wife that he'd "saved the organization," but what he'd really done was destroy the show, because nothing was ever the same after that.

We'd had an opportunity in Cleveland to get John to clean up his act once and for all. If June had had her way, if she'd been able to take John Carter and go back home, I truly think that John would have done anything—even give up drugs—to get his wife and child back. If a certain someone hadn't intervened, everything could have been worked out, but instead, things just started getting worse.

Even though John had seemed to be getting better, in reality he was just getting worse with each passing day. I think that could have only happened with John, because I don't believe another person in the world could have consumed all that he did and lived through it.

The organization was in trouble, and I knew I personally was in trouble, because June and I were allies in the war against John's drug abuse, and we fought him tooth and nail at every turn. I'm not saying that we won many of the battles, because we didn't, and we sure didn't win the war, because John always had the final say. And because John knew that I was very much against his taking drugs, that made me his enemy, and he started to come down on me harder every day. I knew that, but I also knew that, deep down, our friendship was still there; his love for me and my love for him was still there.

John had gone to see our bookkeeper to find out what my income was because he was broke. I told Reba before I left home that I would pay him out of debt; of course, there would have to be a limit to it, but my intentions were good—I would pay him out of debt. Now he was in Nashville trying to find out just how much I was making because he had squandered all his money on drugs and desperately needed my income to support his habit. So when Reba told me that he was in Nashville with E. J., I knew exactly what that was all about. And I knew that disaster was just around the corner.

54

We all gathered in Houston on March 2 to do a private show for a major oil company. Sometime in the middle of the afternoon, John called. I didn't know where he was; the last time I'd heard from him he was in Nashville, and I hadn't talked to him and didn't really know if he would show up for the date or not. He caught a commercial flight from Nashville to Houston, and he hadn't been in his hotel room for more than fifteen minutes when he called.

"Marshall," he said, "I want the Lear jet here tonight to take me home because of John Carter's birthday party." I could tell he wasn't in good shape, but I was at least able talk to him. I said, "You know, John, you've got Braniff Airlines that leaves here tomorrow morning somewhere around nine o'clock, and you could be at your house by noon. If you take the Lear and get there at three o'clock in the morning, there's not a lot you can do except go to bed. You could save thousands of dollars by not taking that Lear jet and just going commercial like everybody else."

"You just don't understand," he said. "John Carter's birthday party is going to start tonight at 3 a.m. and it'll run all day long and the next night and up until the next day. I've got to be there when the party starts tonight at 3 a.m., and I've got to have the Lear jet."

I told him I'd see what I could do and would call him back in half an hour or so. Then I called Executive Jet in Columbus and was told that they had a jet sitting on the ground at Houston's Hobby Airport. I told them what I wanted to do, and they arranged all the details. I called John back and told him the jet would be waiting for him when the show is over.

After that evening's show, I went to my room and changed my clothes, then came downstairs to make sure everything was in order. When he and June got into the limo, John looked back at me with a God-awful, smirky smile that was just terrible. As they pulled away, John stuck his head out the window a bit and looked straight at me until he was so far away that he couldn't see me anymore. I thought that was very strange.

<hr />

I found out the next day while talking to the people at Executive Jet that John didn't fly to Nashville. He'd flown to New York and had gone into hiding because he wanted to get away from everything and everybody. I don't know what happened with June. I think the Lear dropped her off in Nashville and that John stayed on board and continued to New York.

He called Irene Gibbs, his secretary, and dictated a letter that essentially said he was firing me from the band. I received it a few days later by registered mail. Irene is a gracious lady, and later we talked an awful lot about that letter. She said typing it and sending it to me were the hardest things she'd ever done in her life. I thought about putting a copy of the letter in this book, but I decided that wouldn't do anybody any good and would just cause a lot of harm. Let's just say that I know it was the drugs talking, and John said things in that letter that he later regretted.

For all the trouble he went through explaining to me that he had to be in Nashville by 3 a.m. to start John Carter's three-day birthday party, he never even went to the party, if there actually was one. There probably was, but John wasn't there. No one knew where he was when he dictated that letter to Irene.

I was very concerned about June at that point. I didn't know where she was, and I wasn't going to call because I could see things had blown sky high and the partnership that had existed between John and myself even before day one was being terminated. There were some hard days ahead, and I knew it.

I knew that June loved me and that I loved her, and I knew whatever John decided to do was not going to separate us. I feared for her, and I make no bones about that because of what she had already been through, and I was wondering what she was going through now. Plus, I wasn't going to be around to protect her—especially at night and in the hotels where I slept with one eye open waiting for her to call for help with whatever she needed. She knew I would always come to her rescue and I hope I always did. But now I didn't know what was happening, and that concerned me greatly.

The news hit the streets in Nashville and other places the next day. I don't know how, since I hadn't received it yet, but it did, I guess John started talking about it, and the news saturated the industry immediately. The second day after I got the letter, Carl Perkins and his wife, Valda, stopped by my house. I could tell by the look on Carl's face when he got out of his car that he was very uncomfortable, but he had come down to see if Etta and I were all right and if there was anything that he could do, and to find out what had happened.

I told him what we'd been going through, that John had set out to get rid of June and me and was doing a pretty good job of it, because we were the two people who constantly stood between him and what he wanted to do—which was take drugs.

"Gramps, let me tell you what I heard this morning," Carl said. "I went over to W. S. Holland's house to ask him about it, to see what had happened. I pulled up in the driveway and stopped, and W. S. came over and got down on one knee. I rolled down the glass, and the first words I said were, 'What happened between Marshall and John?' And W. S. said, 'Well, he got caught.' I said, 'What do you mean he got caught?' And W. S. said, 'Well, he stole a million dollars and John caught him.'

"'How did he steal a million dollars? He's not handling the money; it's the bookkeeper or Lou Robin that settles up at the box office now. He doesn't do that any more. He doesn't handle the money. How could he have gotten his hands on a million dollars?' And W. S. said, 'Well, I don't know. But however he did, he got caught.'

"'Well, I don't believe a word of it. First of all, Marshall wouldn't do it, and secondly, he didn't have his hands on a million dollars. There's no way in the world that it could have happened.' And W. S. said, 'Well, I can only tell you what John told me, and what he's telling everybody is that Marshall got caught stealing a million dollars, and that's what happened.'"

I called some of my friends in the organization and discovered that, lo and behold, that's exactly what John was telling everybody. I knew that I didn't have to stand for that, because I could prove it wasn't true. You know, I don't really blame the rest of the people in the cast for believing John's tall tales, because they took everything John said as gospel. If he held a meeting and told everyone, "Marshall got caught stealing a million dollars and was terminated," they just accepted it as fact because John had said it and that's all they had to rely on.

Most of the people with the show never did understand John. Of course, they didn't have to deal with him day in and day out, and that's where the difference lay. They didn't have to deal with him, and so they were on the outside looking at John as they knew him. Most of them only knew him from being onstage with him, and they never really saw his darker side when he was blown away on drugs. They didn't know whether he was sober, blown out of his mind, half blown, or whatever, because he was sort of unpredictable and acted differently every day. Most of them thought that was funny, but it wasn't. There's nothing funny about someone who's lost his soul to drugs, nothing at all.

Now that I was no longer with the Tennessee Three, John needed a bass player, and of all the people in the world he could have hired to replace me, he hired Marty Stuart. Now don't get me wrong, Marty Stuart is a very talented musician. He's a fantastic guitar player; he plays fiddle very, very well; and he's probably one of the best mandolin players I've ever heard. However, he'd never played a bass, especially an upright bass.

I had been John's bass player for twenty-six years and played on every hit record Johnny Cash ever made. He recorded many songs after I left the band, but nothing that came close to being a big hit.

I'd also served as the Johnny Cash Show's road manager for twenty-six years and had learned a lot. I learned it the hard way—nobody taught me anything; I just had to improvise and figure things out as I went along. I learned everything that pertained to being a road manager and everything else that goes along with being a general flunky. I called it "keeping the act together."

Everything that Etta and I did went way beyond the job description of road manager.

So whom did John hire to fill that critical role? W. S. Holland, who was a great drummer, always dependable, always on time, and a good guy to have around because he had a great sense of humor. But he didn't know much about the business end of the organization or the ins and outs of setting up a tour, like booking the hotels, airlines, and ground transportation; making out the rooming lists and arranging everyone's travel schedule; and handling the countless details that always arise before, during, and after a tour. He didn't have the experience for the job, and I suspected that he'd be overwhelmed.

In the earlier days of our career, Luther Perkins and I roomed together all the time. After he and his first wife, Bertie, were divorced and he married Margie Higgins, they got a little camper and wanted to travel to a lot of our dates in it. Since Luther was staying with Margie, I took on W. S. as a roommate.

I really liked having someone else in the room with me on the road, because it can get pretty lonesome if you're staying by yourself night after night in a hotel. After a while, though, W. S. started complaining about all the telephone calls I was screening for John and all the activity in the room, and requested a single room. I understood that and told him that would be fine; I'd book him in a room by himself.

I've always admired W. S. for some of the things he could do, and one of them was sleep. If we finished our second show at the Las Vegas Hilton at midnight, he would maybe go to the coffee shop or mess a round a little bit and then head for his room and go to sleep. That cat would sleep the rest of the night and all of the next day, then get up in time to bathe, get something to eat, and go directly to the showroom.

But because he slept almost all of the time he wasn't onstage, he never learned much about the mechanics of touring or the music business, and as a result, he usually didn't know how to do anything if you asked him for help. He was always looked after by someone (usually me) while we were on the road and didn't have to worry about anything. His airline tickets were sent to him, his lodging was taken care of, and he always was given detailed itineraries, which he seldom referred to since it was easier to ask someone (again, usually me) where and when we were supposed to play.

W. S. had no concerns while we were touring because he knew he would be taken care of. And as far as that's concerned, most of the other people in the cast were pretty much the same way. All they had to do was show up and play, and with a few exceptions, none of them would lift a finger to help out in any other area. They had no other worries because they knew I would take care of them like I would my own child—and I did, although at times it was pretty darned frustrating.

—————

I stayed in touch with some of the production people and members of the band, who confirmed my fears about the way things were going with the Johnny Cash Show. As one production person put it, when I asked how Marty Stuart was doing, "We love him to death, but he has got to be the worst bass player that ever stood onstage behind an act."

When I asked about life on the road, one cast member told me, "It's nothing but problems. You can't get in the hotels; you can't get out of the hotels. Sometimes you really don't know what town you're going to. We don't get itineraries. We just play it by ear as to when we're going to leave and how we're going to get there. Out on the road everything is just a mess."

—————

We had always been known as Johnny Cash and the Tennessee Two, and after W. S. Holland joined, it was Johnny Cash and the Tennessee Three. But John decided to change that now that I was no longer with the band. He put together a lineup of eight musicians and called the group Johnny Cash and the Great Eighties Eight. Audiences and critics alike didn't care much for that. The Tennessee Two and Tennessee Three had always had a good following and a fan base all our own. People used to love to come to our shows and talk to me, W. S., and Luther, and later to Bob Wootton. We were a big part of the show.

John once said that he enlarged the band because he wanted to get rid of our sound, because it was holding him back. And he told one musician that one of the reasons I had to go was "because Marshall was a dominant part of the sound" that he wanted to get rid of. That was another "excuse" for letting me go.

About three weeks after I received the termination letter from John, I felt I needed to talk to his attorney, James Neal. James and I had worked together on John's behalf for a long time, and we understood and trusted each other. He was a dear friend, a great attorney, and a good man.

I could tell by the way he talked when I called to set up an appointment that he understood what I wanted to see him about, and he was very gracious and gave me all the time I wanted. After I explained what had happened, I said, "James, we just need to talk about this a lot before we start getting involved." He said, "Well, Marshall, I'm not surprised. He called me when you all played Cohasset, Massachusetts, some time ago and wanted me to write a letter to fire you. I told him absolutely not; I would not do it. I told him that he better reconsider because he was headed for trouble, and he came up with a lot of things that really didn't make any sense, so I just flat told him, 'No, I won't do it.'"

James told me that he recently had seen June on a flight to New York and that they'd had a long talk. "She told me of all the problems," he said. "She didn't think that she could put up with it any longer because she was like a whupped puppy. I can't describe the shape June was in; it was something terrible."

He said June had told him a lot of things that had been going on over the past couple of months, and when she was finished, he'd told her, "When you get back home, give me a call and come in and let's go to work on it." I don't think she ever called him back, because June was determined to make things work if there was any way humanly possible—mainly to save John, because he looked to be on the path to destruction. If the drugs didn't kill him, she was afraid he'd get involved in something else that would, perhaps an automobile accident or something like that. It was only by the grace of God that he was still alive at that point.

I talked to James for quite a while but didn't threaten to file a lawsuit or anything. I did tell him, however, that I wouldn't accept all the so-called excuses John had come up with as his reasons for firing me, because they just weren't true. Plus, I'd heard John had put out the word that I'd been taking kickbacks from airlines and hotels. Those stories were strictly false, and I told James they had to stop because they were devastating to my reputation in the entertainment business, which was impeccable, if I do say so myself. I certainly hadn't done anybody wrong, I hadn't stolen any money, and I hadn't received any kickbacks from anybody.

Being accused of taking kickbacks really bothered me. I had always worked hard to get the best deal possible for us whenever we were on the road, and I can truthfully say that, thanks to my efforts, John very seldom ever had to pay for his suite; it was usually comped. Since we needed up to eighteen rooms for the cast and crew, the hotels were usually happy to give John his two-bedroom suite at no charge. Most times I was also able to get his food comped, as well as the security guard who would sit in the hallway whenever John Carter was in the hotel.

It took a lot of experience and a lot of connections in the travel trade to do things like that. I've been told by people with the organization that the last time I booked hotel rooms for the Johnny Cash Show was the last time John got a free suite on a tour.

As far as the airlines are concerned, Ruth Noble at World Travel and I researched all the carriers and always got the best fares. We once went to Australia and had an entire ton of instruments, amplifiers, and sound equipment to get to the other side of the world. Ticket prices were about the same among the various airlines, but I was able to cut a deal that saved us thousands of dollars in excess-baggage charges. I told the booking agent, "You take the excess baggage for free, and I'll buy the tickets from you." The agent agreed, and a ton of stuff was flown to Sydney at no additional charge. That was about the only thing you could do with airlines to get the best discount. I always strived to get all the discounts I could from the hotels, airlines, and other transportation companies—and all of those savings benefited the Johnny Cash organization.

After a little time went by, people just weren't buying the story that I had stolen a million dollars from John and the organization. Everybody knew better. Actually, the truth was just the opposite: John had stolen Luther and me blind. After the three of us formed our partnership, everything was fine until John's drug abuse starting getting bad. He began using amphetamines in 1956, but he didn't start losing control until the late 1950s and early sixties.

But as his drug use increased and he needed more money to support his habit, John stopped sharing the partnership with Luther and me. After all, he was Johnny Cash and it was his name on the band, not Luther Perkins's name or Marshall Grant's name. Luther and I were equal partners and key parts of the organization, but since John was the headliner, he could do whatever he wanted to do. He had the clout with the promoters, the record company executives, the bookkeepers, and everyone else involved in the business.

And when he stopped sharing the partnership, Luther and I pretty much had to scrape the bottom of the barrel for years just to exist.

———◆———

The time had come to take legal action against John, and I knew it was going to be a long, hard ride. Back in the early days, when we were rehearsing at my house on Nakomis Street in Memphis, I lived two doors down from an attorney named Horace Prierotti. He was a good neighbor and a good man, and about a month after I'd gotten the letter from John, I decided to call him.

"You come right ahead," Horace said when I called and said I needed to talk with him. I showed him the letter and filled him in on what had happened. He looked at me and said, "You know, you don't have to take this." I said, "Well, that's what I'm here for, Horace. I don't really know how to start on this thing because I've never been involved in no litigation. Of all the people in the world, the last person in the world I thought I'd be involved in any litigation with would be my friend John R. Cash. But things have happened. A lot of things have happened, and it would take me a long time to explain all of it to you, but basically you know what's been going on." He said, "Give me a couple of days."

When he called me back, Horace invited me to come down to his house and meet the attorney who would be representing me. Shortly after I arrived, there was a knock at the door and in walked this long, tall drink of water by the name of David E. Caywood. We sat and talked, and after David read the letter, he shook his head and asked, "What kind of documents have you got?" I said, "Enough to prove everything. If we get involved in this thing, for everything that I say I will give you a document that proves that I'm right." He said, "Let me talk to my partners and I'll get back to you."

After about a week, David called and said, "It's time to put this in motion. Start digging up all the documents you've got, anything that will prove your case."

Etta and I started tearing our house upside down. Etta is a pack rat if there ever was one, and thank God she'd kept everything connected to the organization. We dug up so many things, especially documents that helped prove the partnership had existed. She had

304

a little book in which she kept a record of everything—our expenditures on the road, gate receipts we'd earned, travel days, our record royalties, my share of whatever we'd made. She kept track of it all throughout the years. Every time we got a royalty check, Etta logged it in her little book and dated it. These were valid documents, and the more we looked around the house, the more things we kept uncovering.

During that time, I also spent a lot of time with the attorneys, talking at great length about everything that happened and the way that it happened. I started at day one and went right on up to March 1980.

———

I was still worried about June. She sent me word that she was no longer rooming with John on the road. She said she'd told him that he had scraped the bottom of the barrel when he terminated me—that it was just the most uncalled-for and underhanded thing he had ever done—and that he couldn't sink any lower than that.

She went her way and he went his. They still lived in the same house in Hendersonville, but when they went out on the road, they had separate rooms. I knew that was tough for her, and I also knew that somewhere along the line, John would talk her into making up, as he had done so many times before. That happened, although I'm not sure exactly when.

———

One of the worst things about the situation was the effect it had on the religious organizations we had worked with over the years, including Rex Humbard and Billy Graham and their organizations. We had done a lot of Crusades with them, appearing at big arenas and stadiums all over the country.

Well before I got the letter from John, Cliff Barrows and I had been working on a schedule for several upcoming Crusades, many of which Billy Graham wanted John to appear on. John kept fussing that he wanted to be on all of the Crusade dates, but Cliff didn't need him on all of them, a point he kept stressing to me and also to John's secretary, Irene Gibbs. John wouldn't take no for an answer and was adamant about appearing on every date of the three-week tour. Cliff and I were trying to get things worked out when the letter came from John.

When Cliff called me about the tour a few days after that, I told him, "You know, I'm no longer associated with the Johnny Cash organization. I suggest that you work with Irene Gibbs; she's a nice lady, a very thorough person, and she'll deal with you with John." He couldn't understand that and asked me what had happened. I told him flat-out exactly what happened.

"Drugs," I told him. "Cliff, I'm not suggesting that you don't take him on the trip, I'm not suggesting that at all. You be the judge. You need to do a little research and find out what you're dealing with here, because I'm not going to sit here and tell you everything that's going on—I just don't feel right doing that. But you can find out by just making a few telephone calls. Irene Gibbs would be a good one right there, and just go from there."

Cliff called back several times after that to see how I was doing. If Billy Graham ever had the right person in his entourage to handle whatever needed to be done, it was Cliff Barrows. He did for Billy about the same things I had done for John—whatever needed to be done, he would find a way to get it done and then not worry about it.

As time went by, the Billy Graham organization decided to take John off all of the Crusades. Cliff and some of the other people there went to Billy and said that taking John on the Crusades in the shape he was in would be too risky. Billy really liked John, and he wanted to help him, which I knew and appreciated. But taking John off the tours created some problems in the Graham organization, and I was very sorry to hear that, because that is a classy group from A to Z. I can't say enough about Billy and Ruth Graham and Cliff Barrows and all of the people associated with them. They were always straight ahead in everything they did. But John's drug abuse caused a ripple in that organization.

The same thing basically happened with Rex Humbard, because a week after I got the letter, that organization called and wanted to know what had happened. "You know guys, we got a problem," I told them, explaining a little about what was going on without trying to put John down too much. Shortly after that, however, the Humbard group terminated their relationship with John, much to my regret, since I didn't want that to happen and I'm eternally sorry for that.

Word got back to me that John was extremely upset that I called Billy Graham, Rex Humbard, and others and told them about his drug abuse, But that's not true. I didn't call them; they called me. You couldn't explain that to John, however, because that was just something else he could put off on me. I knew he'd look at it that way, so it didn't bother me all that much.

Rumors kept flying around about the bad things that I'd supposedly done. After talking with James Neal and with David Caywood, my attorney, I decided to litigate—to settle the partnership, that is, to prove that it existed. John had decided to terminate our partnership—I had decided to settle it. And I could see it was going to be a long, hard battle.

Over the years, as I've said, we'd pretty much always produced ourselves and did what we wanted in the studio, especially in the early days. The session producers as a rule would just turn the tape machine on and off and every once in a while make a suggestion, but we usually just did whatever we wanted.

Now John decided that he'd use Earl Ball as his producer. We'd hired Earl as a piano player because he could duplicate Jimmy Wilson's sound on the earlier Sun recordings. He was a good piano player, no doubt about it, and a pretty likeable guy, but he always seemed out of place and wasn't very compatible with other people. As it turned out, I think Earl produced the only single John ever recorded that never made it into the Top 100 on the charts.

It was evident that John just wasn't thinking clearly at all. He'd hired someone to play bass that didn't know how to play; he'd hired a road manager who could play drums but otherwise slept all the time; and now he'd hired a producer who didn't know how to produce a record. In his mind, he'd "fixed" the organization—by filling three critical positions with three people who didn't know what the hell they were doing. No, John wasn't thinking clearly at all.

avid Caywood set things in motion. We'd dug up loads of documents and were digging up more, so he knew we had enough evidence to make our case. He wrote Jim Neal and told him that if John would like to talk and try to resolve the situation, we could do that; otherwise, we would have to file suit.

"Let me tell you something, son," I told David. "You're not going to get a response, not from John. He's set in his ways and is so stubborn, and his drug abuse has gone on for so long that, in one sense, when he's blown out of his mind, he's a self-proclaimed God. He feels like he's over everybody in the world. Now, even if you could catch him when he's been completely sober for thirty days, you probably wouldn't hear from him. But I would; he'd call me. But I don't think that's going to happen. So when we set the wheels in motion, you better believe that we gotta go all the way through with it, because I know him too well."

After working on the case for six months or so, we had found, through the discovery process, other documents that proved everything I'd told the attorneys. So, during the last week of December 1980, between Christmas and New Year's, we filed suit. We didn't want any publicity, which is why we chose that time of year, since the attorneys felt most of the media would be more interested in their families and the holidays than in any sort of litigation. I think a couple of small papers picked up on it, but that didn't matter a whole lot.

Although the suit had been filed, the rumors kept coming, and the things John was accusing me of are about as far-fetched as anything could be. When the Johnny Cash Show played Greenville, South Carolina, Lou Robin called my brother Hershel, who lived near that city, and said John wanted him to come to the show because he wanted to talk to him. Hershel went over, and the very first thing John told him was, "You better get in touch with your brother and get him to drop this lawsuit now, 'cause he's gonna be prosecuted for stealing a million dollars." Then he told Hershel I'd been taking kickbacks from the airlines and the hotels and accused me of a bunch of other junk, all of which was a pack of lies.

Hershel called me afterward and was pretty upset. I said, "Man, let me tell you something. You just don't worry about it. A few more of those rumors come by, and I'm going to slap a lawsuit against him for slander, and then we'll let him try to prove it. You just don't worry about it at all."

I told David Caywood what John and others had been saying and doing and suggested that we file a slander suit against them. He felt it would be better, at this point, not to file a slander suit, but instead to write a letter to some of the people who were spreading the rumors and let them know they would be held responsible and accountable for any damage done to my reputation.

That stopped some of the rumors but not all of them. It stopped the people who got the letter from talking, but with John blown out of his mind all of the time now, he just kept coming up with different stories—each of them far, far from the truth—and telling more and more people.

John put out the word that I was suing him for $14 million. I don't know where he came up with that figure, but I must admit that was pretty close to what he probably owed me. I didn't figure it all up, because John's financial records, where they existed at all, were all messed up, even his tax returns. I think he came up with the $14 million figure with the help of some of the people in the office, because according to the terms of our original partnership, that's about what he owed Luther. I really didn't stop to figure out exactly what John owed me, and neither did anyone else, but if he wanted to use that figure, I really didn't have a problem with it. The primary reason I'd filed suit was to settle the partnership.

As time went along, Luther's children got to wondering just how much money John owed him. Luther had remarried after he divorced their mother, so they had to get control of his estate if they also wanted to sue, which they did, because they knew that John owed their father a lot of money and Luther had told them pretty much what had happened. Luther's second wife, Margie, didn't follow through on her part and get everything closed out, so Luther's daughters—Linda, Vicki, and Claudia—were able to get control of Luther's estate away from Margie, because she hadn't closed it out, so it didn't belong to her. Once they obtained the estate, the girls filed suit against John and me as the surviving partners in order to claim Luther's share of the partnership. Things were getting nasty, to say the least.

The girls got the idea that after Luther passed away, it had become a two-way partnership between John and me. They filed for accounting records all the way back to the day Luther died and tried to hold me responsible for half of the partnership. That made things very difficult, because now I was not only fighting with John, one of the best friends I'd ever had, but I also was fighting with the children of another of my dearest friends.

I can't fault Luther's children for doing what they did, because John owed Luther a lot of money. John felt he needed the money more than we did—he needed our money to buy his drugs. We didn't get our share of the partnership for a long time. In fact, Luther and I seldom got any money at all, and when we did, it was usually just the bare minimum—and we had to fight tooth and nail to get that.

From my standpoint, the lawsuit wasn't as much about money as it was about restoring my reputation and everything we had accomplished together as Johnny Cash and the Tennessee Two.

John had tried to take that away, and I felt I had to stand up and fight like a man for what was right. I've always said that if something's right, it's right; and if it's wrong, it's wrong; and there's nothing in between. And I intended to make things right, because that legal battle was caused by one thing and one thing only: John's drug abuse.

58

During this entire time, I really didn't know what I was going to do with the rest of my life. I was too young to retire, but at one point I considered doing just that and staying home with my family and playing with my quarter horses. However, after being in show business for twenty-six years, that was easier said than done.

I started talking with the Statler Brothers, and one day Harold Reid called. "You know, Marshall," he said, "we're coming right by your house—we're going down to Cleveland, Mississippi—why don't you come with us for the weekend?" I said, "You bet!"

They were traveling in two buses at the time and brought both of them to my house. They came inside, and Etta fixed us some goodies, and we sat and ate and joked and talked until it was time to go. We made the show in Cleveland, then traveled to Huntsville, Alabama, and up to Bowling Green, Kentucky, which was the finale of that tour. I caught a flight back home after enjoying a great weekend with my old friends.

Harold and I started talking, and he asked if I was ready to go back out on the road. At that point, I was more than ready. I'd been having a terrible time dealing with being off the road—it was as if someone had reached up and turned off the light and left me in total darkness. I think Etta wanted me to go back out, too, because we were still reasonably young and it was too early to retire. We'd been in the business for a long time and had learned a lot—the hard way, I might add.

I didn't want to go out on the road as a musician. I was strictly a "Johnny Cash musician," just like Luther and W. S. had been. We were the world's greatest "Johnny Cash musicians," but not necessarily the world's greatest musicians, and I wouldn't have been the least bit interested in going on the road with another act to play bass or anything else. I'd have taken up another trade before I would have done that.

The Statlers and I kept talking, and I went out on the road with them a few more times. One day they called and wanted to come to my room to talk. All four of the Statlers— Harold and Don Reid, Phil Balsley, and Lew DeWitt—came down and we talked about the possibility of me going on the road with them as their coordinator. I told them that I would certainly be interested, and we struck a deal right then and there. So, as Willie Nelson's song—which was hot as a firecracker at the time—says, I was "On the Road Again"!

I was really happy and quite fortunate to be on tour with the Statlers. Even though they'd left the Johnny Cash Show in 1973, we were still very close. It was almost as if we'd wrapped up a tour last week and started another one this week. Everything just fell right into place, and we understood one another completely.

They had heard all the rumors about my supposed theft of a million dollars and the kickbacks and everything else, but they knew better and I didn't need to explain any of that to them. Aside from myself, they probably understood John better than anyone else on earth— including his own family. They knew he was capable of doing and saying anything when he was high, if it suited his purpose at the time.

I sort of laid back on my first tour with the Statlers to see how they operated. Harold made it very plain to me when he said, "If you'll notice, Marshall, the things we do are the things you taught us, and we want you to do things for us just exactly the way you did them for John. Just take care of us the way you did John, and do the whole thing." I told him that was good and joked that I wasn't sure if I could change my old work habits. "We don't want you to change," he said.

That began a relationship that worked like a dream. Those guys were professionals in every sense of the word, and I had a little trouble adjusting to that at first, because things with John had been such a mess for so many years that I was used to being surrounded by turmoil. And if you're in that kind of environment day after day, week after week, and year after year, you'll eventually get used to it. Now, however, I was suddenly part of an organization that was the picture of perfection, and whatever I did, they didn't question it because they knew I had their best interests at heart.

I essentially served as the Statlers' road manager, although *coordinator* is a better job description. I coordinated all of their travel arrangements, including booking all the hotels and airline flights when needed, and arranged the travel itineraries and basically handled all other aspects pertaining to the show, just as I had done for the Johnny Cash Show. About the only thing I wasn't doing was booking dates, which Dick Blake International handled.

Everything went so smoothly, it almost got boring sometimes! But, man, I was happy to be out of all the turmoil. It had been really tough, but now, after all those years, I was with a truly professional organization.

For twenty-six years, I'd gone through hell overhauling and patching up vehicles so we could get from one date to another. I'd driven John and June and just about everybody else wherever they wanted to go. I'd lived through John's drug abuse and the trauma surrounding that. I'd had to leave an organization that I helped create. I'd slept on backseats and floorboards of cars. But after all those years, now I was touring with a first-class group, someone else was doing the driving, and I even had my own bunk on the bus! I was in heaven.

They had a great driver in Dale Harmon, and I had it worked out with Dale that whenever we got into a town, he'd call my bunk and I would go into the hotel, get all of our room keys, and pass them out to our entourage. Just as I had done with the Cash group,

I set everything up in advance, and it all ran so smoothly! No muss, no fuss, no fighting—and everybody was always on time. I truly believe the Statler Brothers were the most professional group in country music or any other type of entertainment in the world, and I was so proud to be a part of that.

<hr/>

As time passed, the Statlers and I did some business ventures together. Dick Blake became deathly ill and was unable to continue booking the group's shows, so we formed our own booking agency, American Major Talent. That was sort of new territory for me, because while I'd booked many dates over the years, I wasn't a professional at it, so to speak. However, things quickly fell into place. I started booking all the dates and worked with Al and Chris Zar, our promoters, to line up the buildings, set show times, and handle promotions. I was very heavily involved with the Statlers' career at that point. It was what I was cut out to do.

The five of us being in a business partnership together gave us better insight into what we wanted to do. I'd known Dick Blake for years and loved him to death, and when he booked the Statlers' dates, he'd send them to me and I'd arrange the tour itinerary. Now we started talking about what we wanted to do, how much we wanted to work, and when we wanted to work. We were able to pick and choose the dates and places we wanted to play, and everything was just as upbeat as it could be. The entire organization—the performers, the band, the drivers, the technical crew—was always happy and always on time. It was just amazing, and the best part was—no turmoil!

<hr/>

The lawsuit was in progress, and the attorneys were gracious enough to allow me to work around my schedule. When we'd come off the road after a tour, I'd go to a deposition or do whatever was needed to keep things moving forward. As a result, I never missed a date with the Statlers because of the litigation. John's attorney, James Neal, was very cooperative in scheduling those meetings, as was his associate Bob Sullivan, and the three of us have remained good friends.

Taking depositions was very tough. I hoped and prayed throughout the litigation, and especially during the depositions, that John would come into the depositions in a sober frame of mind and just tell the truth. Being realistic about it, I knew that he wouldn't. I told my attorneys, "If he shows up straight, you'll get nothing but the truth; he will not tell a lie. He may be reluctant, but he'll tell the truth about everything. But if he's strung out in any way, he will not tell the truth; everything he says will basically be a lie."

Unfortunately, for John, he never showed up straight; he was always high enough to tell everybody his cockamamie story. Sometimes it was downright embarrassing. John would tell his version of an incident, but when he was shown a document that proved him wrong, he'd refuse to accept it and wouldn't answer any questions—he would try to totally avoid the subject after that.

It was all very sad, and the saddest part of all was that we'd once sat on the same side of the table and had been allies before he became involved with drugs. Now Johnny Cash and Marshall Grant were sitting on opposite sides of the table, surrounded by high-powered attorneys, fighting one another—and all because of drugs. There's no way to adequately describe the hurt I felt over the whole situation. John, on the other hand, didn't care because he was so high he wasn't thinking clearly. But there's no way he could have faced me if he'd been straight; he just wouldn't have been able to do it.

On a couple of occasions when John was supposed to give a deposition, he didn't show up. The attorneys called his house, and someone there said he'd gone to the deposition, but nobody really knew where he was. My lawyers reprimanded him and reminded him that if he didn't show up when he was supposed to, he'd be held in contempt. But even that didn't stop him—he was determined to do things exactly the way he wanted, and he pretty much did.

<hr />

John's behavior really concerned me, because he was digging himself into a hole that kept getting deeper and deeper. I knew that, somewhere along the line, his attorneys would see through his lies and realize just how bad a position he'd put himself in, and they'd want to negotiate a settlement. I was open to that because I just wanted to put all the unpleasantness behind me. I was perfectly happy working with the Statlers, and the litigation was interfering with the things I wanted to do.

Still, I was absolutely determined to see the lawsuit through, one way or the other, especially since John couldn't come up with any valid reasons for what he had done. Instead, he made up excuses. One was that I had stolen a million dollars; another was that I was taking kickbacks from the airlines and hotels. He even sent his sister Reba Hancock through a travel school to find out how I could be doing it. Reba told me herself that after she'd gone through the school, she told John it was absolutely impossible to get a kickback through an airline, since they're controlled by the government, but of course he refused to believe that.

It got to the point where there were so many rumors being spread about kickbacks that my travel agent, Ruth Noble, got involved. Every time I'd hear one of the rumors, I would call her and tell her what I'd heard and ask if there was anything that wasn't up to par. She would always assure me that everything was open and above board. After I related one particularly ridiculous rumor, she told me, "Marshall, I'll go to the Supreme Court with you, if that's what it takes. There is absolutely nothing true—no way, shape, form, or fashion—about what they're saying."

Ruth also indicated that if the rumors continued, she would slap them with a slander suit. I told my lawyers that both Ruth and I were considering filing slander suits against everyone in the organization except June. They wrote a couple of letters to John's attorneys, and the rumors soon stopped. Those letters really made some people mad, especially W. S. Holland, who had been one of the primary people spreading those false stories.

I was talking to W. S.'s wife one day, although I'm not quite sure why now, and she said, "Why don't you just go on and leave us alone? We're doing fine. You just leave us alone and we'll be OK." That only made me more determined to see the lawsuit through all the way to the end, because if you're any sort of a man at all, you've got to stand up to things like that. And besides, they were employed by an organization that was one-third mine.

The Statlers used different opening acts on their shows, and when they were with Mercury Records, their producer, Jerry Kennedy, told us about a young woman he thought would be a good opener for the group. He had just finished recording her, and when he played the record for us, she just knocked us out. Jerry put me in touch with her management, and after I talked to them a while, we hired that petite woman with the big voice. Her name was Reba McEntire.

I got a lot of criticism from promoters for using Reba because she was pretty much unknown. But she was a hard worker and one of the finest ladies I've ever been around. She was like a daughter and was so cooperative and professional, even though she hadn't been in the business very long. She worked constantly to improve her act, and she'd get up onstage with the band anytime she could.

I started using her exclusively as our opening act—just Reba, on every date. Some of the talent buyers and promoters didn't like

that because she didn't have the name recognition to sell any tickets. Some of them criticized me quite a bit, but I told them, "Look
at it this way: she needs a job, she needs to work, she's a great talent, and somewhere along the line, she's going to make it. I think
I'll just hang on to her and see if I can help her keep her head above
water, and we'll just see what happens."

Reba was the Statlers' opening act for two and a half years, and
then the hit records started coming and her career took off like a
rocket. Just like John had told the Statler Brothers in 1973, we told
Reba, "It's best that you go on your own now; you're ready." He was
right then, and now it was indeed time for Reba to make her own
way in the entertainment industry. Even though it was like losing
a right arm when she left the show, it was for the best, as history
has proven.

We always liked to use female opening acts because they rounded
out the lineup and made it a family show. One was Suzy Bogguss,
who went out on the road with us for about a year.

After her departure, we were booked at the Aksarben in Omaha
in March 1984 for a weeklong stand that included nine shows. We
needed an opening act because the Statlers' set ran about an hour
and ten minutes and we wanted the shows to run about two hours.

I was driving down the interstate in Memphis one day listening
to the radio when the disc jockey played a record by a mother-and-
daughter duo I'd never heard before. I thought they were great, and
as soon as I got home, I called the radio station and found they
recorded for RCA. I called the label's office in Nashville, and they
put me in touch with Woody Bowles, the act's manager.

Woody and his partner, Ken Stilts, another promoter and manager, asked me to work out a deal with them. I called Ken and asked
if the ladies could go to Omaha with us. "Marshall, they don't even
have a band. They just got a record released," he told me. I said,
"Well, put a band together. You gotta start somewhere. You know,
we're looking at seventy-five hundred people per show for nine
shows, and that would be great exposure for them." Then he told
me, "Yeah, but they haven't ever been onstage, just played little
clubs and things."

"The way they sing, work 'em up a little show," I said. "You got a month to do it. Ken—let's just do it." He talked to the pair and called me back to say they wanted to work the date. "Do me up a contract and send it to me and we'll do it," I told him.

The two ladies made it to Omaha and were staying right across the hall from me at the Best Western. When I walked out into the hallway, there they stood. They introduced themselves as Wynonna and Naomi, the Judds.

That night, 7,500 people filled the seats at the Aksarben's main arena, and the girls were really nervous. I talked with them and tried to calm them down, and soon they walked out onstage with their band—the same people who had recorded with them—took their places, and got ready for the curtain to rise. Wynonna peeked out at the audience from behind the curtain and turned to Naomi and said excitedly, "Mama, have you looked out there? I bet there are ten thousand people out there! Mama, we ain't got no business here."

"Oh no, no, no, girls," I said. "You're going to be all right. These people are going to love you." Wynonna said, "Well, I thought it would be some little thing with three or four hundred people." I told her, "Well, there's seventy-five hundred, and you're going to be just fine. Besides, you can't change your mind now. You're already onstage, and I'm getting ready to introduce you. So get ready!"

After I announced them and the curtain opened, we watched the Judds do their very first big professional show, which Woody Bowles videotaped, as he did all their performances. That night, they sat up for two or three hours watching the tape and talking and laughing. They had their guitars and worked on a few things, and the next day they were a little better. The girls did that after every show, and every day they got a bit better. At the end of the run in Omaha, they had become quite professional, and before long they were ready to go out on their own, which they did with great success.

To this day, the Statlers and I are so proud to have been a part of the early careers of Reba McEntire and the Judds. All three of those ladies are class acts, and they really appreciated the opportunities we gave them.

When John was released from the hospital after a few days, he and June decided to go to their home in Jamaica for a while to rest and get away from everything. I called him a couple of times while he was there, and he was doing pretty well, but it was evident that he was very weak.

When I'd seen him in the hospital, after not seeing him for several years, I was shocked at how much he'd deteriorated. He looked terrible, to say the least, and appeared to be almost fifty years older than the last time I'd seen him. That just broke my heart. Here was a man with so much pride and charisma who was so torn down that he looked like hell warmed over. Seeing him in that condition bothered me an awful lot. However, I must say, in all fairness, that John was the only person I know who could have punished himself as much as he did and still been alive. John's only enemies were himself and drugs.

After a week or so, John and June returned to Hendersonville, and we continued to talk on the phone. I called one day, and June told me John was scheduled to go back to the doctor the next day. "Well, I'm coming to town tomorrow," I told her. "I'll just come out there and take you." She said, "Will you do that?" I replied, "I most certainly will! All I have to do is leave here a little bit earlier, and I'll come up there and take him to the doctor." June said she would appreciate the help, "because I'm going to have to be the one to take him, and he's a handful."

I called the next morning as I got closer to town, and June told me, "Come on out. We're cooking breakfast for you." When I arrived, there was an unbelievably big breakfast waiting, and everything on the table was something that neither John nor I should have been eating. We sat down at the table, and I said, "Guys, I love this stuff you got here, but you know something? This will kill you!" John jokingly replied, "Yeah, it will. We know it'll kill you, but this is a very special occasion, and one time ain't gonna hurt nobody."

John could walk pretty well, but he couldn't manage the stairs by himself. I helped him go upstairs, and we went out the back and stood talking and looking over his place until June came up and we headed for the car. I asked John if he wanted to sit in the backseat, which was a little roomier and easier to get into. "Nope," he said, "I think I'll sit up there with you. I sat in that seat a long time with you driving; maybe we'll do it some more." So June jumped in the backseat and off we drove down the interstate.

The three of us were back together again, driving down the highway as we had done for countless thousands of miles. June smiled and said, "You know, Marshall, you're a good driver. John sings pretty good and you play the bass real well—all you'd need would be a good guitar player and you might be able to get into show business. You could call yourself Johnny Cash and the Tennessee Two." I told her, "Hey, that's a pretty good idea! What do think of that John?" He grinned and said, "Let's do it!"

I said, "OK, we'll get together and we'll put us a little group together and we'll see if we can get on Sun Records as Johnny Cash and The Tennessee Two. We might be pretty successful." He laughed and again said, "Let's do it!" We had more fun together than we'd had in years as we made the short run from Hendersonville to Nashville.

We arrived at Baptist Hospital and took John up to see his doctor, who took him right on back into the office. June told me, "When he comes out, I have to see the doctor, so after he comes out, it'll be just a few minutes before we'll be ready to go." I said, "You just take your time. I have a meeting with TNN, but I can call them and postpone it a little bit. It's not a big deal."

John was with the doctor for twenty or thirty minutes, and when he came out he looked very dejected. He walked through the waiting room without saying anything to me or to June and sat down on a little bench across the hall, elbows on his knees, staring down at the floor. I walked over and said, "John, tell me something, I don't know anything about this disease that you have [Shy-Drager syndrome, a progressive disorder of the central and autonomic nervous systems]. I've never heard the name of it before. What's the prognosis of this thing? Do you know?"

John looked up and said, "Well, Marshall, thirty days, sixty days, ninety days, maybe a year." I was stunned. "Oh no, John, you gotta be kidding me!" He said, "No, that's what they told me." That stopped all conversation, and I sat there with him for maybe five minutes, then got up without saying anything and walked back into the waiting room. Two or three minutes later, June came out and we talked a bit before getting the car and going back to Hendersonville.

In the car, June said, "Marshall, would you mind, if you've got enough time, would you like to go by the hospital and see Helen?" June's sister had been in the hospital for about a year with an extremely serious stomach problem, and things didn't look very good for her. I said I'd love to see Helen, and June proceeded to give me directions. We zigzagged around as June said, "Turn left here" and "turn right here," and directly we pulled up in front of a small clinic.

We went to Helen's room where we found her in bed with several tubes running out of her. Her husband, Glen, was there, and we all had a nice visit. John came around a little and even got a little jolly, trying to lift everyone's spirits. June was very sad, but she told Helen, "We just wanted to come by and see you because we know it's been a long time since Marshall had seen you and he was gracious enough to take John to the doctor. But we gotta get back home because he has a meeting." We spent about fifteen minutes visiting with Helen and Glen, and then we had to leave.

The trip back to Hendersonville wasn't as much fun as the one coming in, and hardly a word was spoken. I helped John out of the car and down the stairs to the floor where his bedroom was. We talked a bit there and I said, "Look guys, I've really got to go, but I'll be talking to you often." John said, "Please do."

I thought about John's situation an awful lot, and when I got home I couldn't get him or June off my mind. Johnny Cash was the biggest name ever in country music and had done more than any other five artists I could think of. Legendary recording artist, star of stage, screen, and television—John was what I call an "all-around cowboy." He could do it all.

But now it looked like all of that was gone, never to return. Show business is the hardest business in the world to get into and get out of, and it was devastating to see someone who had been at the very top of the entertainment business, who had spent his life in the spotlight, have to deal with losing all that. Everything was gone, including his health, and now the doctors were telling him he had but a few months to live.

I don't know how he lived with that. I would talk to him and try to sympathize a little, but he would say, "Hey, I'm happy. I've been busy and I'm happy." He would appear on TV talk shows like *Larry King Live* and say things like "Everything is all right; I'm happy. But he wasn't. John enjoyed show business, and he had said many times that being onstage was the highlight of his life. He missed it, he missed it bad, and that was killing him as fast as the disease.

He did try to hang on as long as he could by writing and recording. He wrote some great songs and recorded some decent music. As a matter of fact, he was more interested in writing and recording now than he had been in the previous thirty years. He was very ambitious, and I could understand why: because it took his mind off many of the devastating things that were happening to him. He had signed a deal with American Records in 1994, and they put some stuff out, but he had lost the sound of the Tennessee Two and had absolutely no success recording with studio musicians. He figured out the best thing to do was to perform solo with just his guitar, and that was the best decision he could have made because that acoustic approach was so successful he won a Grammy or two.

⋘∙⋙

Many people have told me that from the time I left the show in 1980, John never drew another drug-free breath. I don't know if that's strictly true, but after his illness forced him off the road, he went to doctors who administered a lot of drugs, although those were prescription medications. At least we didn't have to worry about some outsider bringing John something he didn't need but that he wanted. He got completely off amphetamines.

Old J. R. was back. His health and about everything else was gone, but J. R. was back. And believe me when I say he was back 100 percent. We were the best of friends now; he loved everybody and hated no one in the world. It was a long time coming, but it was such a crying shame that he had to be robbed of his health, his career, and everything else before he got himself straight. The great J. R. "John" Cash was back, and now he had the sympathy of just about everyone on the planet. He was a very forgiving person, and everything was forgiven now.

It was tough to look at John in the condition he was in. His face looked haggard, and the rest of his body had deteriorated as well. No matter what anybody says to the contrary—and I knew John about as well as anybody—drugs did it all.

Anyone trying to get into the entertainment business or con-templating taking any kind of illegal drug should take a long hard look at what drugs did to Johnny Cash. If they could have seen the man toward the end, I don't believe anyone would go down the path he did. Not only did John destroy himself with drugs, he destroyed many of the people who loved him. If a man chooses to take a par-ticular road, so be it, but his choice shouldn't affect anyone else. I've never known anybody who has gone far down the road of drug abuse who has survived it. Drugs will ruin you mentally, physically, and financially, and destroy your family and friends. Take my advice and do as the slogan says: Just Say No.

I've asked myself a million times over the years, What could have been done differently? What could *I* have done differently? What could anybody have done differently? Who should we have talked to? What else could we have done?

The answer is, we did everything we could. Many people who loved John dearly did everything they could to get him off drugs. Rehabilitation centers didn't work. The love of his family and their help and support didn't work. Everything I tried to do didn't work. Actually, John resented anything that anybody did to try to help him beat his drug problems.

Dealing with someone of Johnny Cash's stature and ego is a very difficult thing—superstars generally don't take kindly to people trying to direct or advise them or prevent them from doing something they want to do, even it's something that's harmful to them. John had everyone around him under his thumb, so to speak, and anything that you tried to do to help would come back later to haunt you. We all learned the hard way to just leave him alone. Keep him alive, do anything you could to help, but leave him alone and let him make his own choices.

When John was on drugs, everything turned around 180 degrees. Even if you were his best friend, his wife, his parents, it didn't matter—you became his worst enemy if you tried to get him to stop taking drugs. And by the same token, all those dealers and users and other people who should have been his worst enemies suddenly became his best friends.

<hr />

After John was forced to stop touring because of his health, he spent a lot of time in Baptist Hospital. It seemed that it didn't take anything at all to bring on a bout of pneumonia, and he sometimes would be on life support for days. Everyone would just about give up hope—and there were a couple of times when he had only a trickle of life left in him—but he would always rebound.

I remember one time, when he had just gotten out of the intensive care unit, he telephoned me and asked, in a voice that was so strained it was hard to recognize, if Etta and I would like to go on a long vacation with June and him in their tour bus, just the four of us. That's just the way John was—he thought everybody was free and should be ready to go when he was.

I never did promise him that I would go, since I was still traveling with the Statlers, but I certainly would have made room for that trip if I could have. However, it seemed that John couldn't stay healthy long enough to take it. By that time, he could hardly walk, his eyesight was failing, and his body was deteriorating fast. His mind, however, remained sharp as a tack. While the rest of him was going downhill, John's mind never deteriorated the least bit.

<hr />

Early on the morning of January 19, 1998, I received a call saying that our friend and musical legend Carl Perkins had passed away. Carl had been battling throat cancer and had been hanging on by a thread for quite some time. I called John and June's home in Jamaica, where they were spending a fair amount of time now, to deliver the sad news.

June answered the phone and told me John was outside in the sun. "Hey, don't bring him in," I told her. "just leave him out there. But I want you to give him a message: Carl Perkins has passed away." She said, "Oh, Marshall, just hang on a minute and let me bring him in." About five minutes later, she came back on the line and said, "I told him, but he don't really want to talk about it. He's crying." John loved Carl so much, as we all did, and Carl had been a part of the organization for so long that he was like a brother to all of us.

<hr />

We were beginning to lose people close to us. In the middle of July 1999, I called one day just to talk to John, and he answered the phone, which was very rare. I said, "John, I'm just calling to check on you and see how you're doing." He said, "Well, it's sort of a sad day." We all knew Anita had been in the hospital for a long time and was in very poor health, suffering from rheumatoid arthritis that had destroyed her body. He said, "They're bringing Anita in the house right now."

"Oh, is she coming to stay with you all a little while?" I asked. John said, "Marshall, they've brought her here to our house to die. The doctor said she can't live no more than a couple of days. Every time we move her, we feel another bone break. The pain is so terrible, and there's nothing they can give her for it. The doctor says she can't last much longer." A few days later, on July 29, 1999, Anita passed away.

Mother Maybelle had passed away, Helen had passed away, and now Anita was gone. June was the only member of Mother Maybelle and the Carter Sisters left. At this point, she was in relatively good health; I would say excellent health in view of everything that she had been through over the past couple of decades.

June had recorded an album that John Carter produced for her. Her record label was putting on a big promotional campaign, and she invited a lot of industry people, friends, and family to come out and hear her perform songs from the new album. There was a tennis court behind the house, and they put up a big tent, which they often did when they had parties, and they set up a great buffet for dinner.

June had invited Etta and me to come, and when we got there, thirty or forty minutes before the affair started, the place was packed. There were so many people there that John and I both knew, it was really a great night. And when everyone saw that John and I were back together again and were friends, they were just overjoyed.

June got up onstage to preview her album for the crowd, and then she brought John up to perform some of the songs with her. He worked his way up onstage, which wasn't very easy, and I believe they sang two songs together. When he got through, John was totally exhausted and headed straight for the house, which was about fifty yards away. I saw that he was in bad trouble, so I walked to the house with him. He wanted to rest, so I helped put him in bed and talked to him a while before going back to the party.

People asked me how John was doing, and I told them, "Well, I think he's going to be all right; he's just worn completely out." It was so sad to see how little stamina he had. It had taken nearly all his strength just to make it through those two songs.

<hr>

John still loved to go to his place in Jamaica, but he wasn't able to take a commercial flight because he always had to change planes in Atlanta, and he just wasn't strong enough to do that. A dear friend of his, John Rollins, from whom John had bought Cinnamon Hill back in the seventies (and who has since passed away), had a good-sized Falcon jet. Anytime that John wanted to go to Jamaica, all he had to do was call, and John Rollins and his wife, Michele, would send their jet to a Nashville airport to take him to Jamaica where they arranged the proper transportation to take him to the house.

John went down there often, and that was good. He could fly down and bask in the sun, and that helped him a lot. He could get away from all of the turmoil in the house and around the business as it was closing up, because that was a problem for him, so every chance he got, he would go to Jamaica.

In the latter part of February 1999, Kelly Hancock, Reba's daughter, who was in charge of the House of Cash at that point, called me and said, "Marshall, they're going to do an all-star tribute to John in New York on March sixth, and he'd like you and Etta both to come up." Etta and I discussed it for a couple of days and decided that we wouldn't go, and I called Kelly and told her.

About thirty minutes after I hung up, John called me from Jamaica. His voice was very hoarse. "Marshall," he said, "I don't think Kelly told you the whole story. I want you to come up and play bass for me because I'm going to do two songs." I said, "John, are you sure you want to go to New York and do that show? I didn't know you were scheduled to perform on it." He said, "Well, I'm not. This is going to be my last concert, the very last one with the band. You were there for the very first one that I ever did, and I want you to be there for the very last one, and I want you to play bass on it."

I asked what he was planning to do, and he said, "Would you believe that nobody is doing 'Folsom Prison Blues' and nobody's

346

doing 'I Walk the Line'? That's what I want to do. Those are two of my favorite songs, and I just want you to come and play the upright bass for me."

Etta and I talked about the trip some more because now it had taken a different twist, and we both immediately agreed that we should go. After all, as John had said, we'd been there for the very first show, and if this was going to be his last concert with the band, we needed to be a part of it. I called John back and told him, "Etta and I talked about it, and we would be honored." He said, "Everything will be taken care of, Marshall, you don't have to worry about nothing. Your plane tickets will be sent to you for you and Etta, both first class. You'll have a suite at the hotel, and you'll have limousine service everywhere you want to go. Everything will be supplied, and I'll see to it that it's just that way."

I said, "John, that's not necessary. Are you sure you can do this? Your voice just doesn't sound good enough to go sing on a major TV show, and I don't want you to come off sounding bad, even if it is the last show. It just don't feel right." He said, "Marshall, I'm going to go up there in advance, and I'm not going to speak one word to nobody, even June. If I can get proper rest and not talk to nobody, I can do the show. I can do the two songs as good as I ever did 'em." I said, "Well, John, if you're sure you can do it, that's fine, but to sound like you do right now, I'd just rather that you wouldn't."

He said, "Believe me when I tell you I'm going to rest up, and this bronchitis that I've got, we're gonna treat it. We're gonna put a humidifier in the room, and I'm going to be ready to go. When you get there, I'll be ready to go." I told him that Etta and I would definitely be there.

<hr>

We flew to New York on March 5, and the limousine picked us up at the airport and took us straight to the hotel. When Etta and I walked into the lobby, we saw our old friends Kris Kristofferson and Brooks & Dunn, and we stopped and spoke to them for a bit before going up to our room.

When we came down the next day, the lobby was full of people associated with the show. It was like old times because there were a lot of great people there, including several people from our old entourage as well as a lot of superstars who were appearing on the show. We had all come to pay tribute to John, and that was very rewarding.

No one had seen or talked to John because he was saving his voice, and I think everybody understood the situation. Etta and I certainly did, and even though we knew what room he was in, we never knocked on the door because we wanted him to get himself prepared to do the show.

On March 6, we did a couple of run-throughs with the band for camera positions and so forth, but John didn't come over until later that afternoon for the final rehearsal. When they called Etta and me to come down from the dressing room, I saw John Carter and immediately asked him, "How's your dad?" He said, "We're going right by his room, do y'all want to see him?" I said, "Of course!"

There were several people in the room when we walked in, but lo and behold, when I heard John speak, his voice was crisp and clean and clear. We went down to do the final run-through, and he was great! Here was a group of musicians who hadn't played together in twenty-nine years, but when we walked out onstage, everybody was in sync, felt good, and did their jobs. About halfway through "Folsom Prison," while Bob Wootton was taking a guitar break, John turned around and winked at me as if to say, "Didn't I tell you I could do it?"

That night, all of the great artists did a fantastic job as they performed some wonderful Johnny Cash songs. Nobody tried to copy the sound of Johnny Cash and the Tennessee Two; they played the songs their way, which I thought was fantastic.

The people in the audience didn't know that John was going to be there because his appearance hadn't been advertised. He wanted to go on unannounced. But when the band went onstage, a hush fell over the crowd as they recognized some of us and realized there was a real treat in store for them. Then, with no introduction, we started playing "Folsom Prison Blues," and out walked John.

In all the years that I was with John, I'd never seen such a reception. People jumped to their feet, and all you could hear was hollering and screaming. Flashbulbs were going off everywhere, and I could see that some people were even standing in their chairs.

And when he stepped up to the microphone and said, "Hello, I'm Johnny Cash," they blew the roof off the place. The reception was just unbelievable and continued for a long time. Finally, as he began to sing and his deep, mellow, and very powerful voice filled the studio, they began to calm down—but not much.

There was so much electricity in that building, it reminded me of 1969 and '70, when John was at the height of his career. We played "I Walk the Line" all the way through and he took a bow, then all of the artists on the show joined us onstage as we closed with a group rendition of "I Walk the Line." That was literally the end of the career of Johnny Cash and the whole entourage, and I was absolutely honored to be a part of it.

Etta and I have talked about that show a lot since then. It was probably the highlight of our lives, and I don't mean that in a bright way. I just mean that I don't know what we would have done if we had turned down John's invitation, as we initially had done. I remember that final run-through so well. There were quite a few people in the audience, and during the break on "Folsom Prison Blues," when John walked over to me, I noticed Etta in the audience and June on the side of the stage, both crying their eyes out. They weren't sad; they were just so happy to see John and me standing together again onstage.

———

Now everything was right between John and me. I think we were probably closer at this point than we'd ever been in our lives because we'd learned a lot from the mistakes that had been made, and that had only brought us closer. I'll always regret that Etta and I didn't take his bus and go on the vacation that he'd wanted to go on. Maybe we could have done that if I'd just pushed it a little bit harder, but I sort of let things take their own course, and the trip simply didn't work out.

I was now in Nashville working on the Statler Brothers' TV show, and I called him about every day. During one of our conversations, he asked how the Brothers were doing, and I told him they were doing fantastic. He wanted to know if they could come out and see him, and I said, "Of course! I'll bring them out. When do you want to do it?" He said, "Well, tomorrow."

It was pouring down rain the next day as we pulled through the gates leading to the house. Just like old times, we opened the back door and walked in without knocking. There stood June, and she was so happy to see the Brothers. John was upstairs in his bedroom. He could still walk pretty well, but it took him forever to do anything. When he finally came down, it was a great reunion—this was the first time the Statlers had seen him since he'd performed on their anniversary show.

John called John Carter, who was living across the street at the time, and he came over to join us. June just had to take everyone through the house to see all the pretty things she had. We probably spent two or three hours with John and June, and it was a very enjoyable time.

The Brothers and I went back and started rehearsing for the TV show, which was tremendously successful throughout the 1990s. In fact, everything the Statlers were doing at this time seemed to turn to gold. It was a great time in our lives, even though I couldn't include John in any way. It was very difficult to see him and talk to him knowing that his career had ended and that mine was still going strong. I felt very bad about that, but there was nothing I could do. The Statlers and I were rolling right along, but John was just out of it.

All good things, for one reason or another, have to come to an end. In the summer of 2001, the Statlers and I were in Wisconsin Dells, Wisconsin, and I called the Brothers to my room and told them, "Look, guys, it's getting to be about time for me to hang it up because I feel like I'm forsaking my family. Etta has been through so much in her life since 1954. I've been gone so much, and I just feel like it's time that I spend the rest of my life taking care of my family. I've got two grandbabies and a son and a loving wife who's been through the mill, and it's time for me to hang it up. So I want to tell you that at the end of 2002, I can no longer travel on the road."

I told them that I would do whatever else that they wanted me to do, like book dates for them, but that I just had to get off the road. It was a sad time, and I noticed that Don and Phil had sort of bowed their heads but Harold hadn't. A little grin came across his face and he said, "See there, guys, that's what I want to do."

They started talking about their own retirement from the road, and before we left Wisconsin Dells, they decided they also would do that in 2002. As time went along, we set a final date, which would be October 26, 2002. They wanted to play their final show in Virginia, since it was their home state, and the only building we could find that was suitable and available was in Salem, Virginia, right outside Roanoke.

That last concert by the Statler Brothers was the biggest-grossing date they ever worked in their entire career. That says a lot about the Statlers. They wanted to quit while they were at the top of their game, and that's what they did. The Brothers had been selling out just about every building that we played, so racking up their biggest gross ever at that final date in Salem was the perfect ending to a fabulous career.

The Statlers always took care of business, and I wish them all the best in the world. We remain very close and talk often. Jimmy Fortune has a solo career going, and I'm trying to help him out with that all I can. The Statlers are an institution and will forever be missed by their fans and everyone in the entertainment business.

❦

One of the first people I called after I got back home from the Statlers' last date was John. "Well, John," I told him, "I just wanted you to know that I've hung it up after all these years. We just did our last date, and I just wanted you to know that. You're not alone in your retirement; now we're both retired. And you know, I feel a little bit better about that for some reason or other."

John said, "I understand what you're saying, but you'll be all right, there's no question about that in my mind." Then he added, "I really appreciate you coming up to do the tribute with us. You know, Marshall, the reason I wanted you to come so bad, that was a big show, the biggest show that TNN ever had, and it showed the world that we were back together, that we were friends and that all had been forgiven. So, now we've got a clean slate to work off of." I said, "You're right, and we'll move forward."

It had been evident to me during the tribute to John in New York a couple of years earlier that he was failing pretty fast. He'd built up his stamina, and I was surprised at how good his voice was and how great a job he'd done, but I knew that wasn't going to last. He'd already reached the point of no return then, and now many people were trying to understand just what was wrong with him. But it wasn't a great mystery to me or some of the others who were close to him. I don't think there was another person in the world who could have withstood what John had put himself through with drugs.

The doctors could run all the tests they wanted and come up with all sorts of diagnoses, but the bottom line was drugs. God didn't put people on this earth to withstand what John put himself through. But he wouldn't listen, and you couldn't reason with him, especially if he was high. And if he ever got completely straight, you were very reluctant to talk to him about his problem because it might drive him back to drugs.

John did a few performances after the show in New York, but nothing of any magnitude. He appeared a couple of times at the Carter Fold in Virginia where Jerry Hensley, who lives there, played guitar with him.

John had continued to write songs and was now writing great songs and recording a lot of them for American Records. He didn't write anything that equaled "I Walk the Line," but times have changed a lot since then, and if he'd written some of those songs back in the early days, I'm sure they would have been hits. John was trying to change with the times, and even at this point, when he almost couldn't do anything, his career was still growing. That just goes to show you how loyal his fans are and what an impression he made on the entertainment world.

⟞⟋⟍⟋⟍⟞

Everything in his career and our relationship had come full circle, and I am very happy for that. It does my soul a lot of good to occasionally turn on the TV and see John, Luther, and myself performing onstage. It seems people always have good things to say about the early days of Johnny Cash and The Tennessee Two, and some music scholars tell me that our popularity will last forever. That's one of the reasons I'm writing this book. Johnny Cash and The Tennessee Two, in my opinion, will be around forever, even though John and Luther are both gone. I'm still here, though, and I'm trying to set the record straight. It's been an amazing career, and I really can't put into words just how proud I am of what we did.

I'm equally proud of what I did with the Statler Brothers, even though the two organizations—the Johnny Cash Show and the Statlers—were so different in so many ways. Both were so tremendously successful. The Statlers were great business people, and everything they did was very professional and very polished. John was not a business person, and nothing he did was polished—it was real rough and it was just Johnny Cash. The Statlers did everything by the book, but John threw the book away before it was ever written.

I learned a lot from John over the years, although I probably learned more from watching him do things he shouldn't have done than I did from watching him do the things he should. John could weather any storm and do whatever he wanted, no matter how bad it was, yet somewhere along the line, things seemed to turn to his advantage. With the Statlers, it was their professionalism and business sense that made them so successful.

You learn something every day in show business, and I can truthfully say that if you haven't experienced show business firsthand, you really can't understand it. There are so many people who think they are authorities on the entertainment industry when in fact they haven't lived that life. It sort of rubs me the wrong way to see someone trying to explain to everybody how much he knows about the business when he's experienced nothing. Show business is a very complicated industry to be in, and you can never truly understand just how tough it is unless you've lived it.

When John and I split in March 1980, I was fifty-two years old and it was time to hang up the instrument because entertainment is a young man's game—and that's even more true today. Even though we'd paved the road for so many of the entertainers who followed us, it was time to move into another phase of the business. When I went with the Statler Brothers, I laid down the instrument but became involved in many more things, and that was very interesting. I'll always be thankful that God gave me such a wonderful opportunity when I left the Johnny Cash Show, because the Statler Brothers and I had a terrific relationship, one that I will remember and cherish to my dying day.

I talked to John almost every week on the phone, although I didn't go to Nashville to visit him very often. Even though it seemed he'd declined a little more each time we talked, he was always very positive. We'd talk about the things we used to do, and he'd always laugh, but I could tell he was fading.

It was obvious there wasn't anything that could be done for him medically. All his family or I could do was watch him go away. About the only good part of all this was that John was no longer struggling with a drug problem. And that allowed everything to come full circle for a lot of people, especially the two of us. Once the drugs were gone, the love we had for each other came back, and I'm as proud of that as anything in my entire life.

I couldn't keep track of how many times John was in and out of the hospital at this point. I made countless calls to Baptist Hospital and talked to whoever was in the sitting room about John's health. Many times, he was on life support, but somehow he always managed to come back. He had a strong constitution and faith in God, and while his faith had sort of left him during the drug years, it was very strong and evident in the later years of his life.

I called their house and talked to June a lot, too. I could tell from the sound of her voice that her health was getting bad, as well. That was really tough because I could tell that both of them were leaving us.

I called John in the early part of May 2003 and talked with him at great length, and he told me that June was in the hospital. I didn't know that and asked what was wrong. He said, "Well, she has to have her gall bladder removed. She's having some problems with her gall bladder. Don't worry about it; she'll be fine. She's in good health, and the doctors have assured me that it's just a minor procedure." Some of my friends had undergone gall bladder surgery and were back home in a day, so I wasn't terribly worried.

But when I talked to John a couple of days later, he said, "Well, they found a leaky heart valve, and they have to fix it before they can fix her gall bladder." I said, "What are we talking about here, John? What are they going to do?" He said, "They're gonna have to perform open-heart surgery and replace June's heart valve. But the doctors assure me that it's a routine thing and that she'll be over it in no time at all. She can come back home for a little while and recoup, and then she'll go back in and they'll do the gall bladder."

That bothered me a whole lot because the last time I'd spoken to June, I'd felt that her health just wasn't all that good. Her voice had changed drastically in the last couple of months and was getting weaker every time we talked.

June came through the heart valve replacement very well. She stayed in the ICU for a day and a night, and then they brought her to her room. She was awake and alert, talking to visitors, and seemed to be doing just fine. Regrettably, that night, she suffered a massive heart attack and quit breathing. She was put on life support, and the doctors didn't give John and the kids much encouragement. The family felt that June wouldn't want to be on life support for the rest of her days, and they made the tough decision to remove those "heroic measures." She clung to life for several days after that, but on May 15, 2003, June Carter Cash passed away.

This was very devastating to many people because everyone thought it was John who wouldn't last much longer. We'd been preparing ourselves for that, and we were stunned when June was the first to leave us. But we were going to have to deal with our grief and start worrying again about John.

People from all walks of life were able to come up to the podium and say a few words about June at her funeral. I wanted so desperately to go up there and talk about my old friend, but what I had to say couldn't have been said in a few words.

When the funeral was over, I told Etta, "Let's walk out in the lobby and see if we can say something to John when he comes out." I didn't even try to go down and talk to him during the service. He couldn't see and he couldn't hear too well, so when the girls pushed his wheelchair into the lobby of the church, I bent over him and simply said, "John." He said, "Oh, Marshall, it's so hard; it's so terribly hard." And it was; it was terribly hard.

We spoke for just a few moments, since a lot of people were gathering around, and I told John I would see him later at the cemetery. A few minutes after Etta and I arrived at the cemetery, the girls brought him over in a golf cart, one of them on one side and one on the other. When they were lifting him out of the cart, I offered to help, but they told me, "No, we've been trained to do

this, and it's very, very important that we do it the way we're supposed to."

They set him down right in front of the casket, and one of the
girls turned to me and said, "Marshall, until the family comes, why
don't you sit by him and talk to him?" I sat down and said, "John,
I wanted so bad to get up and say some words about June, but I just
couldn't bring myself to it. I couldn't do it. And there was so much
that I wanted to say."

As John and I sat there and talked, I thought, *Here we are, the
three of us, together again. One of us has gone to Heaven, but the
other two are left behind.* We had been like the Three Musketeers for
so many years, and now John and I were sitting in a cemetery right
in front of June's casket. We probably sat there for fifteen minutes
talking about June, and not a soul bothered us. It was so touching.

The next day I called John to see how he was doing, and he was
in good spirits. He said, "You know what we been doing all day,
Marshall? We got some of the flowers off of June's grave, and we've
been taking them around to nursing homes and giving them to the
people there, and we've enjoyed it so much." He was very upbeat, as
if he had laid a big burden to rest. I guess that was the case because
he'd been through so much in the past few days, and now that everything was over, it was a relief to him.

We continued to talk every day and did a lot of reminiscing. We
talked about things the three of us had done, and I could always get
a little giggle out of him. He was taking June's death well, much
better than I thought he would. I just couldn't believe that he could
live without her. She had been more than a wife, and she had been
through an awful lot with John over the years. However, this too
had come full circle, and they were again very much in love. All had
been forgiven between the two of them. June was his soulmate, his
everything, even though he still had his children. I couldn't understand how John could live without her. But he did—at least for a little while.

It was obvious to me that the end was coming very soon for John.
He just kept deteriorating. He'd lost June, his career (which now
spanned almost fifty years), and he'd destroyed his health with

drugs. He had diabetes, was blind, couldn't hear very well, and couldn't walk. But with all the things that were wrong with him, his mind was sharp as a tack. And this was one of the downsides of his condition: he knew everything that was going on, he knew the shape he was in, he knew everything. Every time I talked to him, whether in person or on the phone, it never ceased to amaze me how sharp his mind was.

He tried very hard not to talk about any of his problems, especially his health. He tried to hang on and keep busy. Often, when I talked with him, he would be writing a song or working out something with his guitar. There were times when, with the help of other people, he'd go out to the little recording studio behind the house and do a little recording.

John was determined to beat the diseases that had invaded his body, whatever they might be. I really think he knew his years of drug abuse had caught up with him. Many people had told him that was going to happen, but he was determined to prove everybody wrong. I honestly think he believed that he could still beat his problems—but I also I think he knew it would be a miracle if he did.

John seemed bigger than life to many people, including myself. But on September 12, 2003, at two o'clock in the morning, the great John R. Cash passed away.

On the day of John's funeral, the Tennessee Three—Bob Wootton, W. S. Holland, and I—walked up to the casket and looked down at him in total disbelief. We didn't think it was possible, but it was a fact. John was gone.

After being in show business for fifty years and seeing how devastating drug abuse can be, I want to say to everyone from every walk of life: if you're thinking about going down the drug road, you're making the wrong turn. As strong as Johnny Cash was, physically, mentally, and spiritually, it was drugs that put him in his grave. And that will happen to anybody that chooses to go down that road. Not only will they put you in your grave, but they'll also destroy your loved ones and associates.

As I've said before, John was the world's greatest teacher, and he's still teaching people from the grave, through his song lyrics or perhaps something he once said or did. I suppose he'll be teaching people right from wrong for many generations to follow.

———

On November 10, 2003, there was a memorial for Johnny Cash at the Ryman Auditorium in Nashville, and John's children asked if I would come and tell the audience a little bit about the beginning, when we started in the business. I was given ten minutes, but I knew it would be hard to explain much about the early days of Johnny Cash and the Tennessee Two.

I got a pretty good ovation when Tim Robbins, the show's emcee, introduced me as an original member of the Tennessee Two, which made me very proud. I knew the applause wasn't so much for me as it was for Luther Perkins and John R. Cash. I took a few bows, waited until the applause stopped, and then started my story. I hadn't really thought about what I was going to say, but I had told the story so many times, I thought I could just wing it. As I got into it, the tale got pretty exciting, and before I knew it, I'd been onstage for twenty minutes. I'm sure the producers and everybody else were pulling their hair out, but when I walked off, I got a standing ovation. I stood offstage, and the crowd kept applauding and applauding, so I walked back out and took a bow or two and then left the stage as the applause continued.

I went back into the audience to sit with Etta and Vivian and watch the rest of the show. As I was taking my seat, Etta asked if I would go to the lobby and get another program. As I got about halfway up the aisle, Vice President Al Gore stepped right out in front of me and he said, "You know, Marshall, you stole the show." I said, "No, Mr. Gore, I didn't steal the show, the story stole the show." Then he asked, "Are you going to write a book?" I said, "I might."

Index

Index

Index

Index

Index

Index

Index